Feminist New Materialism, Girlhood, and the School Ball

Feminist Thought in Childhood Research

Series editors: Jayne Osgood and Veronica Pacini-Ketchabaw

Drawing on feminist scholarship, this boundary-pushing series explores the use of creative, experimental, new materialist and posthumanist research methodologies that address various aspects of childhood. *Feminist Thought in Childhood Research* foregrounds examples of research practices within feminist childhood studies that engage with posthumanism, science studies, affect theory, animal studies, new materialisms and other post-foundational perspectives that seek to decentre human experience. Books in the series offer lived examples of feminist research praxis and politics in childhood studies. The series includes authored and edited collections – from early career and established scholars – addressing past, present and future childhood research issues from a global context.

Also available in the series:

Feminist Research for 21st-Century Childhoods: Common Worlds Methods,
edited by B. Denise Hodgins
Feminists Researching Gendered Childhoods: Generative Entanglements,
edited by Jayne Osgood and Kerry H. Robinson
Theorizing Feminist Ethics of Care in Early Childhood Practice,
edited by Rachel Langford
More-Than-Human Literacies in Early Childhood,
Abigail Hackett
The Early Childhood Educator,
edited by Rachel Langford and Brooke Richardson
Anthropocene Childhoods,
Emily Ashton
Feminist New Materialism, Girlhood and the School Ball
Toni Ingram

Feminist New Materialism, Girlhood, and the School Ball

Toni Ingram

BLOOMSBURY ACADEMIC
LONDON • NEW YORK • OXFORD • NEW DELHI • SYDNEY

BLOOMSBURY ACADEMIC
Bloomsbury Publishing Plc
50 Bedford Square, London, WC1B 3DP, UK
1385 Broadway, New York, NY 10018, USA
29 Earlsfort Terrace, Dublin 2, Ireland

BLOOMSBURY, BLOOMSBURY ACADEMIC and the Diana logo
are trademarks of Bloomsbury Publishing Plc

First published in Great Britain 2023
Paperback edition published 2025

Copyright © Toni Ingram, 2023

Toni Ingram has asserted her right under the Copyright,
Designs and Patents Act, 1988, to be identified as Author of this work.

For legal purposes the Acknowledgements on p. ix constitute an
extension of this copyright page.

Series design by Anna Berzovan
Cover image: Becoming school ball-girl, 2017 © Toni Ingram

All rights reserved. No part of this publication may be reproduced or
transmitted in any form or by any means, electronic or mechanical,
including photocopying, recording, or any information storage or retrieval
system, without prior permission in writing from the publishers.

Bloomsbury Publishing Plc does not have any control over, or responsibility for,
any third-party websites referred to or in this book. All internet addresses given
in this book were correct at the time of going to press. The author and publisher
regret any inconvenience caused if addresses have changed or sites have
ceased to exist, but can accept no responsibility for any such changes.

A catalogue record for this book is available from the British Library.

A catalog record for this book is available from the Library of Congress.

Library of Congress Cataloging-in-Publication Data

Names: Ingram, Toni, author.
Title: Feminist new materialism, girlhood, and the school ball / Toni Ingram.
Description: London ; New York : Bloomsbury Academic, 2023. | Series: Feminist thought in
childhood research | Includes bibliographical references and index. |
Summary: "Applies feminist new materialist ideas to the study of girlhood and the school ball,
building on the social theory of Barad, Bennett, Best, Deleuze and Guattari"– Provided by publisher.
Identifiers: LCCN 2023019427 (print) | LCCN 2023019428 (ebook) | ISBN 9781350165724 (hardback) |
ISBN 9781350165731 (ebook) | ISBN 9781350165748 (epub)
Subjects: LCSH: Teenage girls–Social life and customs. | High school
girls–Social life and customs. | Balls (parties)–Social aspects. |
High school student activities–Social aspects. | Feminist theory. | Materialism.
Classification: LCC HQ798 .I56 2023 (print) | LCC HQ798 (ebook) |
DDC 305.235/2–dc23/eng/20230525
LC record available at https://lccn.loc.gov/2023019427
LC ebook record available at https://lccn.loc.gov/2023019428

ISBN: HB: 978-1-3501-6572-4
PB: 978-1-3502-1527-6
ePDF: 978-1-3501-6573-1
eBook: 978-1-3501-6574-8

Series: Feminist Thought in Childhood Research

Typeset by Integra Software Service Pvt. Ltd.

To find out more about our authors and books visit www.bloomsbury.com
and sign up for our newsletters.

Contents

List of figures		vi
Series editors' introduction		vii
Acknowledgements		ix
1	Becoming school ball-girl	1
2	Entanglements that matter	17
3	School ball-girl matter(ings)	39
4	Once upon a space and time	61
5	Becoming ball-girl-bodies	85
6	Ball-girl-date affections	113
7	Ever after … an ending of sorts	143
References		154
Index		173

Figures

4.1	Once upon a space and time	60
4.2	Ball venue-home-makeup-bodies-laptop-decorations …	70
4.3	Bodies-food-drinks-decorations-home-car-friends-cameras-parents-dates …	75
4.4	Dance floor-balloons-twinkly lights-moving bodies-tables-chairs-seated bodies …	78
4.5	Ball video still sequence	80
5.1	Becoming ball-girl-bodies	84
5.2	Ghost selfie	89
5.3	Beauty products-home-make-up artist-gender norms-nails-polish-jeans-leg-sofa-pink-head-hair-text …	90
5.4	Shoe-shopping-camera	93
5.5	High heels-dresses-legs-feet-nail polish-rug-jewellery-floor …	94
5.6	Walking video still sequence	98
6.1	Ball-girl-date affections	112
6.2	Ball-girl-date mattering	119
6.3	Ball-girl-date-dress-suit-corsage-gendered discourses-photographer-viewer …	123
6.4	Ball-girl-bodies-friends-dresses-decorations-camera …	126
6.5	Sticky affects	129
6.6	Girl-date-ball-entrance-photographer-decorations-camera-lighting-carpet-queue of students-people watching …	135
7.1	Becoming school ball-girl	142

Series editors' introduction

The series *Feminist Thought in Childhood Research* considers experimental and creative modes of researching and practising in childhood studies. Recognizing the complex neoliberal landscape and worrisome spaces of coloniality in the twenty-first century, the *Feminist Thought in Childhood Research* books provide a forum for cross-disciplinary, interdisciplinary and transdisciplinary conversations in childhood studies that engage feminist decolonial, anticolonial, more-than-human, new materialisms, posthumanist and other post-foundational perspectives that seek to reconfigure human experience. The series offers lively examples of feminist research praxis and politics that invite childhood studies scholars, students and educators to engage in collectively to imagine childhood otherwise.

Until now, childhood studies has been decidedly a human matter, focused on the needs of individual children (Taylor, 2013). In the Anthropocene (Colebrooke, 2012, 2013), however, other approaches to childhood that address the profound, human-induced ecological challenges facing our own and other species are emerging. As Taylor (2013) reminds us, if we are going to grapple with the socio-ecological challenges we face today, childhood studies needs to pay attention to the *more*-than-human, to the *non*-human others that inhabit our worlds and the *in*human. Towards this end, *Feminist Thought in Childhood Research* series challenges the humanist, linear and moral narratives (Colebrook, 2013; Haraway, 2013) of much of childhood studies by engaging with feminisms. As a feminist series, the books explore the inheritances of how to live in the Anthropocene and think about it in ways that are in tension with the Anthropocene itself.

The latest edition to the book series is authored by Toni Ingram and entitled *Feminist New Materialism, Girlhood, and the School Ball*. This volume makes an important contribution by inviting readers to engage with the complexities and challenges of the school ball and how gender might be understood through a posthumanist lens. It is a book that invites wonder at what else might be learnt about girlhood, and gendering practices in contemporary school contexts, when the starting place is everyday materialities infused with affective force that shift imaginaries through the telling of lively stories that cause a stutter in our thinking about gender when research is undertaken in different ways. Ingram offers multiple, interwoven and detailed analyses that draw upon her research encounters to provide powerful insights into the complexities of girlhood as it plays out in the neoliberal context of contemporary Aotearoa New Zealand. In paying close attention to the more-than-human nature of how gender is produced in moments – in places – in minute encounters, where bodies, materialities, humans, objects and atmospheres relationally work to disrupt received wisdom. Instead Ingram's writing dismantles, and reconfigures notions of individualized human agency and thereby arrives at rich, illuminating and endlessly complex accounts of gendering practices.

In dialogue with other books in the *Feminist Thought in Childhood Research* series, this volume stresses the significance of situated knowledge, and is invested in interrogating the politics of hierarchies of knowledge in relation to children and educational contexts. Aligned with other books in the series this volume advocates for a more-than-human ontology that holds the potential to challenge Global North, developmental and anthropocentric frames, with a particular interest in the intersection between feminist new materialist, indigenous and affect theories.

The book takes up the invitation offered by the series to rethink not only the politics of what counts as knowledge, but the kinds of research processes and practices that might be necessary to problematize taken-for-granted 'truths' and to take seriously the affective and material actualizations of these in everyday life. In the first book in the series the authors (Osgood & Robinson, 2019) proposed that feminist researchers should 'immerse [them]selves more fully in the intensities, flows, rhythms, affects and forces of children's entanglements with space, place and materiality' (p. 8). Ingram embraces this proposition by taking up a situated feminist approach to attuning to lived experiences in more-than-human worlds. She ultimately shares a passionate account of how research undertaken within a feminist new materialist tradition can generate fresh insights and important lessons that might push the field of childhood studies in novel directions.

Acknowledgements

This book has come into being through a constellation of invaluable people, things, ideas and experiences. A warm thank you to the girls who so generously shared their thoughts, photographs, videos and laughter. Thank you to the liaison teachers who helped facilitate the girls' participation and the principals who kindly opened their school doors to the research.

Two bright stars helped guide the way along this journey. Thank you Louisa Allen for your continual support, encouragement and astute advice. Your work continues to inspire me, as does your commitment to making the landscape of gender, sexualities and schooling a more socially just and positive place for young people. Barbara Grant, I am very grateful for your generosity of time, support and the countless things you do to nurture the brains and hearts of fellow academics. Thank you for welcoming me into the cherished space of the Women Writing Away retreats and for making the world of academia a much brighter place.

My thanks to the Feminist Thought in Childhood Research book series editorial team for helping bring this book to fruition. Thank you, as always, to my friends and family for their love, encouragement and all-round fabulousness. A special mention goes to my parents for setting the example of capability and creativity, and The Committee for the years of friendship and always having great conversation and laughter on the agenda. And to Tamara Nyholt, thank you for being there for everything and anything. Thank you for your unwavering love and support, and everything in-between.

Extracts from Chapter Five are part of a previously published paper: Ingram, T. (2019). Girls and the school ball: A matter(ing) *of* space and time. *Emotion, Space and Society*, 33. https://doi/10.1016/j.emospa.2019.100621

A section in Chapter Six has been explored in more depth in a previously published paper: Ingram, T. (2022). 'I feel pretty': Beauty as an affective-material process. *Feminist Theory*. 23(2), 285–300. https://doi/10.1177/14647001211000015

A section in Chapter Seven is part of a previously published paper: Ingram, T. (2022). (Un)romantic becomings: Girls, sexuality-assemblages and the school ball. *Girlhood Studies: An Interdisciplinary Journal*, 15(2), 71–88.

1

Becoming school ball-girl

School balls and proms are often heralded as an important milestone or 'rite of passage' for high school students. These familiar narratives frequently draw on developmental logic to construct the school ball as a significant moment on a coming-of-age trajectory – a sentiment reminiscent of *Cinderella* where the ball is a turning point or gateway into a new world. For Cinderella, the ball is a pivotal point of transformation from her mundane existence to her 'happily ever after'. Cinderella, of course, is a fairy-tale laced with magic and enchantment, a literary classic from another time and place. This book is interested in how the school ball comes to *matter* in the twenty-first-century schooling context. It too is a tale, one of shimmers and lively entanglements: material things, spaces, ideas and imaginings that collaboratively produce girls, sexuality and the school ball.

While known internationally by various names – the prom, school formal, grad, debs – these events often comprise a familiar landscape involving months of planning and preparation, beauty-body practices, formal dresses and tuxedos, feelings of excitement and anticipation, disappointment and regret. Enduring 'rite of passage' themes can be traced through the legacy of debutante balls: a classed 'coming out' ritual where girls from wealthy families made a formal debut into society (Marling, 2004). These strategic events were fashionable in England from the late eighteenth to early twentieth century, providing parents with the opportunity to facilitate 'beneficial' marriages for their daughters (Richardson, 2020). As British citizens migrated to other parts of the world, so too did the debutante ritual. In America, for instance, the debutante ball gained traction as a means of delineating an emerging upper class in the form of newly wealthy merchants and professionals (Richardson, 2020). Formal balls then moved into the schooling context, and by the 1940s, the high school prom was firmly established in the United States (Marling, 2004).

In Aotearoa New Zealand, school balls are a legacy of colonialism and have become a time-honoured ritual for many senior students. These events are an intriguing blend of contemporary culture and tradition. While they evolve with each generation, they continue to be deeply woven with traditional ideas of femininity, masculinity and heterosexuality (Best, 2000). This book explores the potential of feminist new materialist thought for expanding the scope of 'who or what comes to matter' in this schooling practice (Barad, 2007, p. 35); how we might understand the material-discursive practices associated with the event, the becoming of bodies and sexuality. The school ball is conceptualized as a dynamic assemblage of all manner of 'things' including bodies, spaces, clothing, photographs, hopes and feelings. Through this frame, I explore how shifting entanglements of human and more-than-human forces produce what we come to understand as the school ball-girl. In doing so, the book offers insight into (some of) the many material-affective forces at play in the becoming of gender and sexualities at school. And, in turn, the questions and quandaries this approach opens up for feminist research(ers) interested in the rich material-discursive landscape of gender, sexualities and schooling.

Setting the scene

Schools have long been recognized as key social sites that (re)produce and regulate young people's gendered and sexual identities (Allen, 2005; Epstein & Johnson, 1998; Kehily, 2002; Mac an Ghaill, 1996; Rasmussen, 2006). An important body of work demonstrates the myriad ways gender and sexualities are discursively and materially constituted through a variety of schooling structures and practices, including curriculum and pedagogy (Alldred & David, 2007; Allen, 2005), daily routines and practices (Pascoe, 2007; Youdell, 2005), spatial and material arrangements (Allen, 2013a; O'Donoghue, 2006), school 'rules' and policy (Pomerantz, 2007; Raby, 2010) and peer group relations (Kehily, 2002; Renold, 2005). Sexualities and schooling are a complicated terrain, where young people negotiate a plethora of sexual meanings and positionings on a daily basis. The discourse of childhood 'innocence' (Egan & Hawkes, 2008; Robinson, 2008), for instance, coupled with the idea that student sexualities need to be 'controlled', offer young people multiple, often-contradictory ways for understanding themselves as sexual subjects (Allen, 2007).

Theoretically, sexualities and schooling research has been heavily influenced by the discursive or linguistic turn. The work of Michel Foucault (1976, 1980, 1983) and Judith Butler (1990, 1993) has been instrumental in enabling researchers to examine the various discourses circulating in the schooling environment and how these meanings shape young people's gender and sexual subjectivities. From a Foucauldian (1976) perspective, the school ball can be understood as an institutionalized ritual of governmentality constituted through normative discourses of gender and (hetero)sexuality. School rituals, such as dances, are charged with sexual meanings and increased surveillance of young people's bodies and behaviour (Best, 2000; Pascoe, 2007; Smith, 2014). Existing studies firmly establish school balls as heteronormative spaces where heterosexuality is normalized and privileged as the norm (Allen, 2006; Quinlivan & Town, 1999). For girls, ideas of female beauty, feminine respectability and heterosexuality are intimately connected to the performance and policing of girls' sexual and gendered identities. Dominant discourses may reinforce or sit in contention with other meanings of gender and sexuality constituted within the schooling environment: for instance, the expectation for young people to embody normative gendered discourses at the school ball, such as hetero-desirable masculinity and femininity, might sit in tension with the constitution of schools as non-sexual spaces (Smith et al., 2016).

The feminist motivation for this project stems from my long-standing concern over the enduring regulation of girlhood sexualities within the schooling context. Every year, issues related to school balls and proms emerge in the media: this commentary predominantly focusing on girls. News headlines such as 'Scramble to be the belle of the ball' (Tait, 2014) and 'Frock horror as girls turn up in the same dress' (Eriksen, 2012) offer particular ideas about girls' engagements with the schooling practice. Girls are often constructed as heavily invested in the school ball, for example, excessive spending on dresses and beauty work is a common point of conjecture in the media (Gorrell Anstiss, 2012; Jones, 2013). Enmeshed in this presumed investment is the construction of girls as catty and competitive. The following media quote exemplifies this construction: 'They are like bridezillas ... girls are so quick to turn on each other. It's horrible', states one dress store representative (Gorrell Anstiss, 2012). These accounts are heavily dominated by adult opinion, often stemming from a place of 'protection' and 'concern' for girls' well-being. Sadly, young people's voices are frequently absent in these debates: an issue that fuelled the development of this project.

Media interest also highlights how school balls and proms are powerful sites for the policing of girls' bodies, clothing and behaviour. In the United States, reporting of girls being refused entry to the prom due to 'revealing' or 'inappropriate' dresses continues to prompt international debate and condemnation (Bahou & Orenstein, 2016; Valenti, 2015). In Aotearoa New Zealand, the headline 'Catholic girls' school's strict ball rules: no cleavage, no backless dresses, no taking off shoes and your date must be serious' is another example (Bilby & Gaffaney, 2016). These articles contribute to wider media commentary where school-girl bodies and clothing are continually under surveillance: the reporting of girls being told to lengthen skirts to 'stop distracting male staff and students' is yet another example (Roy, 2016; Rutherford, 2016; Schoultz, 2016). Feminist scholarship has drawn critical attention to the regulation of girls' bodies through school dress codes and peer culture (Pomerantz, 2007; Raby, 2010): discourses of 'appropriate' femininity and moral panic around girls' provocative dress an integral element in this ongoing surveillance.

Dominant discourses of gender and heterosexuality are undeniably potent and enduring forces in how school balls are understood and experienced. Amy Best's *Prom Night* (2000) provides a valuable analysis of young people's experiences of the American prom in relation to dominant cultural understandings. Best argues the prom is primarily constructed as a feminine space, where girls are expected, or perceived to, heavily invest in the occasion: an idea clearly reinforced through media commentary. Attending the prom is often constructed as a central aspect of being and becoming feminine, providing girls with the opportunity to 'solidify and display their feminine identities' (Best, 2000, p. 35). As proms work to secure girls' investments in beauty-body work, girls are required to navigate traditional discourses of femininity that shape what is deemed 'acceptable' and 'expected' behaviour – how girls are expected to look, dress and act. Girls are required to negotiate the fine line between looking 'attractive' yet not revealing too much, the latter falling into the treacherous realm of 'skank' or 'slut'. The policing of girls' sartorial choices through the regulatory 'slut' discourse has been widely documented (Cowie & Lees, 1981; Kehily, 2002; Raby, 2010), and school balls are no exception.

Theoretical tools from feminist post-structuralism and queer theory have been invaluable for exploring young people's complex negotiation of dominant discourses, including both the accommodation of and resistance to pervasive norms. Although the prom can be viewed as a deeply conformist space, young people have the potential to resist or rework dominant meanings to varied extents (Best, 2000): for example, Lee Smith's (2012, 2014) New Zealand-based research highlights how some girls find strategies to subvert and challenge conventional codes of feminine dress and heterosexuality. This work demonstrates how girls do not passively absorb dominant cultural meanings surrounding school balls, such as the notion of the ball as a romantic space (Smith, 2014); instead, within a feminist post-structural frame, some girls have the capacity to resist and rework dominant meanings. Here, agency is located in the human capacity to strategically negotiate discourses of femininity and (hetero)sexuality; therefore, girls can be conceptualized as active and agentic in the (discursive) constitution of their gender and sexual subjectivities (Weedon, 1987).

Alongside a complex discursive landscape, school balls are rich tapestries of material things, bodies, spaces and sensations. It is this materiality – lively (un)predictable matter – that is at the heart of this book and the perspective of the school ball it offers. Drawing on feminist new materialisms, in particular the work of feminist philosopher and physicist Karen Barad (2007), the aim is to explore materiality as co-constitutive *with* discourse in the becoming of girls, sexuality and the school ball. Attention shifts to material objects such as high-heeled shoes, spatial configurations like the dance floor, corporeal practices and affective relations: feelings, sensations and the atmosphere. Drawing on Barad's framework of *agential realism*, the ball-girl is conceptualized as intra-actively becoming through lively assemblages of multiple forces, including but not limited to discourse. This approach does not negate the significance of discourse, but rather entails a reconfiguring of the relationship between discourse and materiality, human and more-than-human, to one of mutual entanglement. I am interested in how this invites a reconfiguring of gender and sexuality as not solely attributable to, or emanating from, the human; instead, might be thought of as an emergent process or becoming, untethered from the human body and identity (Allen, 2013b; Fox & Alldred, 2013).

A central aim of the book is to develop an understanding of *becoming ball-girl* as a dynamic, shifting process, where bodies and femininities are emergent and relationally produced. Central to this endeavour is an interest in the potential of a relational approach for reimagining girls and the school ball in ways that rework or avoid popular constructions, for instance, as a developmental 'milestone' and girls as 'competitive', 'excessive' and highly invested in the ball. I consider how a reconfiguring of gender and sexuality within a new materialist frame might help shift understandings of girls and the school ball beyond the moral panics, romanticized or reductive accounts prevalent in the media (Osgood & Giugni, 2015). These aims are integral to the feminist intentions and politics underpinning the project, including an underlying sense of unease with the developmental and normative logic used to justify the regulation of girls' behaviour and bodies. It signals a desire to ask *what more* might be going on here? (Allen, 2013b; Blaise, 2013). The *more* in this project encompasses all manner of material and affective forces – atmosphere, feelings, intensities and sensations – 'things' that might not be easily explained by the discursive alone. The *more* signals an ethico-onto-epistemological reorientation in how we come to 'know' and 'be' in the world, including who and what comes to matter and how (Barad, 2007).

This feminist project is firmly located within the growing field of educational research drawing on posthumanist and new materialist thought to help (re)conceptualize sexuality beyond a discursive and human focus (see Allen & Rasmussen, 2017; Allen, 2015b, 2018; Garland-Levett, 2020; Renold & Ringrose, 2017a). Drawing on feminist new materialisms, Louisa Allen (2015b) maps 'a "new" ontology of *sexuality at school*' where sexuality is conceptualized as *becoming* via entangled human and nonhuman intra-actions (p. 941, italics in original). Rather than viewing sexuality as purely discursively constituted, that is a subject position(ality), Allen draws on Baradian understandings of matter and meaning to consider how these two elements are co-constitutive in sexuality's becoming. Allen offers a feminist new materialist understanding of sexuality 'as emerging through co-constitutive entanglements of and between meaning, practices, material artefacts, humans and things of all kinds' (2015b, p. 944). Within this framing, sexuality is not something that belongs to an individual (i.e. girl), nor is it a discursive position that individuals 'take up', but rather in Allen's words, 'sexuality at school is a never-ending enfolding of nonhuman, human, practices, objects, affect, motility, discourse, nature, smells, sound and other earthly elements (including those that are unrepresentable in language and/or known to humans' (2015b, p. 951). Applying this idea to girls, sexuality and the school ball, this 'never-ending enfolding' encompasses material-spatial arrangements, such as the school ball entrance, a feeling in the atmosphere, the height of a date or the height of a shoe.

A feminist new materialist ontology of sexuality signals a dynamic open-ended process that blurs conventional boundaries of matter/discourse, human/nonhuman and nature/culture. As a result, neither matter nor discourse, human or nonhuman is privileged, as they are mutually constitutive in the production of sexuality. The nature/culture dichotomy is also destabilized in that sexuality cannot be understood purely as nature (i.e. biologically determined) or culture (i.e. socially constructed) because neither pre-exists the other. Defining sexuality in relation to these binary notions becomes untenable, instead, 'nature and culture emerge in the moment of their coming into relation with each other' (Allen, 2015b, p. 943). The potential of this ontological reconfiguration is a destabilizing of related dichotomies that are premised on a nature/culture divide, such as natural/unnatural, real/constructed and innate/learned (Barad, 2012a). This in turn, helps disrupt the dichotomous logic that often underpins familiar constructions of girls and the school ball found in popular culture and media.

Accounting for more-than-human forces in the becoming of sexuality is an attempt to avoid the anthropocentrism that often pervades sexualities research (Fox & Alldred, 2013) and educational research more generally (Snaza & Weaver, 2015; Taylor & Hughes, 2016). As Hultman and Lenz Taguchi (2010, p. 539) explain, anthropocentric thinking privileges 'humans and human meaning-making as the sole constitutive force' of our world, a positioning they argue to be problematic as it 'reduces our world to a social world and neglects all other nonhuman forces that are at play'. Within sexualities research, an anthropocentric frame of reference privileges the human and individual body as the locus of sexuality, constraining how sexuality is understood and defined (Fox & Alldred, 2013). A new materialist ontology enables things that have gone unnoticed or considered peripheral in sexualities and gender research to become of interest, including space, time and material objects such as mobile phones, clothing and furniture (Allen, 2013a, 2013b; Ringrose & Rawlings, 2015; Taylor, 2013). I am interested in how foregrounding the multiplicity of relations invites understandings of sexuality as at least *materialdiscursive* (Allen, 2015b), thus opening up different questions in relation to girls, sexuality and the school ball; while simultaneously, making more familiar questions redundant, such as those based on humanist framings of subjectivity or agency.

A feminist new materialist approach to the school ball

Across a range of disciplines, including feminist theory, there is a renewed interest in and rethinking of materiality (Alaimo & Hekman, 2008; Barad, 2007; Bennett, 2010; Haraway, 2008; Hird, 2009). For Diana Coole and Samantha Frost (2010, p. 3), the theoretical movement termed new materialism(s) signals a 'returning to the most fundamental questions about matter and the place of embodied humans within the material world'. New materialisms are a diverse and interdisciplinary field, or as MacLure (2015, p. 95) puts it, a 'disparate, yet disparately connected body of work', encompassing varying approaches and conceptual tools for thinking about the productivity and liveliness of matter. As others have noted, the heterogeneity of new materialisms makes it difficult to define or summarize; instead, Elizabeth St. Pierre with co-authors Alecia Jackson and Lisa Mazzei (2016) usefully draw attention to two important conditions that make this form of inquiry possible and necessary: namely, 'an *ethical imperative to rethink the nature of being* and a *heightened curiosity and accompanying experimentation*' (p. 106, italics in original). This book is an attempt towards such curiosity and experimentation; it signals an openness towards different questions in an effort to open up new ways of conceptualizing girls, sexuality and the school ball. This attempt posits curiosity and ethics as entangled, in that 'it is a curiosity about what might be possible that enables us to imagine and create a different, more ethical existence' (St. Pierre et al., 2016, p. 102). This curiosity and experimentation requires new concepts that help 'think and live differently', including what questions we might ask of data and what is possible to 'know' (St. Pierre et al., 2016, p. 106).

The theoretical approach (and indeed curiosity) underpinning the book is indebted to feminist scholarship within the broader field of new materialisms. A range of names denote these theoretical approaches, including new feminist materialism (van der Tuin, 2011), material feminisms (Alaimo & Hekman, 2008), agential realist (Barad, 2003, 2007), relational materialist (Hultman & Lenz Taguchi, 2010) and PhEmaterialisms (Ringrose et al., 2018; Strom et al., 2019). While these various terms signal different theoretical influences and conceptual approaches to new materialisms, they share a commitment to theorizing matter as co-constitutive with discourse, where neither is foundational (Taylor & Ivinson, 2013). Recognizing the force of matter, both human and nonhuman (Bennett, 2010), brings a challenge to humanist framings of agency, human supremacy and separability (Barad, 2007; Braidotti, 2013). Central to feminism is 'a perspective and method that has been about reconceptualizing and reconfiguring the human and what it means to be human' (Osgood & Robinson, 2019, p. 53): this focus remains central in a feminist new materialist approach and this book.

Feminist scholarship offers an important 'commentary on the linguistic turn', which entails a rethinking of the status of discourse and language in research practices (van der Tuin, 2011, p. 271). Barad, for instance, calls attention to the power that has been granted to language and its privileged role in shaping our understandings of the world (2003, 2007). As such, Barad proposes a posthumanist framework for understanding how discursive practices are related to the material world and vice versa, in a way that avoids binary logic and a privileging of one over the other. It is not simply a call to account for matter as well as discourse, but rather a rethinking of how these forces are entangled and co-constitutive in the world's becoming. Reconfiguring the relations between the human and nonhuman, matter and meaning, signals a heightened sense of response-ability for how knowledge gets produced (Barad, 2007; Haraway, 2008). For feminist new materialisms, this entails an ethico-political imperative for opening up fundamental concepts central to feminist theorizing, including ontology, epistemology, ethics, agency and power (Alaimo & Hekman, 2008). How these concepts are understood inevitably shapes how we conceive of our relationship to what it is we investigate, and therefore how we understand how knowledge is produced.

Feminist new materialisms form part of a larger terrain characterized as posthumanism: a 'constellation' of diverse theories, approaches and concepts underpinned by a commitment to destabilizing the centrality of the human in the production of knowledge (Taylor, 2016, p. 6). Posthumanism critiques the notion of human supremacy where 'man is the measure of all things' (Barad, 2007; Braidotti, 2013). In doing so, it destabilizes an assumed distinction between human and nonhuman on which humanism relies. As Barad (2007, p. 136) explains: 'Posthumanism doesn't presume the separateness of any-"thing", let alone the alleged spatial, ontological and epistemological distinction that sets humans apart'. Posthumanism calls into question the privileged position of human separability by reconfiguring understandings of the human as always in-relation with nonhuman and more-than-human forces. For Barad, this signals a posthuman ethics – an ethics of mattering (or worlding) where all bodies, human and nonhuman, come to matter (in both senses of the word). This is not an ethics concerned with the consequences of our interactions with the world as separate entities; rather, it is an ethics of mattering which involves 'taking account of the entangled materializations of which we are a part' (Barad, 2007, p. 384). Crucial to this idea is an understanding of ethics, ontology and epistemology as inseparable (see chapter two for this discussion).

New materialist thinking offers potential in moving feminist theory beyond what has been described as an 'impasse' – a gridlock argued to be a result of the contemporary linguistic turn (Alaimo & Hekman, 2008, p. 1). While a discursive focus has produced complex and important analyses of the connections between power, language, knowledge and subjectivity, this approach is premised on a language/reality dichotomy, in that reality is entirely constituted through language. As a result, materiality such as the ball-girl-body becomes products of discourse. It is a one-way linear process. Feminist new materialisms offer a way of emphasizing the agential force (Barad, 2007) of school ball materialities in an entangled reciprocal relationship with discourse. Acknowledging the force of matter sparks new questions for rethinking girls and the school ball: How does materiality of the body and other matter contribute to school ball experiences and corporeal practices? How might material forces contribute to the production of discourses themselves?

These questions posit discourse not as prior, or separate to the material, rather they become inseparable and co-constitutional, as indicated in the term *material-discursive* (Barad, 2007). The aim is to 'give material factors their due' in the constitution of discourse and reality (Coole & Frost, 2010, p. 3): bodies, corporeal practices, objects, spaces and temporalities are not separate 'things' or passive background to the ball, but co-constitutive in its becoming. In this sense, it is not a 'move beyond' a discursive construction, but a 'move to' a material-discursive understanding of the school ball (Barad, 2014, p. 176). Conceiving matter and meaning as entangled posits nature as inseparable from culture; hence, Barad uses the term 'naturalcultural practices' to signal this inextricable relationship (2007, p. 32). Within the context of the school ball, it means the possibilities for becoming ball-girl cannot be reduced to either nature or culture, as this would presume one is separate from and privileged over the other; thus, arguments that are premised on a nature/culture divide become irrelevant.

New materialist thinking within the field of education has been instrumental in shaping the purpose and development of this book. For the feminist educational researcher, posthumanist and new materialist thought opens up possibilities for exploring educational practices in relational and non-hierarchical ways, where the human, more-than-human and other-than-human are entangled in knowledge production (Allen, 2018; Hackett, 2022; Lenz Taguchi, 2010; Osgood & Robinson, 2019; Ringrose et al., 2019; Snaza & Weaver, 2015; Taylor & Hughes, 2016). Taylor contends, posthumanist research practices 'offer a new ethics of engagement for education by including the nonhuman in questions about *who matters and what counts*' (2016, p. 5, italics in original). The movement termed *PhEmaterialism* (Ringrose et al., 2019; Strom et al., 2019) is an example of the ethical shift away from humanist and anthropocentric logic within educational research, towards a decentring of human subjectivity and human exceptionalism. Bringing together feminist posthumanisms and new materialisms, PhEmaterialism argues 'we need to put theories/concepts to work in education and educational research which can better account for the multiple, entangled, ever-shifting, difference-rich nature of processes of teaching, learning, schooling, and activism' (Strom et al., 2019, p. 2). This movement responds to the call for response-able feminist research (Barad, 2007; Haraway, 2008) that attends to relational, complex and entangled becomings, rather than prioritizing the human as the 'knowing subject'. In short, there is a shift 'from *who* participates in knowledge production to the *what and how*', including material objects and affective forces (Ringrose et al., 2019, p. 11, italics in original).

Within the context of this book, Karen Barad's posthumanist framework of agential realism helps bring the *what* and *how* to the fore. Barad brings together feminist philosophy with quantum physics to offer an ontologically different way of understanding the world. Foregrounding an ethics of mattering, Barad encourages us to think about the human, and indeed the world, as *entanglements*: in their words, 'existence is not an individual affair' (2007, p. ix). Barad's work provides conceptual tools to not only account for the human and nonhuman, but also how material and discursive factors are entangled together in the becoming (or mattering) of the school ball-girl. Barad's concept of *intra-action* is central to this approach as it offers a significant ontological shift in how we conceive the relationship between discourse and materiality, human and nonhuman, space and time: from discrete separate entities to one of mutual entanglement and ontological inseparability (see chapter two for a detailed explanation of this concept). The concept of intra-action offers an expansive rethinking of gender and sexualities from a focus on the human (as a discrete body/entity) towards dynamic becomings and flows involving all manner of forces (Allen, 2015b; Osgood & Robinson, 2019). It entails a reconfiguring of conventional boundaries of the human 'subject', bodies and sexuality. There is a shift from thinking about the human (as subject) and material objects as separate, to emphasizing their entanglement and what gets produced in the in-between. Sexuality, as mentioned, is no longer solely located in the individual human body, but becomes through entangled human and more-than-human forces: In short, it becomes an emergent process (Allen, 2015b).

While the purpose of the project is to explore girls' engagements with the school ball, it attempts to do so in a way that does not wholly centre or prioritize the human. It is not that the human or human actions are ignored; rather, the human is conceptualized in a flattened rather than hierarchical relationship with the surrounding world (Hultman & Lenz Taguchi, 2010). Drawing on the words of Jane Bennett (2010, p. ix), the book seeks to 'highlight what is typically cast in the shadow': material objects, spatial configurations and affective forces. Feminist new materialism establishes all manner of things and forces within a 'confederacy of meaning-making' (Taylor & Ivinson, 2013, p. 666), where meanings are emergent and inseparable from the materiality of the world – both human and more-than-human. The term *more-than-human* is used in the book to refer to the forces, energies and things that are recognized as not human. Lorimer (2013, p. 61) describes the category of more-than-human as 'the embodied, affective and skilful dimensions of our multispecies worlds that often elude research methodologies preoccupied with human representations'.

In relation to the school ball, the more-than-human encompasses all manner of materialities, affects and forces understood to affect and be affected by one another (Deleuze, 1988), as they connect or intra-act (Barad, 2007) in continually shifting assemblages. As such, the human becomes one element amid a confederacy of material-discursive and affective forces that produce girls, sexuality and the school ball. The potential here is a generative and expansive understanding of gender and sexuality as continually remade and reworked, including constraints and capacities (Allen, 2018; Osgood & Robinson, 2019).

Becoming school ball-girl (and structure of the book)

The conceptual project throughout this book is to establish girls, sexuality and the school ball as intra-actively becoming through shifting, dynamic entanglements (Barad, 2007). This entails an ontologically different way of thinking about girls as 'subjects', reconfiguring how we conceptually understand bodies, femininities and subjectivity. Within a new materialist onto-epistemology, humans and other matter are no longer discrete pre-existing entities; instead, they come into being through their relations. The human (and its capacities) are thought of relationally as opposed to being considered an independent, autonomous individual. Here, the girl and ball are no longer separate entities. The girl becomes with the ball and the ball becomes with the girl (Hultman & Lenz Taguchi, 2010): one is not prior to the other. The hyphen in ball-girl denotes this intra-active entanglement.

Dissolving the boundary between the girl and the ball provides openings for rethinking the human 'subject' (i.e. the ball-girl) not as a fixed being but as becoming – a process not a state (Coole, 2013). The ball-girl becomes emergent phenomena (Barad, 2007), and as such, notions of subjectivity extend beyond the individual towards a relational mattering involving an array of forces. It might be thought of as 'a more opened out subjectivity' that exceeds both the human and discourse (Osgood & Giugni, 2015, p. 349). Sexual subjectivity within a new materialist frame does not pertain to a fully formed individual subject, but as 'the conditions of emergence'; these conditions shift and vary depending on the assembled relations (Allen, 2018, p. 130). This encourages us to think about how girls, sexuality and the school ball might come to matter differently, not as independent entities but as thoroughly entangled and emergent.

A feminist new materialist approach to *becoming school ball-girl* reconfigures the human body. Bodies do not have inherent properties or clearly defined boundaries (Barad, 2007); rather, they congeal or emerge through particular configurings at any given moment. To develop this idea, the book explores ball-girl-bodies as continually (re)made via human and more-than-human entanglements of matter, ideas and affects (flows, energies). This means ball-girl-bodies are not solely produced through dominant structural forces, such as discourses of femininity; rather, they become fleeting, contingent and multiple. Through a reconfiguring of the relationship between bodies and material things, the subject/object divide is blurred. I am interested in what this might mean for how we think about gendered bodies and notions of causality and agency: for example, simple cause and effect logic becomes untenable within new materialist thought as it is premised on a subject/object divide. Humanist notions of agency as located within the individual also no longer make sense. Instead, agential realism offers a dynamic reconfiguring of causality and agency, where gendered bodies, capacities and constraints become emergent and open-ended. Conditions of (im)possibility are dynamic, continually reconfigured and reconfiguring.

In thinking about femininities, it is easy to centre the human – this study is indeed concerned with girls and the capacities they have within the school ball space. However, rather than conceiving girls, bodies and femininities as stable or fixed entities/identities or purely discursively produced, becoming ball-girl is a dynamic shifting process where bodies and femininities are relationally produced. Thinking about femininities not as something we 'are' but as *becomings* enables an understanding of femininities as multiple, messy and nonlinear. They are open-ended, never complete or closed. A central idea is *becoming school ball-girl* does not reveal a true or authentic femininity or identity; rather, it is a making and unmaking of bodies through entanglements of things, forces, discursive practices, histories and desires. This approach marks a shift in focus, from what a ball-girl *is* to what a ball-girl can do and become, and what forces are implicated in these dynamic becomings.

To do this work, the book draws on a research project conducted in Aotearoa New Zealand focusing on the discursive and material forces that produce girls, sexuality and the school ball. Forty-one girls voluntarily took part in the study, sharing their ideas and experiences of the ball through a range of visual and verbal methods, including participant-generated photographs and video, group discussions and individual conversations. As the school ball is an event for senior students, research participants were in their final two years of secondary schooling – Year 12 and 13 (aged 16–18 years) – from two state-funded urban secondary schools (Years 9–13): one school was co-educational and the other an all-girls school. Both schools comprised diverse ethnic and socio-economic student populations. Participant ethnicities were self-identified and included Māori, New Zealand European/Pākehā, Sri Lankan, Chinese, Korean, Indian, European, NZ/German and European/American. The marketing for the research would have appealed to students identifying as 'girls', and participants did not need to disclose whether they were transgender or cisgender. Similarly, participants were not asked to disclose details regarding sexual orientation, although during the conversations, participants spoke about current relationships, which included both male and female partners.

In order to explore the becoming of the school ball-girl through dynamic entanglements, the following questions are central: What are the possibilities for becoming ball-girl if matter is taken into account? How do human and more-than-human relations limit and extend ball-girl becomings? And, how do entanglements of material-discursive and affective forces produce particular ball-girl capacities: actions, feelings and desires? The next chapter outlines the theoretical and conceptual tools crucial to exploring these questions, including agential realism and the concept of intra-action (Barad, 2007), the notion of sexuality-as-assemblage (Allen, 2013b; Fox & Alldred, 2013) and theories of affect (Ahmed, 2004b; Deleuze, 1988). I consider how these concepts enable an understanding of *how* matter comes to matter in the emergent becoming of girls, sexuality and the school ball. The discussion explains the onto-epistemological shift entailed in a feminist new materialist approach and how it reconfigures the relationship between discursive practices and materiality, where matter and meaning become inseparable. Establishing the entanglement of materiality and discourse, I explain how the school ball and ball-girl emerge as phenomena produced through dynamic processes of intra-activity (Barad, 2007). It is an onto-epistemological approach that establishes an inseparable relationship between being and knowing, where entangled research relations are implicated in the production of phenomena.

Chapter three brings together media commentary, fairy-tale and academic scholarship that inform current understandings and perceptions of girls and the school ball. Continuing the discussion in this opening chapter, I examine the ways school balls and proms have previously been theorized and the dominant understandings that cohere around these events. Specific attention is given to theoretical approaches for understanding the materialization of girls' bodies (Butler, 1990, 1993; Barad, 2003). I consider how Barad's posthumanist performative approach extends the work of Butler to theorize materiality as co-constitutive with discourse in the materialization of ball-girl-bodies. The discussion highlights how feminist new materialisms and theories of affect offer a different approach to thinking about girls' bodies and 'agency' than previous analyses of the school ball. Attention moves away from a solely human focus (and the idea of bodies having agency) to explore the ways forces that circulate in an assemblage produce capacities and constraints.

Chapter four offers a rethinking of the school ball in relation to time and space. Rather than a fixed space or moment in time, the chapter brings together the Baradian notion of *spacetimemattering*, the concept of assemblage (Bennett, 2005; Deleuze & Guattari, 1987) and theories of affect (Deleuze, 1988), to conceptualize the school ball as a continual process of becoming. I consider how the school ball is intra-actively produced through multiple spaces and temporalities, troubling the idea of the school ball as a milestone or discrete moment in time along a 'coming of age' trajectory (Best, 2000). Space, time and matter emerge as entangled forces, co-constituting what we come to understand as the school ball. In mapping the relations in-between time, space and matter, the chapter blurs the conventional borders of the school ball as an isolated spatial-temporal event. This opens up ways of thinking about girls and this schooling practice that reworks or avoids popular narratives, including reductive or developmental logic used to justify the regulation of girls' behaviour.

The material-discursive and affective entanglements that produce the ball-girl-body are brought to the fore in chapter five. With a focus on beauty-body practices as material-discursive intra-activity, the chapter considers how relations limit and/or extend the capacities of ball-girl-bodies. It is a relational opening-up towards the 'what else' a ball-girl-body might do and become (Manning, 2013; Holford et al., 2013). Rather than fixed processes or something simply done *to* bodies, beauty-body practices can be thought of as multi-linear and affective matterings involving human and more-than-human forces. I consider how Barad's (2007) posthumanist performative approach to bodies highlights the materiality of the body and other matter as active forces in the becoming of ball-girl-bodies. The chapter argues there is no essential ball-girl-body; rather, bodies are material-discursive phenomena continually becoming through dynamic affective relations.

Popular cultural constructions of proms and school balls are infused with themes of romance. Chapter six brings together a feminist new materialist ontology of materiality (Barad, 2007; Bennett, 2010) and sexuality (Allen, 2015b; Fox & Alldred, 2013) with theories of affect (Ahmed, 2004b; Deleuze, 1988) to examine the affective relations in-between ball-girls and their dates. Ball-girl-date encounters are conceptualized as dynamic sexuality-assemblages of material objects, bodies, spaces and affects. Material things such as high-heeled shoes and photographs, affective-spatial 'hot spots' like the dance floor and school ball entrance, are considered vital forces in ball-girl-date encounters and the becoming of sexuality. A particular focus of the chapter is how affective relations produce ball-girl capacities – actions, feelings and desires – opening up a space for understanding ball-girl-date relations beyond a human and discursive focus.

Coalescing the central themes and ideas of the book, the final chapter does some of the traditional work of a conclusion yet is also an opening to new possibilities. I consider how a new materialist ontology entails an open-ended potential for the ball-girl and for research more generally. Conceptual framings of 'newness' and 'endings' are explored in relation to a feminist new materialist onto-epistemological framework, where an unknown and unending potential is inherent in this approach. The chapter considers the generative potential of feminist new materialisms for research involving young people, gender, sexualities and schooling – the invitations and openings such an approach might bring.

2

Entanglements that matter

Materiality is central to our world. We coexist in a lively world of matter, where forces swirl and shimmer, push and pull. New materialist scholarship attends to materiality in ways that foreground matter's dynamism (Barad, 2007; Bennett, 2010); rather than being passive, materiality entails 'an excess, force, vitality … that renders matter active, self-creative, productive, unpredictable' (Coole & Frost, 2010, p. 9). Recognizing the liveliness of matter is integral to a new materialist ethico-onto-epistemological understanding of the world. As Barad (2008, p. 122) argues: 'It is vitally important that we understand how matter matters': how matter is generative and productive in the world's becoming. Taking this call as the chapter's starting point, the coming discussion establishes the theoretical tools that help orient the book's attention to matter, including Barad's (2007) framework of agential realism, assemblage theory (Bennett, 2005; Deleuze & Guattari, 1987) and theories of affect (Ahmed, 2004b; Deleuze, 1988; Gregg & Seigworth, 2010). I outline key conceptual tools that enable a relational conceptualization of girls, sexuality and the school ball, that is not restricted to humanist and anthropocentric understandings or representational logic. Key to agential realism is a reconfiguring of the relationship between ethics, ontology and epistemology to one of inseparability. I consider the productive possibilities this offers for reworking conventional boundaries and dualisms associated with girls' bodies, sexuality and the school ball; the implications this has for notions of agency, causality and subjectivity; and the pertinent questions this raises for feminist politics and critique.

Feminist new materialism: conceptualizing the 'new'

Feminist research has long been interested in the material structures that shape the lives of girls and women. The established materialist feminism that emerged out of western Marxism (Hennessy & Ingraham, 1997), for instance, was concerned with the materiality of women's lives (i.e. material living conditions) structured through factors such as class, age and race. What might be considered distinct in the emerging analyses of material feminism or new materialisms is 'a keen interest in *engagements* with matter' (Hird, 2009, p. 330, italics in original). The 'new' here, is the conceptualization of matter as animate or agentic, rather than inert or background to human activity (Taylor & Ivinson, 2013). Accounting for matter as an agentive factor in processes of materialization (Barad, 2007) brings attention to the relationship between nature and culture, matter and discourse, human and nonhuman; and more broadly, raises questions about the nature of being, causality and responsibility.

While feminist theory is argued to be undergoing a 'material turn' (Alaimo & Hekman, 2008, p. 6) how 'new' a material focus is has been a point of debate (Ahmed, 2008; Davis, 2009; Irni, 2013; Todd, 2016; van der Tuin, 2008). Jones and Hoskins (2016) remind us that indigenous ontologies do not differentiate 'culture' from 'nature'. In Aotearoa New Zealand, for instance, entanglements of human and nature are embedded in traditional Māori thought. Ontologically, human beings and the natural world (e.g. rivers and mountains) are entangled in mutually constitutive relationships. Taylor and Ivinson (2013, p. 666) urge us to 'remember that the subject/object split inflicted by the legacy of Descartes is a western ontological problem exported via colonialism'. Within indigenous ontologies, the 'identity of "things" in the world is not understood as discrete or independent, but emerges through, and as, relations with everything else' (Jones & Hoskins, 2016, p. 80). While new materialisms might signal a rethinking of, and renewed attention to matter, we are reminded to treat this 'newness' with caution (Osgood & Robinson, 2019), amid the risk of colonizing, appropriating or ignoring indigenous cosmologies (Todd, 2016). When qualifying the 'newness' of new materialism, perhaps then, as St. Pierre, Jackson and Mazzei (2016, p. 100) succinctly note, 'the descriptor "new" does not necessarily announce something new but serves as an alert that we are determined to try to think differently'. For this research, it signals a 'different starting point' (Truman, 2019, p. 2) that attends to the more-than-human and liveliness of matter in the becoming of girls, sexuality and the school ball.

Amid debates of 'newness' also lies a question of whether feminist new materialisms are an extension of or radical break away from feminist post-structuralism (Davies, 2016; Osgood & Robinson, 2019). Post-structural theory has been invaluable for feminist researchers interested in the production and regulation of gender through discursive practices (Weedon, 1987). Butler's (1993) theory of gender performativity, for instance, has been vital in enabling an understanding of gender as a *doing*, rather than an attribute of individuals. This has provided feminist scholarship productive means for illustrating how young people are active in the constitution of their sexual and gender subjectivities, both accommodating and resisting discursive norms (Blaise, 2005; Davies, 1989; Kehily, 2002; Renold, 2005; Walkerdine, 1990; Youdell, 2004). As mentioned in the book's opening chapter, feminist post-structuralism and queer theory have been instrumental for identifying the discursive forces that shape how school balls are understood and experienced: for instance, how school balls are heteronormative spaces where dominant discourses of heterosexuality shape expectations and behaviour (Allen, 2006; Quinlivan & Town, 1999). Young people can be understood to both promote and subvert heterosexual discourses in various ways. Male students attending the school ball frequently use homophobic humour to police and promote heteronormative codes (Smith, 2015); yet, there are also occasions where young people, particularly girls, subvert and challenge heteronormative ideals by wearing clothing that does not conform to traditional feminine norms, such as a suit, or through non-heterosexual public displays of affection (Smith, Nairn & Sandretto, 2016). Feminist post-structuralism enables understandings of the competing discourses at play in the constitution of gender and sexual subjectivities. In this framing, there are no essential qualities of femininity and masculinity; rather, gender is dynamic and multiple – an idea that resonates with a new materialist approach.

Challenging the idea of feminist new materialism as a 'definitive cut' from the past, Osgood and Robinson (2019, p. 10) note the 'traces and entanglements', or in Barad's (2010, p. 240) terms, the 'dis/continuities' within feminist philosophy that shape understandings of childhood and gender. Fox and Alldred (2017), Osgood and Robinson (2019) among others, recognize the rich legacy of feminist thought that has informed new materialisms including post-structural scholarship. In a Baradian sense, we might think of this work not as prior or separate, but intra-actively entangled with/in new materialist thought. Hence Barad also expresses discomfort towards the adjective 'new' used in the term new materialisms, in their words: 'The "new" not only ignores matter/ing's inherent historicity but also assumes a progressive notion of time that is explicitly challenged in agential realism' (Barad & Gandorfer, 2021, p. 27). As Barad explains, 'there is no moving beyond, no leaving the "old" behind. There is no absolute boundary between here-now and there-then' (2014, p. 168). In an interview with Malou Jaelskjær and Nete Schwennsesen (2012, p. 16), Barad uses the term 'dis/continuity' to signal a way of thinking about change that does not presume it is 'either more of the same or a radical break'. For Barad: 'Dis/continuity is a cutting together-apart (one move) that doesn't deny creativity and innovation but understands its indebtedness and entanglements with the past and the future' (2012, p. 16).

An important point made by Barad is continuity and discontinuity are not dichotomous; instead, the relationship is one of 'agential separability, each being threaded through the other' (2007, p. 236). This also means dis/continuities are not limited to the past and present, as the future is inextricably enfolded. Here, I am mindful feminist new materialist thought is experiencing its own becoming. Following its own logic, it is something that is not, or can never be, fully formed. This book draws on new materialist thinking not to dismiss insights from feminist post-structuralism (e.g. the power of discourses in the way ball-girl-bodies are understood or deemed 'acceptable'); rather, I am interested in how feminist new materialist ideas might enhance understandings of gender and sexuality in ways that attend to the vitality of matter within material-discursive processes of becoming. In an interview, Bronwyn Davies describes this potential as enabling 'the things that were happening, and have been happening in post-structural theory, to be taken a step further' (cited in Osgood & Robinson, 2019, p. 54). This 'step further' entails an emphasis on how matter comes to matter (in both senses of the word), signalling a posthumanist ethical commitment for our role in who or what comes to matter (Barad, 2007). Here, there is a dual understanding of the verb 'to matter' in both a material and meaning sense: for instance, bodies 'matter *as matter*; they matter because they are important but they exist through their material *mattering*. Bodies therefore *are* discursive practices themselves, and they are inseparable from the environments in which they move, shape and express themselves' (Hickey-Moody et al., 2016, p. 2016, italics in original). This takes us back to Barad's conceptualization of matter and meaning as inseparable.

Ethics, politics and critique

Conceiving matter as lively and productive disrupts the conventional idea that agents are exclusively human. It fosters an attention to 'things' that affect girls and the school ball, which may not be able to be explained discursively: for example, the way entanglements of girls' bodies and high-heeled shoes can produce affects that may exceed a discursive rendering (see chapter 5). We are encouraged 'to think relationally with other beings/matter' in a move towards a flattening of human/nonhuman and material/discursive hierarchies (Taylor &

Hughes, 2016, p. 2). Instead of situating discourses of gender and sexuality at the centre, materialities and more-than-human relations are recognized as productive, co-constitutive forces in the becoming of the school ball-girl. For feminist researchers, this offers 'possibilities to reconfigure what we think we see and what we think we know' about gender and sexualities (Osgood & Robinson, 2019, p. 6). For example, reconceptualizing the relationship between school ball materiality and discourse as co-constitutive offers a push to my thinking – a relational reorientation towards what gets produced through entanglements of discourses of beauty and femininity, the material body and other matter.

The possibilities and limits of new materialisms for feminist theory are a source of ongoing debate (Ahmed, 2008; Frost, 2011; Hinton & van der Tuin, 2014; Osgood & Robinson, 2019; van der Tuin, 2008). Central to these debates are questions surrounding the compatibility and configuring of feminist politics with/in new materialist orientations (Bargetz, 2019; Hinton & van der Tuin, 2014; Kirby & Wilson, 2011; Revelles-Benavente et al., 2019). Debbie Epstein, for instance, argues new materialism's 'micro focus on *matter* has the potential to trivialize or obscure larger concerns of inequality (e.g., sexism, racism, homophobia, transphobia)' (cited in Osgood & Robinson, 2019, p. 52). Barad characterizes their work as grounded in questions of ethics and justice, not as an additional concern or layer we add to questions of matter, but as 'always already threaded through the very fabric of the world' (Barad in, Dolphjin & van der Tuin, 2012, p. 69). When asked in an interview what their work has to do with feminism, Barad succinctly articulates 'everything': 'I have been particularly interested in how matter comes to matter. How matter is itself felt. This is a feminist project whether or not there are any women or people or any other macroscopic beings in sight' (Barad in, Dolphjin & van der Tuin, 2012, p. 59).

Attending to the force of matter entails a rethinking of agency as relational and emergent via multiple human and more-than-human forces. As a result, agency is not aligned with human intentionality or subjectivity (Barad, 2007). This decentring of human agency contributes to concern new materialisms might depoliticize research and erase power imbalances. Barad recognizes the apprehension a relational understanding of agency might bring: 'I know some people are very nervous about not having agency localized in the human subject, but I think that is the first step—recognizing that there is not this kind of localization or particular characterization of the human subject is the first step in taking account of power imbalances, not an undoing of it' (Barad in, Dolphjin & van der Tuin, 2012, p. 55). Agential realism poses an understanding of power relations, ethics and politics that are not confined to the domain of the human.

For Barad, in order to understand the workings of power 'an understanding of the nature of power in the fullness of its materiality' is required (2003, p. 810). This entails not only a rethinking of power, but also the notion of dynamics, through the concept of intra-activity, which I return to shortly.

While agency is reconfigured and the human no longer privileged, feminists engaging with feminist new materialisms argue that an ethico-political focus remains central to this work (Osgood & Robinson, 2019; Revelles-Benavente et al., 2019). Drawing on Kristeva (1981), Davies (2020, p. 30) reminds us that various feminisms 'can be called on in different situations' to undertake 'quite different, but complementary work'. This does not mean approaches are mutually exclusive or should be pitted against one another; rather, for Davies, it offers choice 'in response to the work that needs to be done', depending on the time and context (2020, p. 30). Concern with ethics, power and justice continues to be central to feminist scholarship. So is an interest in the politics of knowledge production. For new materialisms, politics is inseparable from a sense of responsibility: 'a need to account for how and what it is that we, feminists, participate in materialising' (Hinton & van der Tuin, 2014, p. 4). Both Haraway (2008, 2016) and Barad (2007) call for research that is *response-able* for our role in constituting who or what comes to matter. Barad advocates for 'a posthumanist ethics, an ethics of worlding': ethics is about 'responsibility and accountability for the lively relationalities of becoming of which we are a part' (2007, p. 392). In this framing, ethics is emergent in the entanglement of knowledge, being and doing.

A new materialist approach involves a shift from a place of critique, to one of reconstruction (Osgood & Robinson, 2019) and creative experimentation (MacLure, 2015): a capacity that might appeal to feminist scholars who feel a sense of unease or disinterest with conventional mobilizations of critique, where 'being "critical" is construed as a practice of unmasking, demystifying, exposing error or dispelling illusion' (MacLure, 2015, p. 97). Scholars both within and beyond the field of new materialisms (Barad, 2012a; Edwards & Fenwick, 2014; Latour, 2004; MacLure, 2015) call for a reconceptualization of the nature of critique that often underpins qualitative research. Barad (2012a, p. 49) notes how critique is often 'over-rated, over-emphasized, and over-utilized, to the detriment of feminism'. For Barad, critique can be problematic, as it often resembles a 'destructive practice meant to dismiss, to turn aside, to put someone or something down – another scholar, another feminist, a discipline, an approach' (2012a, p. 49). Hence, it becomes a negative and distancing practice.

Questions surrounding the relationship between new materialist politics, critique and feminism are ongoing (see Allhutter et al., 2020; Bargetz & Sanos, 2020). Brigitte Bargetz and Sandrine Sanos (2020, p. 502) argue the 'move beyond "conventional" or negative forms of critique embodies a "longing for agency" (Bargetz, 2019), which maps out a future-oriented narrative that, in turn, promises a new and, hopefully, more realist politics'. Although, this potential is not unproblematic, in that they also caution the narrative of moving beyond critique 'risks ignoring the work of attending to power and difference for imagining the world otherwise. It also implies overlooking the complicated ways in which ("conventional") critique may still be useful for the acknowledging and undoing of power relations' (Bargetz & Sanos, 2020, p. 508). This leads Bargetz and Sanos (2020, p. 511) to the question: 'How might we productively mine the thought-provoking insights of new feminist materialisms in terms of reconfiguring the political without abandoning critique?'

Critique in a conventional sense becomes untenable within new materialist thought as judgement often relies on representation and binary logic (MacLure, 2015), such as true and false, good and bad. MacLure notes critique is problematic for new materialists as 'it *arrests* things – stitches them up, pins them down or closes them down, in the rage to expose error and the rush to pronounce judgement' (2015, p. 101, italics in original). This study of the school ball was not motivated by a desire to make a critical judgement whether the schooling practice is 'good' or 'bad' for girls. We already know school balls are heteronormative spaces that (re)produce gender and sexual norms. My goal is to explore the intricate relational dynamics of girls' experiences, including that which is messy, contradictory or (un)expected. Here, the focus is relationality and process – intricacies that cannot be easily 'pinned down' by conventional mobilizations of critique. Feminist new materialisms are grounded in 'a politics of entanglement' (Truman, 2019, p. 9), and as such, demand a rethinking of critique. This rethinking occurs at an epistemological and ontological level: In MacLure's words:

> Critique must be *immanent* – caught up with the movements and process in which it is entangled. It must be transversal: able to follow, or sense, the multifarious connections and intensities and coalesce in events, rather than sniping from its particular dugout at other disciplines and paradigms. It must be oriented towards eventualities that cannot be foreseen, and where the usual privileges of human agency, and the linearity of cause and effect are not in play.
> (2015, p. 105, italics in original)

Building on the work of Donna Haraway (1997), Barad proposes a practice of diffraction rather than critique: a method of 'reading insights through one another in attending to and responding to the details and specificities of relations of difference and how they matter' (2007, p. 71). Diffractive readings are detailed, ethical engagements attuned to the relational nature of difference. Barad draws on the physical phenomenon of diffraction to convey this idea: the bending and spreading of waves (water, sound or light) that occurs when waves encounter an obstruction – when waves overlap, diffractive patterns are produced. Barad explains how diffraction or interference phenomena can be observed in daily life in the form of ocean waves pushing through a gap in a barrier, such as rocks or breakwater: as the waves push through, a diffractive pattern is produced, perhaps observed as concentric half circles. We might notice diffraction phenomena produced by light waves in the form of colour – the rainbow swirl of colours on a soap bubble, the iridescent shimmer on peacock feathers or the wings of a butterfly – the swirling changing pattern of these colours is a diffraction effect (Barad, 2007). The concept of *shimmer* and *shimmering* can be found across varied theoretical disciplines and applied in different ways (see Malone et al., 2020; Rose, 2022). In this book, the term *shimmer* is used in a diffractive sense. It also alludes to a soft sparkle of data that 'glowed' and reached out to grasp me (MacLure, 2013b). This idea also resonates with affect theory (Seigworth & Greig, 2010), where the term *shimmer(s)* can signal a liveliness and potentiality of intensities, 'a sharpening of attention to the expressivity of something coming into existence' (Stewart, 2010, p. 340).

Barad is interested in the notion of diffraction and its methodological potential for recognizing and responding to the effects of difference. It is in this vein, Barad suggests, diffraction patterns can be thought of as 'patterns of difference that make a difference' (2007, p. 72). As a methodological tool, a diffractive reading differs from critique in that texts/approaches are 'respectfully read *through* each other in a relational way, looking for creative and unexpected provocations', as opposed to an approach that uses 'an atomistic binary logic to compare one with the other' (Murris & Bozalek, 2019, p. 873, italics in original). Diffractive readings entail an ethics of entanglement; thus, critique in a new materialist framing always begins 'in the middle of things' (MacLure, 2015, p. 97). Or as Edwards and Fenwick put it, is about 'working *through* practices and not simply *about* them' (2014, p. 3, italics in original). Here, objectivity does not involve separation and representation; rather, objectivity entails accountability to the specific matterings or materializations of which we are part. It requires an approach that is attentive to, and responsive to, the specificity – the finer details – and vitality of material entanglements. Shortly, I discuss Barad's agential realist framework as a productive tool towards this endeavour.

Before doing so, I briefly return to the earlier point on the dis/continuities between feminist post-structuralism and feminist new materialisms. Thinking about the relationship between 'old' and 'new' sexualities research (i.e. previous research utilizing a feminist post-structural approach and emergent research drawing on new materialist thinking), Allen (2017) draws on a new materialist ontology and Barad's notion of diffraction, to explain how current thinking about sexuality is not a move beyond previous ideas as they are inextricably (intra-actively) entangled. When different theoretical approaches to sexuality research are conceptualized diffractively – as coming together to create an emergent diffractive pattern – 'past' and 'new' research findings overlap, and boundaries become indistinguishable. This is an interesting way to think about past and new knowledge. Drawing on Barad's reconfiguration of time, Allen (2017, p. 155, italics in original) explains how 'it casts uncertainty over the possibility that any*one* will produce something distinctly new again, at the same time as it maintains newness is perpetual: "There is nothing that is new; there is nothing that is not new" (Barad, 2014, p. 168)'. This perspective is pertinent in relation to claims of 'newness' or assumptions of leaving 'the old behind'. Previously established understandings of the school ball as a heteronormative and gendered space are inseparable from this project and my own feminist motivations for embarking upon it.

Thinking–doing with Barad

A feminist new materialist framework, informed by Barad, entails a fundamental recasting of ontology and epistemology. Barad (2003; 2007) uses the term *onto-epistem-ology* to recognize the interdependent and intertwined relationship between being (ontology) and knowing (epistemology). The separation of epistemology from ontology establishes an inherent difference between human and nonhuman, matter and discourse, subject and object. Instead, Barad argues the practices of knowing and being cannot be separated from one another and are mutually implicated: as such, onto-epistem-ology can be understood as 'the study of practices of knowing in being' (2007, p. 185). In Barad's words 'we do not obtain knowledge by standing outside of the world; we know because "we" are *of* the world' (2003, p. 829). Lenz Taguchi (2010, p. 51) explains 'Being-*of*-the-world' is different from 'Being-*in*-the-world' (where matter and organisms are kept apart), or 'Being-in-*discourse*' (where everything is constituted by collectively constructed discourse). 'Being-of-the-world' is an entangled state of interdependence where knowing comes from a direct material engagement with the world. As such, humans can be understood as material objects *of* the world, just like any other beings and matter (Barad, 2007).

Drawing on these theoretical understandings, this book applies an onto-epistemological worldview to understanding *becoming* in the school ball setting. In this frame, our ways of being in the world depend on our knowing of it, and our knowing depends on our being (and continuous becoming) in the world (Lenz Taguchi, 2010). Here, our meaning making is dependent on the material world around us; we are not separate to the world but part of it in a process of mutual and intra-dependent becoming. Ethics are integral to this project. Indeed, Barad would term this framework ethico-onto-epistemology: an entanglement of ethics, ontology and epistemology. Theorizing the school ball through an ethico-onto-epistemological framework acknowledges the entangled research relations that shape and reshape the phenomena of the school ball and the knowledge produced. As mentioned in the previous chapter, Barad argues language has been afforded 'too much power' in how we come to understand and represent the world (2007, p, 132). In response, Barad's agential realist framework provides an elaboration of performativity where 'matter is produced and productive, generated and generative', challenging the notion of materiality as either a given, or a mere effect of human agency (2007, p. 137). Instead, matter is in an entangled agentive relationship with other matter, including humans, and through these entangled relations new becomings emerge.

A key conceptual tool for agential realism, and for this book, is Barad's notion of *intra-action*. The concept differs from 'interaction', which describes the relationship between distinctly separate bodies and entities. Intra-activity, on the other hand, is 'the mutual constitution of entangled agencies' (Barad, 2007, p. 33), which refers to a relationship between organisms and matter (human and nonhuman) where there are no distinct boundaries. Instead, they are in a state of intra-action – a material-discursive process where agencies emerge through their intra-action rather than precede it. In other words, they emerge as an effect of their mutual engagement. In thinking about the school ball, the human and more-than-human emerge through, as a part of, their entangled intra-actions with everything else (Lenz Taguchi, 2010). For Barad: 'To be entangled is not simply to be intertwined with another, as in the joining of separate entities, but to lack an independent, self-contained existence' (2007, p. ix). The school ball event itself, girls, discourses of femininity and all manner of materialities are not individual pre-existing elements, they only become 'distinct' in relation to one another through intra-active relations of entanglement.

Throughout the book, the term *entanglement(s)* is used in the Baradian sense, denoting these intra-active and co-constitutive relations: for instance, the becoming of the ball-girl is an intra-active entanglement of bodies, things, discourses, spaces and practices. Theorizing the ball-girl as human and more-than-human entanglements can work to dismantle the privileged position of human separability. The concept of entanglement can be applied to not only the becoming of school ball and ball-girl, but to the becoming of the researcher and the research itself. The knowledge that is produced in the book is an entanglement of theory, methodology, participants, data and researcher. When research is considered an entanglement, there is no division between the world and the separate observer – the 'knower' and the 'known' (Barad, 2007; Lenz Taguchi, 2013).

In contrast to representational logic which assumes there is a primary reality out there to be found, and that it can be accurately represented through language (St. Pierre, 2013b), 'materialist ontologies prefer a "flattened" logic (De Landa, 2002; Hultman & Lenz Taguchi, 2010) where discourse and matter are mutually implicated in the unfolding emergence of the world' (MacLure, 2013a, pp. 659–660). This means language no longer holds an elevated position of giving meaning to the world; instead, language is one element within an array of entangled forces and intensities. As opposed to data being a reflection of 'reality', data enacts *ball-girl becomings* produced via assembled material-discursive relations. Therefore, there is no revealing or uncovering the 'truth' of data, but 'an uncovering of *a* reality that already exists among the multiple realities being enacted in an event' (Lenz Taguchi, 2012, pp. 274–5, italics in original). In the context of this book, data does not represent a single or definitive 'truth' about girls and the school ball, rather data enact multiple ball-girl 'realities'.

To be able to examine the school ball through myriad entanglements, it is necessary to produce provisional 'cuts' or separations between the 'object' of inquiry, the researcher and theory. Barad (2007) explains the enactment of agential cuts separate *what* is researched from *how* it is researched. This cut is not a separation in a permanent sense, but agential separability: a 'cutting together-apart (one move)' (Barad, 2014, p. 168): or put another way, 'a cut that differentiates-entangles' (Barad, 2014, p. 175). A specific intra-action (of which the researcher is part) enacts an agential cut effecting a separation between 'subject' and 'object' (Barad, 2003). As there is no ontological separability between the observer and the observed, the notion of agential separability is vital as it allows for the possibility of being able to separate something out for analysis. What is particularly pertinent is 'different agential cuts materialise different phenomena' (Barad, 2007, p. 178) or different accounts of the school ball.

A fundamental element of intra-action is a dynamic reworking of the relationship between discursive practices and material phenomena in the relational becoming of the world. The term *material-discursive* signals an intertwined and mutually constitutive relationship – they exist simultaneously and continuously intra-act in an on-going production (Barad, 2007; Lenz Taguchi, 2010). As Barad explains:

> Neither discursive practices nor material phenomena are ontologically or epistemologically prior. Neither can be explained in terms of the other. Neither is reducible to the other. Neither has privileged status in determining the other. Neither is articulated or articulable in the absence of the other; matter and meaning are mutually articulated.
>
> (2007, p. 152)

The idea that materiality and discourse (matter and meaning) are mutually implicated in the dynamics of intra-activity opens up understandings of how materiality affects our discursive understandings, just as much as discursive understandings affect the material reality around us (Lenz Taguchi, 2010). It is in this vein that Barad's theory of *posthumanist performativity* builds on the important work of Butler (1990; 1993) and Foucault (1976; 1980) to account for materiality and the discursive as co-constitutive forces in processes of materialization. The reciprocal relationship differs to post-structural analyses where the material (e.g. the body) is constituted through discourse, but not the other way around (i.e. in Barad's reading of Butler's theory of materialization). If intra-actions are simultaneously material and discursive in an entangled relation, we can understand why Barad suggests agential realism provides an elaboration of 'how discursive practices matter' (2007, p. 135). For this project, it means ball-girl becomings are not limited to accommodating or resisting (pre-existing) discursive norms. Conceptualizing reality and materiality as discursively produced establishes a material/discursive dichotomy. In contrast, within a new materialist approach both discourse and materiality are accounted for, not as two distinct elements, but as inseparable. As such, the material/discursive binary is potentially dissolved (Allen, 2015b): hence the hyphenated term *material-discursive* (Barad, 2007) is used to signify this ontological understanding.

Barad's posthumanist performative approach enables a shift in focus from the materialization of the ball-girl as a product of discursive practices (i.e. produced and regulated via discourses of femininity), towards recognizing materialities and the more-than-human as dynamic productive forces in the becoming of the ball-girl. This expansive relational approach encourages attentiveness towards physical bodies, clothing, high heels, sensations, gut feelings, photographs, atmosphere, corporeal practices and spatial configurations like the school ball entrance and dance floor. In Barad's words: 'Material conditions matter, not because they "support" particular discourses that are the actual generative factors in the formation of bodies, but rather because *matter comes to matter* through the iterative intra-activity of the world in its becoming' (2008, p. 140, italics in original). It entails an ethical reworking of materiality and discursive practices to one of mutual entailment, illuminating understandings of the material-discursive constraints, conditions and practices that produce girls and the school ball.

Conceptualizing the school ball-girl as phenomena

Drawing on Karen Barad's agential realist framework, this book develops an understanding of the school ball and ball-girl as *phenomena* produced through agential intra-actions. In an agential realist sense, phenomena are constitutive of reality and it is through specific intra-actions that phenomena are produced. This means phenomena (the school ball and ball-girl) do not simply exist 'out there' in the world; rather, they are iteratively (re)materializing with each intra-action. As a result, 'functions' or properties of things can no longer be assumed or taken for granted. Instead, it is through agential intra-actions that the boundaries and properties of specific school ball relations or 'components' become determinate and that particular embodied concepts become meaningful (Barad, 2003). An important implication of conceptualizing the ball-girl as phenomena is a reconfiguring of notions of identity and identity formation. If 'individuals' (i.e. the ball-girl) materialize through intra-action as opposed to being a pre-existing entity/identity, then the ball-girl does not begin with a set of given or fixed differences; rather, differences become made and remade through intra-active processes of mattering. This complicates fixed and categorical notions of identity. What might be considered identity formation becomes a contingent ongoing process, which has implications for conceptualizing not only gender and sexuality but also factors such as race and class.

Within a Baradian frame, material-discursive conditions can be understood to performatively produce relations of class and cultural identity (2007). This does not mean girls become class-less or race-less; rather, new materialisms entail an ontological shift in how difference is understood: for example, in the context of sexuality education, Allen (2018) argues 'cultural and religious difference should not be understood as an essentialized distinct set of identity attributes, but that these play out as a consequence of relational *intra-active becomings* that cannot be known in advance' (p. 12, italics in original). Within an agential realist framework, separation and differentiation only exist within phenomena, which is why Barad calls phenomena 'differential patterns of mattering' (2007, p. 140). This means a new materialist approach does not begin with conventional (pre-existing) identity categories attached to particular bodies nor do bodies have inherent meanings; this includes identity categories such as queer or heterosexual, hence the identification or categorization of girls' sexual identities (as pre-existing) becomes less important.

As mentioned, agential cuts materialize different phenomena or different accounts of the school ball. Agential cuts enable understandings of how ball-girl-bodies are produced (or emerge) in classed, gendered and raced ways. The agential cuts enacted in this book aim to bring sexuality and gender to the fore, thus shape the perspective it offers. While factors related to ethnicity and class are entangled in assemblages, the emphasis on the mattering of gender and sexuality has placed limits on the attention given to the intra-active becoming of class and race. That is not to suggest this is not possible; for instance, Michael Hames-Garcia (2008) engages with Barad's theoretical tools to theorize race as intra-actively produced, arguing the importance of taking into account the agential material human body when attempting to explain racial phenomena. Not in the sense that bodies have inherent meanings, which would be antithetical to Barad's approach to bodies; rather, for Hames-Garcia, it is about accounting for the agential capacity of material bodies as co-constitutive in the process of racial formation.

Critiques of new materialism draw attention to the potential erasure of identity politics and the elision of race more specifically (Ahmed, 2012; Irni, 2013). Questions regarding how race can be understood and analysed within new materialist frameworks are ongoing (see Hinton et al., 2015; Hinton & Liu, 2015). Peta Hinton and Xin Liu (2015) address the question of what has potentially been abandoned in new materialist discourse with specific attention to race. Adding further texture to these critiques, the nature of abandonment is explored from within a new materialist frame, a positionality that involves working 'from inside the space and "object" of critique (new materialism), using its texts and conceptual vocabulary' (Hinton & Liu, 2015, p. 129). The authors highlight the potential paradox and (im)possibility of new materialist abandonment, in their words, 'the movement of abandonment appears to be more like that of a doubling or enfolding, perhaps a dis/locating of/from some*thing*/itself, without ever being able to perform a "pure" cut that creates the possibility for absolute separation, and absolute alterity' (p. 137, italics in original). As mentioned earlier, the idea of 'leaving behind' or 'moving beyond' does not make sense in a new materialist frame, which complicates notions of abandonment if based on a temporal and spatial separation. This does not negate these important political questions surrounding the affordances and limits of new materialisms; rather, it is a matter of opening up critiques and questions within a new materialist frame.

Returning to a reconfiguring of identity, Barad (2014, p. 173) suggests: 'The key is understanding that identity is not essence, fixity or givenness, but a contingent iterative performativity'. This has important implications for conceptualizing agency and causality. If individual entities do not pre-exist intra-action, then it becomes impossible for the human or more-than-human to act on their own or have independent agency. This offers a departure from the notion of the intentional and autonomous human subject, in this instance, the ball-girl. As opposed to agency being an attribute of someone or something, for Barad, 'agency is a matter of intra-acting; it is an enactment' (2003, p. 826). In this framing, agency is not an attribute at all, it 'is "doing" or "being" in its intra-activity' (Barad, 2007, p. 178). Therefore, agency is no longer aligned with human intentionality or subjectivity, and matter is no longer considered inert and passive. Although, it is not simply a matter of saying material things have individual agency; rather, agency is an emergent quality produced in the entanglements of human and nonhuman. All manner of things become important, and the potential of agency is not foreclosed or restricted to human action or intention. Causal relations are not conceived of as relations between isolated objects where one distinct entity affects another (i.e. linear cause and effect); this is impossible as there is no subject/object divide. Instead, cause and effect emerge through intra-activity which entails a sense of indeterminacy and open-endedness.

Within an agential realist account of the school ball, intra-actions continually reconfigure what is possible. Barad suggests there is a vitality and sense of aliveness to intra-activity and as such agency never ends or 'runs out'. In Barad's words, 'intra-actions always entail particular exclusions, and exclusions foreclose the possibility of determinism'; this means intra-actions can be understood as 'constraining but not determining' (2007, p. 177). While this opens up possibilities for becoming ball-girl, this does not mean 'anything or everything [is] possible at any given moment' (2007, p. 177). Instead, bodily capacities and constraints are continually reconfigured through the dynamics of intra-activity – particular ball-girl becomings may be opened up or blocked depending on the material-discursive relations. When agency is no longer the domain of the subject, we have a wider scope to (re)imagine what the ball-girl can do and become.

The school ball assemblage

As an assemblage, the school ball is more than a simple collection of forces or elements; rather, it is the relations or capacities emerging through entanglements that are of particular interest. The concept of *assemblage* from both Deleuze & Guattari (1987) and Bennett (2005; 2010) is employed to focus attention on particular affects and capacities within entangled relations. Bennett (2010, p. 23) describes assemblages as 'ad hoc groupings of diverse elements, of vibrant materials of all sorts. Assemblages are lively, throbbing confederations'. In this framing, it is about exploring what the assemblage *can do* or produce that offers new possibilities and imaginings: for example, ball-girl-body capacities are understood as emergent via an array of entangled human and more-than-human forces: perhaps high-heeled shoes, ball-dates and gender norms (see chapter 5); or a raft of relations within sexuality-assemblages involving ball-girl-date encounters (see chapter 6). The focus is not simply on what things and forces make up various school ball (sexuality) assemblages, but what gets produced in the entanglements – capacities, constraints, sensations and desires.

To focus attention on emergent relational matterings, the concept of assemblage is brought together with Barad's notion of intra-action. In Baradian terms, insights from these different theoretical ideas are *diffractively* read through one another (see also Lenz Taguchi, 2012; Jackson & Mazzei, 2012). While Barad does not explicitly use the Deleuzo-Guattarian notion of assemblage, the concept is argued to be 'compatible' with Barad's posthuman performativity and concept of intra-action (Ringrose & Renold, 2016, p. 222), and has been utilized together in a number of studies for varying purposes (Bodén, 2016; Ivinson & Renold, 2013; Mazzei & Jackson, 2016; Renold & Ivinson, 2014; Ringrose & Renold, 2014). Together, they can foster a 'close examination' of the particular ways in which phenomena emerge through human and nonhuman entanglements (Bodén, 2016, p. 40).

Methodologically, Mazzei and Jackson (2016) bring these concepts together to offer a new way of conceptualizing *voice* in educational research. Instead of thinking about voice as 'spoken words emanating from a conscious subject', they theorize a 'posthuman voice' emerging 'within the material and discursive knots and intensities of the assemblage' (Mazzei & Jackson, 2016, p. 1). Inspired by Deleuze and Guattari's concept of *Body without Organs*, Mazzei theorizes a *Voice without Organs:* 'a voice thought as an assemblage, a complex network of human and nonhuman agents that exceeds the traditional notion of the individual' (2013b, p. 734). It is a voice without a subject; there is no individual person or participant in an interview to which a single voice can be linked – everything is entangled. This methodological understanding of voice underpins the verbal fragments entangled in this book. Brief details follow each fragment including the method through which the fragment was generated (i.e. group or individual conversation, video diary), the number of voices within the fragment (including the researcher) and their school year level (year 12 or 13); however, comments are not attributed to individual names/persons, nor are the comments from the researcher differentiated from participants.

While theorizing from Deleuze and Guattari are increasingly 'put to work' (Lenz Taguchi, 2012, p. 267) with new materialist theorists such as Barad and Bennett, the compatibility of the philosophies of Barad and Deleuze is not uncontested: Hein (2016), for example, suggests that while Deleuze's work is often used alongside new materialist theorists, in particular the work of Barad, their ontologies and understandings of matter fundamentally differ. Hein argues, 'Deleuze's work can be seen as emphasizing force and creation, whereas Barad's work can be seen as emphasizing indeterminacy and intra-action' (2016, p. 137). Although as Bodén (2016, p. 44) suggests, 'if "the real" in posthumanism is already understood as multiple', then multiple ontologies are not only operating on the same plane of thinking, 'but also produce new versions of the real in their encounters'. While Deleuzian and Baradian theories may come from different traditions, there is the potential to read texts diffractively into each other (Barad, 2007; Lenz Taguchi, 2012; Murris & Bozalek, 2019) or plug one text into another (Jackson & Mazzei, 2013) to produce new ways of theorizing and performing research practices (Lenz Taguchi, 2012).

Plugging the concept of assemblage and intra-action into one another enables a focus on the emergent properties, capacities and intensities produced in school ball assemblages. This approach can open up understandings of the school ball that do not rely on cause and effect logic (Blaise, 2013): for example, the idea that certain things or practices will have a negative/positive effect on the ball-girl. Within an assemblage, neither elements nor the production of new ideas is pre-determined; therefore, it is impossible to know or predict what assemblages can do or produce. Conceptualizing the school ball as dynamic assemblages of material things, practices, spaces and imaginings moves the focus 'from the rational human intentional actor to a wider posthuman field of power relations' (Ringrose & Rawlings, 2015, p. 11). Within a posthumanist frame, it is about attending to 'what happens when heterogeneous things intra-act with force and affect' (Jackson & Mazzei, 2016, p. 105). As opposed to independent things affecting something in a linear cause and effect manner, it is the assemblage itself that produces intensities and capacities. These capacities are conceptualized as *affects* (Deleuze, 1988),

Theories of affect (Ahmed, 2004a and 2004b; Deleuze, 1988; Gregg & Seigworth, 2010) are invaluable for exploring the intricate and productive workings of assembled relations, such as how sensations, intensities and emotions can shape actions and capacities in the school ball setting. As Gregory Seigworth and Melissa Gregg explain: 'Affect rises in the midst of *in-between-ness*: in the capacities to act and be acted upon' (2010, p. 1, italics in original). Affect can be understood as an emergent force that can prompt movement, action or thought. Although, as Seigworth and Gregg (2010, p. 2) note, likening affect to a force does not imply it needs to be forceful, as it includes 'the subtlest of shuttling intensities: all the minuscule or molecular events of the unnoticed'. This research employs a posthumanist approach to affect (Mulcahy, 2012; Ringrose & Renold, 2016), where affect is also more-than-human – it is spatial and atmospheric circulating in-between bodies, things and spaces. Affect can be felt when you walk into a room (Anderson, 2009); it may be registered as a bodily feeling, but it can also exceed the body and the human. One example is how the affective atmosphere of the school ball – a buzz – can be felt and sensed bodily, yet it exceeds the individual human ball-girl body (see chapter 4). Here, affect does not belong to specific bodies but flows intra-actively, thus drawing attention to relationality, process and the in-between. This approach understands a body's capacities to act, feel and desire as produced via relations of affect (Fox & Alldred, 2013). The decision to take a date or not to the ball, for instance, is conceptualized as emerging through flows of affect within assemblages (see chapter 6). In this sense, the 'decision' to take a date shifts from the autonomous agentic ball-girl towards all manner of lively affective relations.

Importantly, affects are not tethered to human intention or agency, nor are they wholly reducible to discursive practices.

Within affect theory there are different approaches to the meaning and relationship between affect and emotion. Making a distinction between the two concepts, Massumi (2015, p. 5) clarifies emotion as a partial expression of affect: 'the way the depth of that ongoing experience registers personally at a given moment'. In this framing, affect can be 'captured' or 'qualified' as emotion, yet affect can also exceed or escape emotion. Seigworth and Gregg clarify affect as 'visceral forces beneath, alongside, or generally *other than* conscious knowing'; for them, affects are 'vital forces insisting beyond emotion' (2010, p. 1, italics in original). In this book, emotion is conceptualized as part of an 'affective flow that produces bodies and the social world' (Fox, 2015, p. 1). As such, attention turns to what emotions do (Ahmed, 2004b), what actions they perform and what e/affects follow. Affect is understood as material (Mulcahy, 2012), in that it 'registers on the body' and 'affects' other bodies (MacLure, 2010, p. 284), yet it is more than human: for example, the affective atmosphere of the school ball can be felt and sensed bodily, yet it exceeds the individual human (ball-girl) body. I am interested in how affect (including what is felt as emotion) is productive – it does something. Affect flows through and in-between assemblages in complex ways; it is not free flowing but cut through with power relations (Deleuze & Guattari, 1987). In this sense, affect is political in that 'power is an inextricable aspect of how bodies come together, move and dwell' (Zembylas, 2007, p. xiv). The affective flow of power is a productive force in the becoming of the ball-girl, both limiting and expanding what is possible.

Deleuzian concepts of assemblage and affect have been brought together by Fox & Alldred (2013) to establish an anti-humanist sociology of sexuality. Like Allen (2013b), Fox and Alldred propose a new materialist ontology of sexuality in an attempt to disrupt the anthropocentric gaze often evident in sexualities research. Their approach understands sexuality not as something attributable to bodies or identities but 'the affective flow within assemblages of bodies, things, ideas and social formations' (Fox & Alldred, 2013, p. 770). This work draws attention to the sexual capacities this flow produces in bodies and collectivities. What I find enticing about these new understandings offered by Allen (2013b, 2015b), and Fox and Alldred (2013) is the broadening of factors and forces that are at play in the production of sexualities: the human, more-than-human, the material and discursive. Examining the school ball via a new materialist ontology of sexuality reconfigures not only how we understand sexuality, but also the array of forces that form sexuality's becoming.

Sexuality-as-assemblage

As discussed in the introductory chapter, this book is underpinned by a new materialist ontology of sexuality, which reconfigures not only how we understand sexuality but also the array of forces that form sexuality's becoming. Here, we can think about sexuality with the concept of assemblage. Conceptualizing sexuality-as-assemblage is a productive way of moving the location and focus of sexuality away from the body and the human (Allen, 2013b; Fox & Alldred, 2013; Holmes et al., 2010; Lambevski, 2005). A sexuality-assemblage can comprise all manner of material-discursive, human and more-than-human forces. As Allen (2013b, p. 125) explains 'sexuality-as-assemblage enables an understanding of the sexual which is more than discourse, discrete bodies and their identities and occurs in the spaces between intra-acting human and non-human entanglements'. It is not about 'being' but 'becoming' and it is through the intra-action of the components of the assemblage that the becoming of sexuality occurs (Allen, 2013b). Similarly interested in conceptualizing sexuality-as-assemblage, Fox and Alldred (2013, p. 769) view sexuality as 'an impersonal affective flow within assemblages of bodies, things, ideas and social institutions, which produce sexual (and other) capacities in bodies'. Within both of these depictions of sexuality-as-assemblage, there is a sense of sexuality that encompasses multiple factors and forces, relationality and affective flows. These insights are productive for thinking about the becoming of sexuality through school ball assemblages, where sexuality does not derive from the human (i.e. ball-girl or date) nor is it reduced to discursive ideas associated with proms and balls, such as themes of heterosexual romance.

Conceptualizing sexuality-as-assemblage reconfigures the notion of sexual identity away from an individual and pre-existing body/entity. It is through affective flows – the capacity to affect and be affected (Deleuze, 1988) – that sexual identities, desires, subjectivities, masculinities and femininities are produced (Alldred & Fox, 2015). As mentioned earlier, participants in the research were not required to disclose their sexual identities or orientation. Through the course of conversations, however, several participants did share details of previous and current romantic partners; these included queer and heterosexual relationships. In relation to the school ball, dates included female and male friends, girlfriends and boyfriends, set-up dates and ball-swaps (see chapter 6 for more details). One of the aims of the book is to explore how dynamic assembled relations within sexuality-assemblages produce emergent capacities, constraints and desires. Many of these examples include relational forces that were present *only* for girls who took male dates. Bringing these dynamics (and related constraints) to the fore should not be construed as a normalization of heterosexual couplings at the ball, nor should it be presumed attending the ball with a male date represents a heterosexual identity; rather, it draws attention to the micropolitics of heterosexual school ball dynamics – the affective flows which produced certain (im)possibilities and limitations for girls attending the ball with a male date.

A new materialist ontology of sexuality also has implications for conceptualizing pervasive structural forces surrounding school balls, such as heteronormativity. As Alldred and Fox (2017, p. 668) explain, the notion of sexuality-as-assemblage 'steps back from a structural analysis of power. While not underplaying the territorializing forces of pervasive social norms such as patriarchy and heteronormativity, in this ontology, these forces are understood as produced and reproduced locally via actions and events'. Within this frame, it is the sexuality-assemblage that is productive of all phenomena; therefore, there are no pre-existing units of analysis or deterministic causal factors. For Barad, 'structures are themselves material-discursive phenomena which are produced through the intra-action of specific apparatuses of bodily production marked by exclusions' (2007, p. 237). Heteronormativity might be thought of as a product of boundary-making practices in the intra-action of material-discursive forces, including heterosexual norms and expectations. Sexuality-assemblages are argued to 'bridge "micro" and "macro", private and public, intimacy and polity, and establish the capacities for individual bodies to do, feel and desire' (Alldred & Fox, 2015, p. 4). Importantly, a sexuality-assemblage is not a stable or fixed entity, but continually in flux. While relational forces can work to constrain bodies and desires, there is always the possibility of becoming otherwise.

Drawing on Baradian understandings of agency, Allen (2018) recognizes agency in a sexuality-assemblage as something that resides in the intra-relations of elements in the assemblage, as opposed to being a property of bodies and entities. In Fox and Alldred's (2013) thinking around sexuality-assemblages, they replace the concept of human agency with the Deleuzian ontology of affect (Deleuze & Guattari, 1987; Deleuze, 1988). Affect can be understood as the capacity to affect and be affected. An affect is a 'becoming' that can be defined as a change of state of an entity or its capacities: these changes may be physical, psychological, emotional or social. Affects can produce capacities (in bodies), and affects are capable of producing further affects within assemblages (flows of affect). Within school ball sexuality-assemblages, both human and more-than-human relations affect one another, and it is these relations of affect that produce ball-girl capacities and create conditions of possibility. These understandings enable resistance to be theorized in ways that do not suggest essentialism or individual agency, thus attempting to avoid questions of structure and agency (Allen, 2015b; Fox & Alldred, 2013).

In Bennett's (2005) thinking about agency and assemblages she proposes the idea of distributive agency, where agency is not centred in a single living being but an assemblage of living and non-living 'vibrant matter' (Bennett, 2010, p. 3). The notion of agency of assemblages draws attention to the distributive and composite nature of agency, which includes nonhuman actants. As such, agency crosses the human-nonhuman divide. Bennett proposes 'bodies enhance their power *in* or *as a heterogeneous assemblage*' (2010, p. 23, italics in original). Capacity or potentiality for action is distributed across an 'ontologically heterogeneous field', as opposed to being solely attributable to, or emanating from, a human body or human effort (Bennett, 2010, p. 23). Thinking about the agentic power of human-nonhuman assemblages moves us beyond human-centred notions of agency to a distribution of agentic capacities among beings, entities and forces. Understanding agency as distributed and emerging via entangled relations reconfigures how we understand the ball-girl, both as a 'subject' and what the ball-girl can do and become. As Alldred and Fox (2017, p. 658) explain, 'it is not an individual body but the sexuality assemblage that is productive of all phenomena' and establishes 'the capacities of individual bodies to do, feel, and desire'.

The theoretical tools discussed in this chapter offer an ontologically different way of conceiving the human subject. For Barad, subjectivity is produced through intra-action, in that individuals materialize through intra-activity. From this understanding, girls are not a pre-existing entity with inherent boundaries, but rather are continually constituted through specific iterative intra-actions. This brings us back to the idea of *being-of-the-world*; individuals, in this instance girls, along with all manner of 'things' emerge through, and as a part of, their entangled relations (Lenz Taguchi, 2010). Humans and human bodies are considered (emergent) material objects of the world, just like any other beings and matter. This idea leads us into the next chapter and the possibilities for understanding the materialization of girl bodies in relation to the school ball.

3

School ball-girl matter(ings)

This chapter brings together fairy-tale, media commentary and academic scholarship to inform current understandings and perceptions of girls, bodies and the school ball. It is an enfolding of 'things' that might conventionally be thought of as background to the study; however, onto-epistemologically, a background is never neutral or passive. This enfolding of previous research, fairy-tale and cultural constructions of balls and proms bring together a collection of discursive practices, imaginings, commentaries and opinions. These 'constructions' are conceptualized as *matter(ings)*: dynamic articulations/configurations of the world (Barad, 2007). School ball matterings are produced through entanglements of research practices, theoretical frameworks, discourses, tradition, public concern and opinion, space and time. Specific attention is given in the chapter to theoretical approaches for understanding the materialization of girls' bodies (Butler, 1990, 1993; Barad, 2003) and the potential Barad's post-humanist performativity offers for (re)conceptualizing the mattering of ball-girl-bodies and agency. Different versions of phenomena emerge depending on relational forces, perhaps how something is researched, its theoretical or contextual framing and audience. The aim of the chapter is to bring together differential matterings, not as separate to the research, but as threaded through the particular version of 'reality' the book offers.

The fairy-tale ball

'You wish you could go to the ball; is it not so?'
'Alas, yes,' said Cinderella, sighing.
'Well,' said her fairy godmother, 'be but a good girl, and I will see that you go
Run into the garden and bring me a pumpkin.'

Charles Perrault, 1697
Cinderella

Cultural imaginaries of balls and proms are interwoven with fairy-tales like *Cinderella*. There have been many incarnations of Cinderella over the years, the earliest potentially dating back to ninth-century China (Dundes, 1988; Hennard Duthiel de la Rochère et al., 2016). At times, Cinderella has been known by a different name: Basile's *La Gatta Cenerentola* (1634–36) and the Grimms' (1857) tale of *Aschenputtel* are two examples. The Brothers Grimm version is a somewhat grisly affair where the stepsisters cut off their heels and toes, and birds deliver justice by pecking out their eyes. One of the most familiar versions of Cinderella is based on Charles Perrault's (1697) *Cendrillon*. This adaptation introduces the fairy godmother, the pumpkin and the glass slipper. It is the version most recognizable in Walt Disney's 1950 animated film (Dir., Geronimi et al.) and Little Golden Book (1950; 1998), and the story most familiar from my own childhood. In the Walt Disney tale, the ball is the pivotal moment where Cinderella and her life are transformed. With the help of the fairy godmother – and of course, a touch of magic – Cinderella attends the grand palace ball. Here, she captures the attention of the handsome prince, who like everyone at the ball is struck by the beauty of this mysterious girl. As the story unfolds, Cinderella's identity is revealed and she goes on to receive her heart's desire: the prince and her 'happily ever after'.

The Cinderella story is a common 'rags to riches' theme that continues to permeate popular culture. The plots of movies and novels often follow a well-trodden path: a girl (or on the rare occasion, a boy), whose beauty and worthiness is unrecognized, undergoes a transformation to emerge from oppression with triumphant reward – often in the form of beauty and romance. In these stories, 'true' beauty and worthiness ultimately prevails. Steeped in traditional discourses of femininity, tales of Cinderella often portray ideals of feminine beauty, romance and 'good girl' femininity (Shannon, 2015). While the early versions from Perrault and the Brothers Grimm have narrative differences, both tales 'set a model of comportment' where girls are 'gentle, pious, and good' (Zipes, 2016, p. 360). In the Cinderella fairy-tale, feminine beauty is inextricable from ideas of recognition, appreciation and self-worth. Cinderella's ultimate happiness is linked to Prince Charming: the love and attention he bestows on Cinderella affords her the recognition and ultimately the rightful destiny she deserves.

Fairy-tales like Cinderella have long been the subject of feminist critique (Dworkin, 1974; Leiberman, 1972; Minard, 1975; Rowe, 1986; Yolen, 1977). Writing over forty years ago, Rosemary Minard (1975, p. viii) described fairy-tale heroines like Cinderella as 'insipid beauties waiting passively for Prince Charming'. Similarly, Karen Rowe (1986, p. 209, italics in original) argued 'fairy tales perpetuate the patriarchal *status quo* by making female subordination seem a romantically desirable, indeed an inescapable fate'. Offering a more considered view of Cinderella, Jane Yolen (1977, p. 22) distinguishes 'America's Cinderella' (i.e. Disney influenced by Perrault), from its historical folklore lineage, which she refers to as 'the true Cinderella'. Yolen (1977, p. 26) argues feminist criticism should be aimed at the 'caricature' Cinderella, such as Walt Disney's; this 'coy and condescending' version offers a 'pitiable and useless' Cinderella, in contrast to the 'shrewd' and 'witty' Cinderella of the old tales.

Forty years on, fairy-tales continue to be a source of debate, consternation and inspiration for feminist writers; possibly, because they remain a lucrative source of material for media and entertainment conglomerates such as *The Walt Disney Company*. Disney princesses like Cinderella continue to be critiqued for creating and perpetuating 'princess femininity' in girls (Shannon, 2015): a socially constructed femininity that accentuates particular beauty ideals (slimness, made-up faces), a kind and gentle demeanour, and a lack of ambition and action. Erin Shannon (2015) argues princess femininity is an unattainable goal; therefore, girls are continually destined to fail. As a result, consuming these movies is argued to have a profound effect on girls as they enter adolescence. In this framing, cultural texts such as fairy-tales are conceptualized as separate or other to the girl. This is evident in arguments such as Shannon's, which are premised on a one-way linear cause and effect relationship; that is, fairy-tale princesses affect girls in particular ways, more often than not negatively. Cause and effect logic is premised on a clear subject/object divide, each element distinctly separate to the other. Within a new materialist account, however, this theorizing becomes untenable as distinct entities are no longer recognized (Barad, 2007). The relationship between girls and literature shifts from one of opposition or one-way cause and effect, to a mutual co-constitutive relationship. In this approach, girls' bodies and literature, such as fairy-tales and magazines, emerge or become through their relations.

Tree o'mine, O tree o'me,
Shiver and shake, dear little tree
Make me a lady fair to see,
Dress me as splendid as can be.

Joseph Jacob, 1916
The Cinder-Maid

Cinderella is a story of metamorphosis, not just for Cinderella and her animal friends, but the tale itself. It is a story continually rewritten, translated, adapted and transformed – a story continually becoming through ongoing matterings of time, space, cultural motifs, creative flair and feminist critique. The fairy-tale's enduring life and continual regeneration has been attributed to its 'inherent and seemingly inexhaustible ability to adapt to ever shifting social and cultural contexts' (Orme, 2016, p. 215): from children's and young adult books where Cinderella is a boy (Cole, 1987) or a cyborg (Meyer, 2012), through to adult fiction and erotica (Swann, 2016), the Cinderella story continually becomes anew. Queer and feminist rewritings of Cinderella offer a departure from familiar themes and dominant cultural norms. Emma Donoghue's *The Tale of the Shoe* (1997), for instance, reconfigures traditional representations of (hetero) romance, gender roles, beauty and desire (Riggs, 2016); or Margaret Atwood's subversive use of fairy-tales in her novels, such as *The Edible Woman* (1969), where the lead character is saved *from* the prince rather than *by* the prince (May-Ron, 2016). Feminist retellings of Cinderella include plot variations often motivated by a desire to create strong and intelligent female protagonists: for instance, 'a girl's feistiness' might replace the fairy godmother's magic as the catalyst for change and freedom (Bottigheimer, 2016, p. 28).

Cinderella's penchant for multiple retellings shows no sign of waning; neither does the academic interest surrounding it. Since the advent of feminist fairy-tale critiques in the 1970s, an increasingly nuanced view of the relationship between gender, feminism and fairy-tales has emerged (Hennard Duthiel de la Rochère et al., 2016; Haase, 2004; Joosen, 2011; Warner, 2014). As Donald Haase (2004, p. 31) notes, the 'the intersection of feminism and fairy-tale studies created a powerful synergy that has dramatically and permanently affected the way fairy-tales are produced, received, studied and taught'. This synergy can be applied to the context of this book, where a feminist new materialist approach sparks new questions surrounding the fairy-tale ball. Throughout the study, Cinderella has shimmered around the edges, at times catching my gaze, tugging at my thoughts. These nudges sometimes sparked by a participant comment, '*you get to feel like a princess*', something on television or a conversation with a friend. As the theoretical framings of the research developed, so did my thinking around Cinderella. Initially, I was drawn to destabilizing this cultural figure and the ideas of femininity and girlhood that pervade popular constructions of the school ball. Yet, new materialisms encourage my thoughts to wander elsewhere, to notions of metamorphosis, enchantment and magic (Warner, 2014). My attention is drawn to the mice, the shoe and the pumpkin; how these nonhuman, sometimes inanimate things, are integral to the tale. Mice become footmen and a pumpkin transforms into a grand golden coach. A glass slipper becomes a pivotal object in

Cinderella's 'transformation'. What intrigues me is how these happenings – these magical moments – go unquestioned in a fairy-tale. As Marina Warner (2014, p. 21) explains 'no one in a fairy-tale is taken aback when rocks and trees and streams and waterfalls act under their own volition or shape-shift from one form into another'. We readily accept shoes can be made of glass, animals can speak and inert objects have active power.

With these ideas in mind, an alternative way of 'reading' or thinking about Cinderella is entangled in this book. Cinderella fragments enact relationally entangled socio-historical traces of femininity, enchantment and affect. Prose from Cinderella stories are enfolded with academic analysis of fairy-tales, new materialist ideas and visual data. These enfoldings form part of a collection of *data snaps:* data-researcher (thinking-doing) encounters. The word 'snap' is used here in an emergent, lively sense – they are a mattering produced through entanglements of researcher, participant, digital tools and other (un)known material and affective forces. Data snaps might be thought of as 'data-in-the-making' (Springgay & Zaliwska, 2015, p. 138) that emerge from my questioning of data (what it can do) and my relationship with it. I am inspired by Mirka Koro-Ljungberg's call for researchers to engage creatively with data, to find our own 'methodological amplifiers, interpretive ruptures, and creative spaces' (2012, p. 808). This call for engaging creatively with data is motivated by a desire not to capture what data 'is' or what it means, but rather to consider 'what else can we do with data; and what does it do to us?' (Koro-Ljungberg & MacLure, 2013, p. 220).

This twist on the usual framing of Cinderella expands how we might think about Cinderella beyond a discursive reading and ideas of traditional femininity. The book does not ignore discourses related to the fairy-tale; indeed, they are entangled in ball-girl becomings; rather, it is a way to add another perspective – a shimmer – that might create space for different thought or feeling. We might think of these snaps through Barad's (2007) concept of diffraction where the photograph, prose and academic text are read through one another to produce something new. At other times, data snaps may work to interrupt our usual 'perceptive style and habits of seeing' (Jackson & Mazzei, 2012, p. 134): for example, a blurring or layering of images may disrupt or subvert an anthropocentric gaze by making it is impossible to discern an individual (human) body or bodily features (see chapter 5). For me, data snaps are an attempt to 'open up data, to *diffract it*, and to imagine what newness might be incited from it' (Lenz Taguchi, 2012, p. 270, italics in original). This 'newness' does not refer to new meanings about girls and the school ball; rather, it signals an interest in data 'for what it produces, how it moves and for how it can be lived and sensed by researchers' (Benozzo et al., 2013, p. 309). Like Cinderella, I find myself as researcher co-implicated in the becoming of data.

Proms, girls and the media

Silence fell, the dancers stood still, and the violins stopped playing as all the guests gazed at the beauty of the unknown princess. A murmur ran all around the room. "Oh, how lovely she is!"

Charles Perrault, 1697
Cinderella

Themes of the fairy-tale ball are not confined to folklore or pages of children's picture books: their tendrils are deeply woven through contemporary media and popular culture. Recalling the media headlines mentioned in the opening chapter, girls are frequently constructed as highly invested in the school ball, which allegedly leads to excessive and competitive behaviour. These portrayals are often underscored by developmental logic and the perception the ball is an important 'milestone' for girls as they 'progress' towards womanhood: as one media article articulates, 'for girls, there's something magical about throwing up your hair, slipping into a pair of heels and having your date show up in a tux. It turns a girl into a woman' (Tay, 2007). Much of this media commentary is produced by adults and heavily dominated by adult opinion. So too is the plethora of prom marketing produced annually, yet unlike much of the mainstream news media, it is girls who are the intended target market or audience. Prom articles and advertising are a common feature in teen magazines, offering detailed tips from finding the 'perfect dress' through to the finer points of being 'prom ready'. There are publications solely devoted to the prom, such as *Seventeen Prom*: the entire issue providing inspiration for planning the 'best prom ever'.

Existing research identifies three prevalent themes in the articulation and marketing of the high school prom: (heterosexual) romance, the framing of the prom as 'the night of your life' and the potential for 'perfection' through physical beautification (Mazzarella, 1999, p. 98). Dominant discourses surrounding the 'perfect prom', gender roles, dating and consumption are offered to girls through both article content and advertising. The importance of planning is heavily emphasized, from 'purchasing the right products' to avoiding 'promdate fashion blunders' (Mazzarella, 1999, p. 107); here, physical beauty and the need to 'dazzle' a date is an imperative. Not confined to print media, prom tips and survival guides are an increasingly popular topic for YouTube videos and blogs. The unrelenting publication of these 'how to' articles and videos suggest the prom continues to be a lucrative market for magazine publishers, hair and beauty salons, florists, hotels and caterers, limousine services and fashion retailers. In the United States alone, proms generate billions of dollars in annual revenue: a figure that continues to grow (Anderson, 2012).

Previous scholarship highlights girls' complex and nuanced negotiation of dominant ideas found in prom magazines, such as 'the perfect prom', the expectation to engage in body and beauty work, and heterosexual romance (Zlatunich, 2009). Challenging the construction of girls as particularly vulnerable to the influence of media, Nichole Zlatunich's (2009) work opens up a space to think about the relationship between girls and the media as one of negotiation, rather than girls simply being 'oppressed' by these texts. Glimpses of resistance include not attending with a male date or borrowing a dress as opposed to investing time and money into purchasing something new. Girls are understood to actively negotiate meanings as opposed to passively absorbing the dominant ideas about beauty, romance and heteronormativity. Zlatunich situates girls on a 'continuum of negotiation and resistance', with some girls having the ability to reject traditional gender norms more than others (2009, p. 371). She argues girls employ 'strategic selectivity' when reading prom media, meaning they are able to 'pick and choose' what they like from the text and ignore the rest, signalling some level of resistance to the dominant meanings being offered (Zlatunich, 2009, p. 355). While maintaining a clear subject/object divide between girls and magazines, this argument destabilizes a simplistic and presumed negative effect media has on girls (i.e. a one-way linear relationship).

The idea that young people demonstrate agency to negotiate dominant prom discourses resonates with Amy Best's (2000) *Prom Night*, a US-based study examining young people's engagement with dominant cultural understandings of the high school prom. Although Best viewed the prom as a deeply conformist space, she argues it is also a site where young people are able to disrupt dominant cultural understandings. Young people do not merely passively absorb the meanings offered to them through prom culture; rather, they have the potential to resist and rework (to a limited extent) these dominant meanings in order to constitute their experiences in alternative ways. Like the work of Zlatunich (2009) and Smith (2014), Best's analysis locates agency within the human subject, in their ability to potentially resist or rework dominant discourses of femininity and sexuality: for example, some students found ways to partially reject or resist the traditional 'trappings' of the event through the use of style and dress, or 'playful' tactics such as irony and parody. Some girls challenged their school's emphasis on modesty and propriety, in terms of both clothing and sexual expression. Ironically, girls used practices that work to structure their expressions of femininity as potential means of resistance, signalling these moments of resistance were constrained within the prevailing organizations of gender and heterosexuality.

Ontologically, this book offers a different approach to thinking about the school ball, girls and agency. Rather than conceptualizing agency as something the girl might have or wield, 'agency' emerges intra-actively (Barad, 2007) through human and more-than-human relations. A feminist new materialist conceptualization of agency opens a space for thinking about the force of matter (e.g. bodies and clothing), not as passive objects wielded by an agentic human (i.e. a girl using clothing to subvert traditional discourses of femininity) but as active and lively (Bennett, 2010). This liveliness is not attributed to, or an extension of, human will and action. Ball-girl becomings emerge via entanglements of human, more-than-human, material and discursive forces. Therefore, the possibilities for becoming ball-girl are not limited to accommodating or resisting dominant discourses of femininity. It also offers a reframing of the relationship between girls and popular constructions of the ball that emerge in the media. If discourses are no longer prior to becoming ball-girl (as they are now entangled), there can no longer be a presumed boundary between girls and the media that a relationship of 'negotiation' or 'strategic selectivity' might suggest. Instead of a clear subject/object (i.e. girl/media) divide, media discourses and cultural narratives form part of the material-discursive entanglements that produce the ball-girl. As such, the project considers how this reconfiguring might provide openings for reimagining girls in ways that destabilize or escape common tropes found in the media and popular culture, such as notions of the ball as a romantic space. A feminist new materialist approach allows me to ask what more might be going on here?

Prince Charming

'Would you care to dance?' a deep voice behind her asked.
Cinderella whirled around. It was the prince! And although he wasn't as tall as he claimed in his palace bio, she was pleased to see that he was generically handsome.

Laura Lane and Ellen Haun, 2020
Cinderella and the Glass Ceiling

Deeply connected to notions of the 'perfect prom' are themes of heterosexual romance (Mazzarella, 1999; Zlatunich, 2009; Best, 2005). A quick Google search yields topics from finding your 'perfect date' to 'crazy romantic promposals'. As mentioned, proms and school balls are heteronormative spaces where heterosexuality is presumed and reinforced (Allen, 2006; Best, 2005). The normalization of heterosexuality shapes what is considered 'natural' and 'acceptable' in these contexts, such as the expectation to attend the event with a partner of the opposite sex. This expectation has been maintained through policies, including the banning of same-sex dates (Wade, 2011), or students being required to visit the school counsellor in order to bring a same-sex partner. It is heartening to note, schools in Aotearoa New Zealand have come under fire for these heteronormative practices; this critical commentary fuelled by student petitions and complaints to the Human Rights Commission. In 2013, New Zealand school principals were warned they would be in breach of the Human Rights Act if they restricted students' choice of partner (Tait, 2013). This has resulted in a significant shift in school 'rules' surrounding school balls in Aotearoa; although, the freedom to bring a partner of your choosing continues to be constrained or enhanced by peer culture and the climate of the school (Smith, 2015).

Popular culture and media, both in New Zealand and internationally, often portray school balls as a romantic space for young women. In contrast to culturally constructed idea(l)s, New Zealand-based research has shown girls do not necessarily view the ball as romantic space for them personally (Smith, 2014). Instead, the study found it was male participants who were more likely to constitute the ball as a space of heterosexual romance, contradicting the portrayal of the ball as a night of 'storybook romance' for young women (Smith, 2014, p. 82). Like Zlatunich (2009), Smith's (2014) work suggests young women are not simply passively taking up discourses of romance and normative femininity presented in magazines, movies and media. Drawing on theoretical tools from queer theory and feminist post-structuralism, Smith (2015) notes how male students in particular, reproduce discourses of hegemonic masculinity when discussing the idea of taking same-sex partners to the formal: homophobic humour, for instance, was commonly used by boys in both the single-sex and co-educational schools to police and promote heteronormative codes.

While heteronormativity is argued to be a dominant force in this setting, Smith's continued work with Karin Nairn and Susan Sandretto (2016) highlights how young people subvert and challenge this heteronormative space, albeit in limited ways. Young women had a larger capacity to subvert normative codes of gender compared to males, for example, through challenging conventional codes of feminine dress or girl couples seen dancing together and kissing. These findings illustrate how young people are both complicit in and disruptive of normative heterosexuality in the school ball environment. In their examination of the school ball as a heteronormative space, Smith and co-authors do not conceive of space as something concrete but something that is fluid, complex and discursively produced, which means gendered displays have the capacity to (re)produce space. As such, behaviours that enact dominant gendered scripts reproduce school balls as heteronormative social spaces, for example, heterosexual couples kissing and touching on the dance floor. Alternatively, gender performances may subvert or transgress the heteronormative space of the school ball, such as same-sex couples kissing at the formal, or the wearing of clothing that contravened 'typical' gendered dress, like a girl wearing a tailcoat. In sum, the school ball is considered an important social space where young people can challenge heterosexual/homosexual and masculine/feminine binaries to varying extents.

The current project draws on a new materialist ontology of sexuality and the notion of sexuality-as-assemblage to explore the complexities and dynamics within ball-girl-date encounters (see chapter 6). In doing so, it asks how a relational approach might invite different ways of thinking about normative structures such as heterosexuality? More specifically, when sexual capacities, desires and inclinations are not individually located but relationally produced, what possibilities might this open up for rethinking dominant expectations or perceptions associated with the ball, such as the (un)importance of a ball date or notions of the ball as a romantic space? The aim is not to explicate the heteronormativity that pervades these schooling practices – this has been widely established; rather, I am interested in extending existing understandings by considering how feminist new materialisms open up avenues for exploring the material dimensions of regulatory practices, including relational forces associated with heterosexuality.

The matter(ing) of girls' bodies

But her great toe could not go into it, and the shoe was altogether much too small for her. Then the mother gave her a knife, and said, 'Never mind, cut it off; when you are queen you will not care about toes; you will not want to walk.'

The Brothers Grimm, 1857

Aschenputtel

In developing a feminist new materialist understanding of the becoming of ball-girl-bodies, it is useful to consider how female bodies have previously been theorized, particularly within the context of gender, sexualities and schooling. More broadly, feminist research has persuasively shown how dominant discourses shape the ways female bodies are understood, experienced and regulated. The work of Foucault (1980; 1983) has been particularly useful for feminist analyses of the power relations evident in the disciplinary practices on the female body (see Bartky, 1990; Bordo, 1993). From a Foucauldian perspective, discourses work to structure the ways in which bodies are disciplined and understood, for instance, female bodies are regulated in accordance with social and cultural ideas of beauty and femininity. This includes the way women actively regulate their own bodies and those of others through, for example, bodily ideals of slimness (Bordo, 1993).

Influenced by the work of Foucault, Judith Butler (1990; 1993) explored the relations between gender, subjectivity and the materiality of the body. Butler's theory of gender performativity understands bodies as continually constituted through practices that mark them as male or female. In this approach, gender is conceptualized as a product of styles and techniques, such as dress and adornment, as opposed to being an essential quality of the body. For Butler, gender is a matter of 'doing' – it is the performative effect of reiterative acts. Butler (1993, p. xii) links gender performativity to the materialization of bodies in that regulatory norms work in a 'performative fashion to constitute the materiality of bodies and, more specifically, to materialize the body's sex'. Theoretical understandings offered by Foucault (1977) and Butler (1990; 1993) recognize the inseparability of the body and discourses of gender and sexuality. Here, the materiality of the body is understood and shaped through discursive meanings. Theorizing the body in this way has been a deliberate attempt to shift the focus from the biological body to wider cultural, social and historical factors (Frost, 2011; Grosz, 1994). This approach has opened up possibilities for understanding gender, sexuality and the body beyond biological reductionism and essentialist categorizations of the 'nature' of the female body. Butler's theorization of the heterosexual matrix (1990) has also been invaluable for highlighting heterosexuality as a pervasive (discursive) force in the constitution of 'appropriate' performances of masculinity and femininity at the school ball, including bodily dress and comportment (Smith, 2014).

For feminist researchers, Butler's approach has been instrumental in highlighting how schooling practices play an active role in the surveillance and regulation of girls' bodies (Allan, 2009; Happel, 2013; Pomerantz, 2006; 2007; 2008; Raby, 2010; 2012; Renold, 2005; Youdell, 2005; 2006). School dress codes are one example of the myriad ways schools regulate girls' clothing and bodily exposure. In Shauna Pomerantz's (2007) analysis of girls' style and clothing, school dress codes are considered one of the many invisible practices that schools employ to organize young women's sexuality and femininity. Sartorial rules shape girls' understandings of what is deemed 'appropriate' in relation to their bodies and the schooling environment: for example, what aspects of their bodies are considered 'acceptable' to be seen and what 'should' be hidden. Through the regulatory practice of school dress codes, certain forms of female sexuality are normalized, such as 'good girl' (white, middle-class, heteronormative) femininity (Pomerantz, 2007). School dress codes that promote modesty are argued to perpetuate the idea of girls' bodies as dangerous and needing to be controlled (Lesko, 1988). The policing of girls' prom dresses or girls being told to lengthen their skirts to 'stop distracting' male students and teachers (Roy, 2016; Rutherford, 2016; Schoultz, 2016) are typical examples of the way girls' bodies continue to be constituted as 'dangerous' and 'problematic' in the schooling environment.

Schooling practices, such as dances and school balls, foster the regulation and surveillance of girls' bodies. At these events, the presentation and deportment of girls' bodies comes under intense scrutiny from peers and adults alike. Previous research highlights how female students attending the school ball feel more harshly judged than their male peers (Smith, 2012). Girls are required to dress and present their bodies in accordance with the 'acceptable' norms of this social situation: for instance, the wearing of a dress and make-up are constituted as 'normal' and expected practices for girls. The parameters of what is expected at the school ball may also differ from what is deemed 'acceptable' in other schooling spaces: for example, school uniform rules governing hair and the wearing of make-up at school. By highlighting these discourses, we can think about the ways dominant meanings are attributed to the bodies of girls: how bodies are constituted as 'intelligible' or 'non-intelligible' in relation to feminine beauty ideals (Butler, 1990).

Barad's posthuman performativity

Once upon a time, though it was not in my time or in your time, or in anybody else's time

Joseph Jacob, 1916
The Cinder-Maid

Extending the work of Butler, Barad offers a different understanding of the materialization of the body and the relationship between discourse and materiality. In contrast to a linguistic or discursive approach, Barad calls for feminists to 'take account of *how the body's materiality*–for example, its anatomy and physiology–*and other material forces actively matter to the processes of materialization*' (2003, p. 809, italics in original). Barad's framework of agential realism provides the basis for their posthumanist performative account of the production of material bodies. In Barad's reading of Butler, they suggest Butler's theory of performativity is limited as it 'ultimately reinscribes matter as a passive product of discursive practices' (2007, p. 151). It is not that Butler denies the materiality of the body, but by conceptualizing matter as a product of discourse, Barad argues this 'fails to recognise matter's dynamism' (2007, p. 64). Offering an alternate approach, Barad conceptualizes matter (i.e. the materiality of the body and other material forces) as an active force in the process of materialization. To do this, Barad offers a new understanding of the relationship between discursive practices and material phenomena. For Barad, discursive practices are 'material (re)configurings of the world', and it is through these continual (re)configurings that boundaries, properties and meanings are differentially enacted (2007, p. 151). The idea that discursive practices are *material (re)configurings of the world* means discursive practices are always material, just as materiality is always discursive: this mutual entailment occurs through the dynamics of intra-activity. The concept of intra-activity dissolves a conventional divide between the material/discursive (or nature/culture). As such, Barad suggests it avoids reinscribing the nature-culture dualism, which they would argue Butler's account inadvertently enacts.

Employing Barad's posthuman performative account of the materialization of bodies, this book offers an alternative understanding of girls' bodies in relation with discourses. There is a shift from thinking about the discursive limits of girls, femininity and the school ball, to consider 'the "material limits": the material constraints and exclusions, the material dimensions of agency, and the material dimensions of regulatory practices' (Barad, 2007, p. 192). I consider how this approach provides openings for understanding how matter might play a part in producing and maintaining discourses that limit or constrain ball-girl becomings. Moreover, how might material forces potentially reconfigure discursive ideas of femininity associated with the school ball? What is distinct here is rather than a linear model of causation where power relations (and discursive practices) produce the body in particular ways, the relationship is reciprocal and multi-directional. I consider how not privileging the discursive over material, the possibilities for considering 'who or what comes to matter' (Barad, 2007, p. 35) become much wider. This further extends Butler's theory of materialization, which Barad suggests, exclusively focuses on human bodies and social factors. For Barad, the focus is not solely on the materialization of human bodies but the materialization of *all* bodies – human and nonhuman.

An agential realist approach offers a different way of thinking about how the ball-girl-body might be understood, produced and experienced. Barad understands bodies not as objects with clearly defined boundaries and properties, but as 'material-discursive phenomena' (2003, p. 823), where bodies emerge through intra-active relations of multiple elements. Barad's theoretical ideas are being increasingly drawn on to explore girls' bodies in relation with schooling environments (Lenz Taguchi & Palmer, 2013; Ringrose & Rawlings, 2015; Ringrose & Renold, 2016). In contrast to thinking about bodies as purely discursively produced, these studies are premised on ontological understandings of the body that emphasize relationality. Lenz Taguchi and Palmer (2013, p. 671), for instance, explore 'the entanglement of architecture, materialities, bodies, discourses and discursive practices' in the co-constitution and enactment of girls' school related ill- and well-being. In their work, 'things' often perceived as 'the fixed material backdrop of human agency' are (re)considered 'strong co-constitutive agents' (Lenz Taguchi & Palmer, 2013, p. 672). Rather than thinking about the body of the girl as an object with inherent boundaries and fixed properties, Lenz Taguchi and Palmer draw on Barad's ontological understanding of girl bodies as *phenomena*. Through this framework, girls' ill- and well-being are conceptualized as 'material-discursive intra-active enactments' (Lenz Taguchi & Palmer, 2013, p. 673): A 'panicking girl body' is understood as 'an event of an entanglement of multiple performative agencies' (Lenz Taguchi & Palmer, 2013, p. 673), including discourses, embodied practices and materialities such as schooling spaces.

In an analysis of bodies, objects and classroom spaces, Taylor (2013, p. 689) draws on Barad to develop 'a material feminist analysis of the body in the "fullness of its materiality"'. Taylor's analysis highlights how objects such as clothing do 'powerful yet usually unremarked material-discursive work … in installing gendered practices through their entanglement with bodies and spaces' (2013, p. 698). Chapter five engages with these ideas to conceptualize girls' bodies as phenomena (Barad, 2007) emerging through the material-discursive and affective entanglements of beauty-body practices. The discussion highlights the materiality of the body and other matter, such as high-heeled shoes and fake eyelashes, as co-constitutive in the becoming of the ball-girl-body. The ball-girl-body has no ontological status prior to its relational or intra-active production

(Barad, 2007); therefore, it is the relations that produce the phenomena of what we come to understand as ball-girl-bodies. Underpinning this approach is a shift in focus from what a body *is* to how bodies *become*.

Body as becoming

Slowly, the pumpkin turned into a fancy coach. "What we need next are some fine, big – mice!"
At the touch of the wand Cinderella's little friends turned into handsome horses. Then the old horse became a fine coachman. And Bruno the dog turned into a footman

Walt Disney, 1950
Cinderella

Researchers have become increasingly interested in thinking about the body in terms of *becoming*, rather than *being* (Budgeon, 2003; Coffey, 2013; Coleman, 2008, 2009; Fox, 2012; Grosz, 1994; Ivinson & Renold, 2013). Employing Deleuzian and feminist theory, Rebecca Coleman develops a feminist approach to understanding bodies as *becomings*: In Coleman's words 'the term "the becoming of bodies" refers to a conviction that bodies must be conceived as processes which are constantly moving rather than as discrete, autonomous entities' (2009, p. 1). For Deleuze, a body is not an independent entity but in process – always becoming through the connections it makes with multiple and different bodies (human and nonhuman). Bodies are no longer autonomous bounded beings but are constituted relationally, which means the girl body does not pre-exist relations but becomes via continual and open-ended connections with other bodies, things, ideas and practices. In this framing, the body is inseparable from its relations with the world (Deleuze, 1992), and the binary distinction between subject (i.e. the girl) and objects is no longer viable. Bodies are assemblages of all manner of things, human and more-than-human, and it is through these entangled relations the body is constituted or becomes.

Both Deleuze and Barad propose a relational perspective of bodies. In a Baradian framing, we can think of bodies as intra-actively becoming via an array of forces. Here, there is no ontological separation between bodies, discourses and other relations. I draw on Barad to conceptualize the ball-girl-body as becoming in particular material-discursive configurings in any given moment. Ball-girl-bodies are agential in that they materialize through intra-actions, and 'it is through specific agential intra-actions that the boundaries and properties of the "components" of phenomena become determinate and that particular embodied concepts become meaningful' (Barad, 2003, p. 815). What emerges as ball-girl 'femininity', for instance, is unstable performative phenomena (an enactment) rather than a fixed attribute of bodies.

An important aspect of a Baradian approach to bodies is they do not have inherent properties or clearly defined boundaries. They congeal or emerge through particular configurings at any given moment, which means ball-girl-bodies are fleeting, temporary and unfixed. This framing helps move understandings of ball-girl-bodies beyond discursive subject positionings and understandings of femininity, to a conceptualization of bodies as materializing via the productive entanglements of matter, practices, affects and other relational forces. This means bodies are emergent, contingent and multiple as they are continually (re)made via human and more-than-human matter, corporeal practices, ideas and affects (flows, energies). The ball-girl-body as matter is not a fixed substance; rather, it is a 'substance in its intra-active becoming' (Barad, 2003, p. 822): a form of iterative congealment that is on-going, continually becoming anew. In other words, it is not that the ball-girl-body has relations with other things; rather the ball-girl-body *is* the relations (Coleman, 2009), and it is by examining these relations that new understandings of the ball-girl might emerge.

As mentioned, femininity is not ascribed to bodies and identities (i.e. a fixed identity or quality that one can reveal or solidify) but emerges via intra-active entanglements. This approach enables an understanding of how ball-girl femininities might reinforce, supersede or potentially rework pre-conceived discursive boundaries, such as the expectation to engage in beauty-body work. Coole (2013, p. 455) describes a new materialist becoming as 'ineluctably multiple and complex; variegated, folded, labyrinthine; and multi-dimensional and multi-scalar'. She explains how 'entities, structures, objects all emerge as unstable, indeterminate assemblages that are composed of and folded into smaller and larger assemblages'; therefore, they are continually reconfigured by their 'encounters with other provisional constellations' (2013, p. 455). This prompts us to think about the 'subject' (i.e. ball-girl) not as a pre-existing entity but as an assemblage or material-discursive phenomena. Ball-girl femininities are material-discursive becomings – they are multiple and open-ended.

In this research, ball-girl femininities are enacted through agential cuts (Barad, 2007) that differentiate and entangle bodies, imaginings, clothing, discourses, beauty-body practices, high heels, feelings, dates and spaces, among other forces.

In the following chapters, visual and verbal data perform these provisional and temporary cuts producing a 'temporal freezing of the phenomenon' (Bodén, 2015, p. 195): for example, a photograph enacts an agential cut that brings material forces to the fore (bodies, objects and spatial configurations); or verbal fragments from a conversation might be considered a provisional cut (Bodén, 2015) that can allow analysis of elements of a phenomenon (imaginings, memories, laughter and ambivalence). Or put another way, data enact specific material-discursive assemblages through which the school ball-girl becomes.

Girls' bodies, 'agency' and affect

'I actually didn't buy these glass slippers myself,' explained Cinderella. 'They were a gift and it seemed rude not to wear them.'
'When I think a gift is ugly I just throw it away,' said the Prince.
'They were my only option,' said Cinderella. 'I don't own a pair of shoes.'
'Not even boat shoes?' asked the Prince. 'Or those ones with the red bottoms that ladies love?'
'I sleep in a fireplace,' she quipped. 'How would I know anything about gender-normative footwear?'

Laura Lane and Ellen Haun, 2020
Cinderella and the Glass Ceiling

Feminist analyses that employ a Butlerian/Foucauldian approach to bodies have largely understood agency as inseparable from subjectivity and that the individual operates as an effect of power, for instance, through discursive formations (Coole, 2005; Frost, 2011). If the subject is constituted through discursive practices, then agency lies in the potential for discourses to be undermined, subverted and reworked. This conceptualization of agency has enabled researchers to document girls' subversive and resistant practices to hegemonic gendered and sexual scripts (Allen & Ingram, 2015; Gonick, 2003; Harris, 2004; Hauge, 2009; Kelly et al., 2005; Renold & Ringrose, 2008). In this body of work, girls are recognized as social agents who both participate in and challenge gender inequalities. For example, in Rebecca Raby's (2010) analysis of school rules, girls can be understood to both reproduce and contest school dress codes and the regulation of normative gender and sexuality. Raby's study showed many girls were critical of school dress codes and how they were enforced; yet at the same time, they were scornful of their female peers who wore revealing clothing. Raby suggests girls simultaneously challenge, reproduce, negotiate and strategically use the meanings constituted through this regulation. These findings not only highlight the fine line girls are required to negotiate between 'attractive' and 'provocative', but also demonstrate how girls actively negotiate the contradictory discourses of girlhood through simultaneous resistance and reproduction.

As detailed earlier in the chapter, girls negotiate dominant discourses of femininity in the context of the school ball and prom: a negotiation that often includes both accommodation and resistance. In these analyses, agency coheres around human action, for example, girls' behaviours or speech that challenges pervasive structural norms. A feminist new materialist approach offers a rethinking of girls' bodies and agency beyond notions of human will and intentionality (Barad, 2007; Bennett, 2005). Agency does not reside in the individual subject or restricted to possibilities of human action; instead, capacities are produced through particular material-discursive configurations. As such, Barad argues the space for agency in an agential realist account is larger than Butler's performative account would allow: 'Cut loose from its humanist orbit' (Barad, 2007, p. 177), agency is distributed over nonhuman and human forms. In a similar vein, Bennett's (2010, p. 21) theory of *distributive agency* offers an understanding of agency as a 'confederation' of human and nonhuman forces within assemblages. These new materialist framings of agency undermine an anthropocentric approach, which emphasizes humans as exclusively productive of the social world (Fox & Alldred, 2017).

Feminist new materialist framings of agency open up understandings of the capacities of girls' bodies in connection with other matter (Hultman & Lenz Taguchi, 2010; Ivinson & Renold, 2013; Renold & Ivinson, 2014; Ringrose & Renold, 2016; Taylor, 2013). In Hultman & Lenz Taguchi's (2010) relational materialist approach, they draw on Deleuze (1990) and Barad (2007) to think about agency as a quality emerging in-between different bodies, for instance, a girl and sand. Agency does not belong to either but emerges through their mutual engagements and relations involving muscles, hands, the force of gravity, grains of sand, surface areas and buckets. This approach troubles the notion of a distinct human/nonhuman and subject/object divide. As opposed to a subject that is 'autonomous, unitary and coherent', the subject emerges or becomes as 'an effect of an event on a relational field' (Hultman & Lenz Taguchi, 2010, pp. 531–2). Engaging with these ideas, ball-girl capacities are understood as emerging through entanglements: for example, chapter six explores how sexuality-assemblages produce particular bodily capacities for the ball-girl (Fox & Alldred, 2013). Sexual (and other) capacities are not produced by, or located within, an individual agentic subject; instead, capacities emerge via flows of affect within assembled relations.

The idea of bodies as processes (i.e. becoming) rather than stable entities invites a shift in focus from what a body *is*, to what a body can do (Coleman, 2008; Deleuze, 1988). For Deleuze (1988), bodies are defined not by what they are but by their affective capacities. These capacities are not pre-existing but are produced via relations within assemblages. From Spinoza's *affectus*, Deleuze and Guattari theorize affect as 'an ability to affect and be affected': a pre-personal intensity that can augment or diminish a body's capacity to act (Massumi, 1987, p. xiv). If bodies are defined by their capacity to affect and be affected, then affect 'refers to what bodies are and are not capable of' (Mulcahy, 2012, p. 13). In this study, relations of affect create conditions of possibility for what a ball-girl-body can do and can become. This way of thinking about bodies resonates with an agential realist approach in that ball-girl bodily capacities are not limited to discourse, nor do they derive from an individual human body. Characterizing 'the turn to affect' in body-studies, Blackman & Venn (2010, p. 9) suggest theories of affect offer a 'rethinking of the concept of embodiment' which 'take us beyond discourse and the social construction of bodily matters'. While affect can be registered bodily as intensity (Mulcahy, 2012), affect is not restricted to, or contained within, the human subject or body. Affect is relationally produced; therefore, the capacity of a ball-girl-body can 'never be defined by a body alone but is always aided and abetted by, and dovetails with, the field or context of its force-relations' (Seigworth & Gregg, 2010, p. 3). In this sense, ball-girl bodily capacities become emergent and open-ended – never fixed or pre-determined.

Conceptualizing the ball-girl-body as intra-actively becoming through relational forces (including affect) reconfigures notions of agency and resistance. Bringing together a new materialist approach to the body with Deleuzian theories of affect, Fox and Alldred (2016, p. 125) theorize 'the resisting young body' where bodily capacities for 'resistance' are produced relationally, rather than being an agentic quality pertaining to the individual body. Their relational perspective of power and resistance draws on Deleuzo-Guattarian theories of affect, assemblage and territorialization, enabling them to explore 'the affectivity of young bodies, and the flows and intensities that produce … what young bodies can do, feel and desire' (2016, p. 125). Replacing a conventional understanding of (human) agency with a focus on the capacity to affect and be affected (Deleuze, 1988) enables Fox and Alldred to theorize 'resistance' as an affective movement within assemblages. Attention moves away from a solely human focus (and the idea of bodies having agency) to explore the ways forces circulate in an assemblage to produce capacities for human bodies. This resonates with an agential realist framing of agency as a quality that emerges in between multiple relations (Barad, 2007). I draw on these ideas to conceptualize ball-girl bodily capacities as shifting from moment to moment, depending on the material relations and affectivities within the assemblage. As such, it is impossible to know in advance what a ball-girl-body might do or become.

I began this chapter by thinking about how different versions of phenomena emerge depending on what or who is entangled with the research (Bodén, 2015). The enfolding or *cutting together-apart* of academic scholarship, media and fairy-tale in this chapter has produced particular configurations or understandings of girls, bodies and the school ball. These different perspectives (or matterings) are formed through theoretical frameworks, research methods, literary style, context and audience, folklore, history, public concern and commentary. This collection of academic studies, media and fairy-tale might conventionally be considered in the past; however, the ontological foundations of the research would suggest 'the past is never finished ... we never leave it and it never leaves us behind' (Barad, 2007, p. ix). As such, this research does not have a clear beginning, nor is there an end to previous studies, literature and media commentaries that are entangled in the becoming of the research.

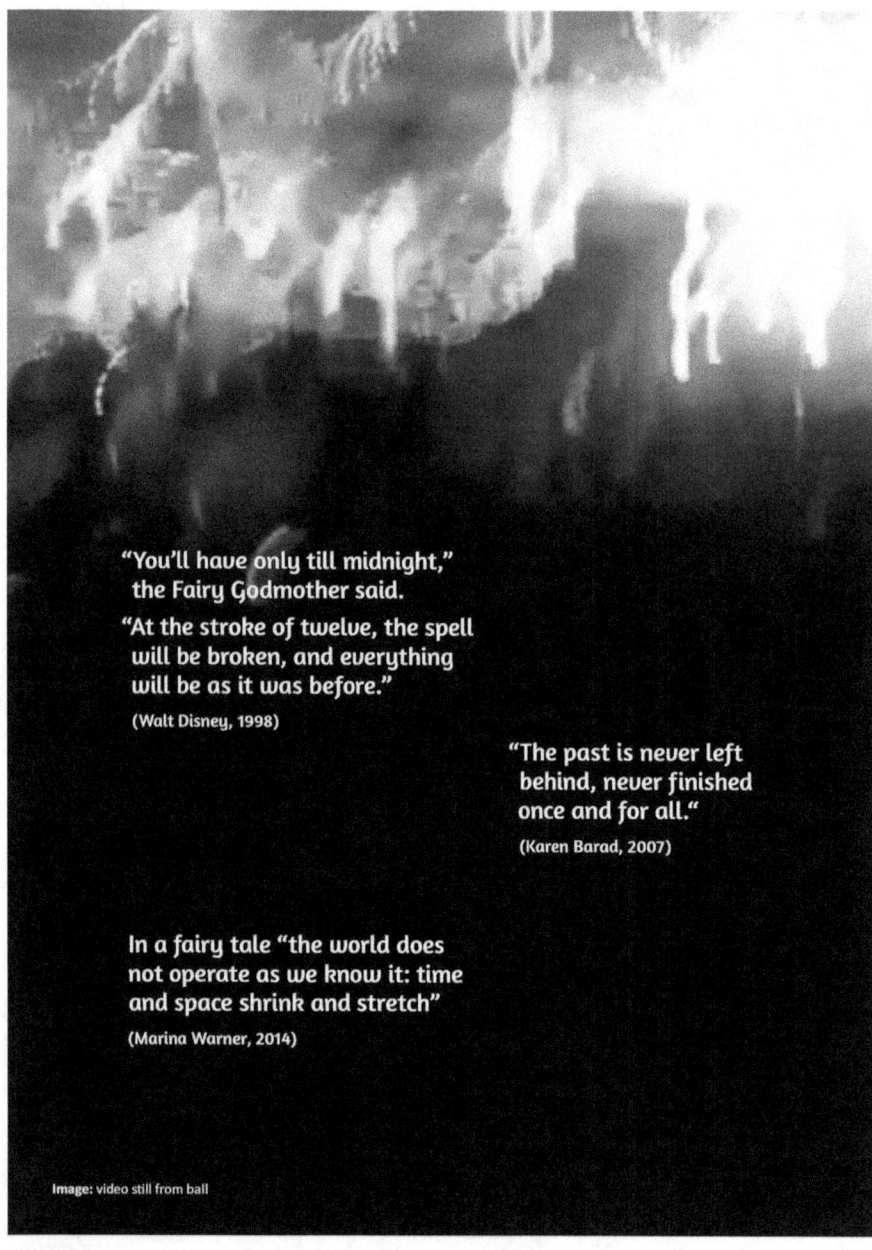

Figure 4.1 Once upon a space and time.

4

Once upon a space and time

Unlike fairy-tales, where time can shrink, bend and stretch (Warner, 2014), conventional time is usually considered linear – made up of discrete consecutive moments. The notion of the school ball as 'a night to remember' (Tait, 2014) on a coming of age trajectory echoes this linear perspective of time. Temporality and time are powerful constructs that shape understandings of childhood and 'growing up'. The idea of the ball as a social ritual that 'turns a girl into a woman' (Tay, 2007) resonates with developmental thinking where young people undergo a stage-delineated process of maturation. Feminist scholarship has drawn critical attention towards the way developmental logic can reinforce gender norms, shaping what is perceived as expected behaviour for gendered child bodies (Blaise, 2005, 2013). When attending the school ball is portrayed as a 'normal' step in social development towards adulthood, this can work to reinforce or naturalize the dominant meanings of gender and sexuality that surround this practice. It also reproduces a sense of significance and value of the event as 'the most important occasion on the social calendar for year 11, 12 and 13 students' (Murray, 2012, p. 10). As mentioned in the introductory chapter, pervasive themes in the media fuel the presumption or expectation that young people, in particular girls, will be heavily invested in the event. The school ball is often constructed as 'one night' confined to, or defined as, a few hours in which girls inhabit the physical space of the school ball venue: a notion that can be used to idealize the event as an important milestone, yet also drawn on as a means to critique girls' investments, for instance, perceived excessive spending for just 'one night'. Confining the event to the 'official' school ball time and venue places spatial-temporal limits on who or what plays a role in this schooling practice, and importantly, shapes how girls are constructed and understood.

This chapter brings together the Baradian notion of *spacetimemattering*, the concept of assemblage (Bennett, 2005; Deleuze & Guattari, 1987) and theories of affect (Deleuze, 1988) to rethink the school ball in relation to space and time.

Rather than an isolated spatial-temporal event, the school ball is understood as a continual process of becoming through shifting entanglements of space, time and matter. Crucially, the ball-girl is not a separate entity situated *in* school ball time and space, but entangled *with* space, time and matter. This approach differs to developmental thinking which tends to separate the human body from the environment (Blaise & Pacini-Ketchabaw, 2019). Within an agential realist framework, space is no longer a discrete place or 'container' in which humans inhabit (Barad, 2007); rather, space is produced through an array of entangled relations, including material configurations, time, histories, memories, affect and movement. This means space, time, matter (including the ball-girl) are co-constitutive and mutually emergent, which works to destabilize conventional spatial-temporal boundaries that often underpin reductive or developmental logic used to justify the regulation of girls' behaviour.

Drawing on Barad (2007), I consider how the 'past', 'future' and the 'now' are threaded through multiple school ball spacetimematterings unsettling a linear notion of time. The discussion draws attention to the way girls' memories, hopes and imaginings enact the 'past' and 'future' as already part of the 'present'. Here, the ball-girl is produced through intra-active relations, where space, time and matter are overlapping co-constitutive forces. From an intra-active perspective, time and age are produced through shifting and dynamic entanglements of human and more-than-human relations that produce (un)predictable effects (Hohti, 2015). This means time is no longer a neutral outside parameter upon which to measure young people's lives, including what is deemed 'appropriate' gender and sexual behaviour or 'development'. Entanglements of spacetimematter also include an array of affective forces (feelings, intensities) that circulate in-between bodies, practices and imaginings: for example, 'effort' is conceptualized not as something emanating from the human, but as a powerful affective force that emerges in the entanglement of things, discourses and embodied practices. As an affective force, effort creates a sense of 'build-up', producing feelings of anxiety, excitement and boredom. These entanglements highlight the affective materiality of atmospheric space and the force it exerts in the becoming of sexuality and the school ball-girl.

Theorizing entanglements of space and time

The ideas developed in this chapter are premised on an understanding of time and space as relational and entangled (Barad, 2001; Massey, 1994). From the field of human geography, Doreen Massey's (1992) influential work posits an understanding of 'space-time' in which time and space are inseparable. Moving beyond conceptualizations of space as static and subsequently opposed to, or devoid of, time, Massey argues space is constituted out of social relations. Relations are inherently dynamic, and as such it becomes impossible to conceive of space as a 'flat' or static surface. The conceptualization of space as produced through social relations means space is imbued with power relations, something Massey refers to as a kind of 'power-geometry' (1994, p. 149). Social relations of space are interpreted and experienced differently, depending upon one's positioning within them, thus constituting the plurality or multiplicities of space-time. In this framing, space is always in the process of being made and remade, it never ends or closes. Massey's theorizations are particularly productive in thinking about the relationality, multiplicity and openness of space and time. Rather than being independent or separate 'things', space and time are dynamic and relational forces in the becoming of the school ball.

Barad's (2007) agential realist framework similarly takes a relational approach to space and time, by thinking about time and space as produced through the dynamics of intra-activity. This means time is not understood as a given externality or a 'succession of evenly spaced individual moments', nor is space merely a 'container' for things/people to inhabit; rather, the dynamics of intra-activity constitute the making and marking of space and time (Barad, 2007, p. 180). If temporality is constituted through iterative intra-actions, then time only makes sense in the context of specific phenomena. What this means is time is no longer universally given but articulated or made through various material practices (Dolphijn & van der Tuin, 2012). For Barad, spatiality is also produced through intra-activity. It is intra-actions that enact specific boundaries; therefore, the ongoing material (re)configuring of boundaries continually (re)structures spatial relations. Importantly, this continual (re)making of space and time suggests intra-actions do not occur *in* space and time but are *of* space and time.

A crucial aspect of a Baradian understanding of space and time is it displaces the usual sense of time as chronological. What we take to be 'past', 'present' and 'future' are no longer separate or sequential; rather, they are entangled with one another. Barad describes the making and marking of time as a 'lively material process of enfolding' where 'the past and the future are enfolded participants in matter's iterative becoming' (2007, p. 181). This means there is no inherent determinate relationship between 'past', 'present' and 'future', nor do they follow one another in a linear fashion. In the entanglement or intra-activity, the 'past' is no longer determined or pre-existing, nor does the 'future' progressively unfold;

rather, the 'past' and 'future' are continually reworked through the dynamics of intra-activity. These temporal entanglements pose a dynamic reconfiguring of temporal constructs often associated with childhood, such as 'growing-up', development and youth. Time is no longer static or linear, but a relational force in ball-girl becomings.

Within an agential realist framework, matter is productive and implicated in the production of space and time, a process Barad refers to as *spacetimemattering* (2007). Space, time and matter are produced together in one ongoing movement – they are overlapping, intertwined and co-constitutive forces. This theorizing posits matter not as a fixed substance but as a 'dynamic intra-active becoming' (Barad, 2007, p. 170). Barad's reframing of space and time as spacetimemattering offers a way to think about spatiality and temporality as co-existing forces in the becoming of the school ball-girl. Bodies (the ball-girl for instance) are not located or positioned within school ball space; rather bodies, space and time are materialized through the dynamics of intra-activity, more specifically spacetimematterings. Establishing the entanglement of space, time and other matter blurs conventional spatial and temporal borders of the school ball. Rather than a fixed space or moment in time, the school ball is continually becoming anew. This reframing provides openings for understanding the ball-girl differently; rather than conceptualizing the school ball as a 'coming of age' ritual, ball-girl becomings are constantly reconfigured by multiple and nonlinear spacetimematterings.

Re-mattering the school ball: past–present–future

Following Barad, the 'past' and 'future' are considered intra-actively entangled in girls' enactments of the school ball and mutually implicated in the becoming of the ball-girl. The past and future are key components in the school ball spatial-temporal assemblage in that they are always already part of the 'present'. Vestiges of the past and future permeate participants' talk about the school ball: memories of seeing older sisters go to school balls; perceptions of the ball imbued with history, movies and fairy-tales; the hope that the ball will be special and memorable. In a Baradian sense, we might think of it as 're-turning (to) the past', not a returning as in reflecting on the past, but a 're-turning, turning it over and over again, tasting the rich soil from which ideas spring' (Barad, 2014, p. 184). Rather than time unfolding in a linear fashion, girls' imaginings of the ball, their expectations and memories, move across, beyond and in between past, present and future. The following fragments enact this flow of multiple tenses and temporalities:

So what are the positive things about the ball?
The dancing [laughter], like the dancing would probably be the best bit
And like, the excitement of like getting ready
Yeah [multiple]
Getting ready, the pre-ball and taking photos all together is so good
Mmm [multiple]
Like that bit is exciting
Yeah the photos are pretty good
You kind of like have talked about it your whole lives kind of thing, like going to your ball
Yeah seeing my sister go to hers, like, I was always like 'oh I want to go to my ball'
Yeah, so exciting
(Year 13, focus group, 3 voices)

How long have people been talking about the ball?
About half way through last year [laughter]
Since Year 9! When you're in Year 9, I know lots of students, I was one of those students, don't judge me [directed towards other participant], like they look forward to, they see the ball as part of becoming a senior, and they look forward to it because everyone talks about it, they see it happening, they see their big sisters or they see photos and they're like oh this is a really big glamorous event, when is that ever going to happen again? Like, I think that's why people try so hard, you get to pretend that you're sort of famous, do all the glamorous glitzy stuff at the cost of spending so much money
(Year 12, focus group, 3 voices)

The multiple temporalities and spaces enacted include references to childhood, beginning high school, balls attended by siblings, preparations, getting ready, the evening of the school ball and the sharing of photos after. Tenses and temporalities shift within each fragment, times seeping through one another: what the ball is, *'part of becoming a senior'*, was, *'you kind of like have talked about it your whole lives'*, and will be, *'a really big glamorous event'*. The past and future materialize via girls' memories, both actual and potential. The past surfaces as girls recall looking forward to and talking about the ball since childhood or the beginning of high school (Year 9 – four years prior). Seeing older sisters attend the ball or viewing ball photos on social media fuels this anticipation. One voice declares *'being one of those students'* who have looked forward to the ball since beginning Year 9. Memories enact not only the past but also the future, in that the school ball holds the promise of potential memories. The ball is considered a rare event and therefore *'memorable'* and *'special'* for some girls: as one participant notes, *'when is that ever going to happen again?'*

Traces of history, tradition and fairy-tale emerge in girls' imaginings of the school ball. These perceptions are material-discursive entanglements that can include discourses of 'princess femininity' and unattainable goals of beauty and perfection (Shannon, 2015), beauty-body practices and related financial and economic implications, feelings of excitement and ambivalence. The following fragment is one example:

> *I've got sort of high expectations but then 'cause I'm helping organise it, I'm sort of like … mmm … maybe not*
> *Expectations in what kind of way?*
> *Like 'cause you see all this American commercialised stuff and then you like think it's going to be like the movies, and then you're like, my ball must be like that*
> *Mmm [multiple]*
> *I think everyone is sort of different, like some people are fine with spending, having quite a low budget and making it work, but some are like 'oh this is the dream'*
> *Go all out*
> *Go all out and be a princess*
> *Yeah [laughter]*
> *And that's ok*
>
> (Year 12, focus group, 4 voices)

Residue from childhood stories and movies emerge in comments such as *'you think it's going to be like in the movies'* and *'go all out and be a princess'*. Images from television and fairy-tales enter the assemblage as 'material-discursive imaginaries' (Lenz Taguchi & Palmer, 2013, p. 680). A participant notes how *'American commercialised stuff'* can influence perception and expectations of the ball, which may connect with pervasive themes of perfection found in prom media and the expectation to engage in beauty-body work (Mazzarella, 1999; Zlatunich, 2009). Yet at other times, historical resonances were a relational force entangled with feelings of uncertainty and critique:

> *Well it doesn't really appeal that much, it just seems a bit you know, materialistic and the reason behind it has sort of gone with the years as well, like, it just doesn't have the same value that it used to. It's, I don't know, also it's really expensive and I don't know whether I care enough to spend that much money*
> *Mmm*

And it's ridiculous the amount of worth people put into things like this, cause yeah
For one night, it's a bit too much, I put worth into it, but not that much worth
(Year 12, focus group, 3 voices)

Ripples of history emerge in this fragment where imaginings of the school ball are imbued with historical resonance: one participant declaring the ball was 'materialistic and the reason behind it has sort of gone with the years'. School balls in Aotearoa New Zealand have been a tradition for senior students for many years (Tay, 2007; White, 2007). The history of the event is not prior and past, but rather materializes in and as current balls. Historical legacies of the event are part of the array of ideas and concepts that form the contemporary school ball. In the previous fragment, vague historical notions of the ball infuse current imaginings: 'it just doesn't have the same value that it used to'. As such, the participant was undecided as to whether she was going to attend the ball and if she cared enough to 'spend that much money'. Feelings of anticipation, excitement and ambivalence are intra-actively entangled with memories, imaginings and expectations:

I'm definitely going. I'm really excited [laughter]
Same
So you always knew you wanted to go?
Yup, I always like looked at everyone, they posted their ball pictures and I just always thought, oh my gosh! I really want to go, get all my make-up done and look really pretty
Even when I first started high school, I was like oh my gosh, yes this is like the start of when I'm going to be able to go to the ball, high school is when you go to the ball, this is exciting
[agreement and laughter]
[groan] Oh my gosh
[laughter]
So this is your first ball. Do you know what to expect? Or what do you hope for?
I'm not expecting much, I'm completely opposite, I didn't like, never thought about the ball, it's just like, Meh [shrugs shoulders], yeah I might go, it's more the fact that everyone is going that I might go, like if a few of my friends weren't going I'd just hang out with them instead
(Year 12, focus group, 4 voices)

In this fragment, mutual enthusiasm for the ball, '*oh my gosh! I really want to go*', mixes with a lack of enthusiasm, '*it's just like, meh, yeah I might go*'. The utterance '*meh*' and accompanying shoulder shrug conveying a sense of ambivalence towards the ball. The participant explains how she has very low expectations and, like some others, did not wish to spend a large amount of money on the occasion. As the first two participants laughed and talked about looking forward to the ball since starting high school, the third lets out an audible groan and accompanying 'oh my gosh': the tone manifesting a sense of bafflement and friendly mockery. This affective bodily response is an example of the materiality of language where 'language is in and of the body; always issuing from the body; being impeded by the body; affecting other bodies' (MacLure, 2013a, p. 663). As the groan issues forth from her body, I imagine her eyes rolling in accompaniment; both affective bodily responses to her peers' animated and enthusiastic talk about the ball. The participant's groan and 'oh my gosh' evoked laughter from the 'enthusiastic' participants, further adding to the flow of affect (Fox, 2013).

The phrase 'oh my gosh' was uttered by all three girls during the conversation, but for some it enacted a sense of enthusiasm and delight. 'Oh my gosh' moments can be understood as an affective response of the body (Mulcahy, 2016); the affective force, perhaps excitement or ambivalence, varied depending on other entangled relations. Bodily entanglements of language (MacLure, 2013a), such as laughter, groaning and exclamations 'meh' and 'oh my gosh' produce feelings and sensations that circulate in and among this discussion: humour, anticipation, excitement, bewilderment, indifference and jovial mockery. These sensations or affective forces articulate the material force of language and its entanglements with body and matter (MacLure, 2013a), opening up ball-girl matterings in ways that are not wholly constrained by discursive forces, such as presumed excitement or investment in the school ball.

School ball as becoming: one night and more

Developing an understanding of the school ball as becoming, the school ball moves across, beyond and in-between multiple temporalities (i.e. past-present-future) and multiple spaces. As such, the school ball is not merely 'one night' confined to, or defined as, a few hours in which girls inhabit the physical space of the school ball venue. Rather, the school ball is produced through material-discursive relations, and depending on the relations the school ball can be both one night and much more. School ball preparations and 'build up' are conceptualized not as separate to the school ball (in time or space), but as spacetimematterings through which the school ball and ball-girl become. Preparations encompass an array of human and more-than-human matter, places, discourses, ideas and imaginings, all of which are implicated in the production of space and time; thus, not only expanding the conventional boundaries of the school ball but the scope of who or what comes to matter.

Within a new materialist ontology, it no longer makes sense to view the school ball as an isolated temporal and spatial event – a configuration that underpins enduring constructions of the ball as an important milestone towards adulthood, yet is also used to diminish or critique girls' investments in the event (i.e. excessive for 'just one night'). Spatial-temporal boundaries are blurred: there is no longer a clear divide between the lead-up to the ball, getting ready on the day, the actual ball itself, post-ball conversations and the viewing/sharing of photos. Instead, they are relational intra-active forces that collaboratively enact the school ball. The following fragment enacts this blurring of temporal and spatial boundaries as girls discuss school ball preparations and their parents' thoughts about the ball:

> *My mum liked coming around with me and trying on the dresses and stuff, and then but my Dad is like 'why is this so expensive?' Because it's the school ball! 'It's just a disco' [imitating Dad's voice]. It is not just a disco. He doesn't understand what it means to a girl*
>
> *I went away with my Mum and we got the dress together, I paid for it and when we got back I showed it to my Dad, and he asked 'how much did that cost?' and when I told him he was like 'that is so expensive', but I didn't really think about it*
>
> *You said he doesn't get what it means to a girl, so what does it mean? What doesn't he get?*
>
> *It's just like one thing, but for a girl it's like all the preparation, all the organisation, it's all build up, so for someone to just say 'oh it's just one night', yeah it's just one night, but it's one night of the result of everything that's happened: all of the pressure, all the organisation, all the prep, all the hair, make-up, and yeah*
>
> (Year 12, focus group, 3 voices)

In this enactment, the school ball is more than an isolated spatial-temporal event with clear boundaries, that is, the school ball venue or a clearly defined point in time. As one voice explains, *'it's just one night, but it's one night of the result of everything that's happened'*: the pressure, organization, preparations and other forces. These elements are not independent of the ball, they are intra-active forces in its becoming. Preparations are a particularly salient and material aspect of the school ball: shopping, choosing what to wear, planning hair and make-up, pre-ball preparations, organizing dates, transport and post-ball activities. These preparations (and financial obligations) can begin months in advance and extend across numerous spaces: school classrooms, girls' homes, cars and public transport, shopping malls, beauty/hair salons and online spaces such as retail websites and social media platforms. They involve multiple human bodies, including friends, parents, siblings and professionals such as hairdressers and make-up artists, paid and unpaid labour, financial investment, commitment of time and energy. These material-discursive relations continually (re)configure the school ball and the ethico-political implications of who or what matters in its becoming.

Figure 4.2 Ball venue-home-makeup-bodies-laptop-decorations ...

This image comprising four participant photographs enacts multiple temporalities (hours, days, months before the ball), spaces (girls' bedrooms, bathrooms, the school ball venue), human and more-than-human matter (make-up, nail polish, furniture, bodies, decorations). A new materialist engagement with these photographs encourages the multiple spaces, temporalities and more-than-human matter to 'rise to the surface' (Allen, 2015a, p. 12). The caption indicates some, but not all of these entangled relations. Engaging with these photographs diffractively (Allen, 2015a; Hultman & Lenz Taguchi, 2010), the materiality of these 'things' overlaps with discourses of femininity, participant comments, preparations and responsibilities, and my own memories of attending the ball (both as a teenager and as a researcher). A photograph (top-right) shows the day of the ball; a human body (participant) sitting in a chair at home; another body (her sister) leans in; a lip pencil-hand configuration applies make-up. I recall the participant feeling pleased her sister did her make-up as she 'trusted her' more than someone she did not know. Another image (bottom-left) depicts a bottle of red nail polish enveloped by a hand with bright red nails; light glints off the thumb nail; the nail-polish-hand configuration casts a shadow on the wooden surface where another small bottle of polish rests; the participant has added the text 'painting nails night before the ball'.

A member of the school ball committee shared a photo (bottom-right) taken during a visit to the school ball venue a few months prior to the ball. The image shows the conference centre, table centrepieces that will be used on the evening; these material elements entangled with responsibilities and time commitment of being on the school ball organizational committee. When I look at this image, I recall the evening of the ball – the atmosphere, lighting and decorations – I am surprised it is the same place. Another image (top-left) depicts an array of make-up, a laptop and desk; a participant has added the text 'make-up time' to the image. The material objects and text in this photograph overlap with ball preparations, beauty-body practices and ideas of feminine beauty. Emerging through entangled relations, the school ball becomes a never-ending enfolding of spaces, temporalities, objects, discourses, memories, histories and affective forces. It is a material-discursive and affective process that is always in process of becoming. This means the emergence of space is multiple and fluid, never closed or complete. Importantly, it is the assembled relations that create possibilities and constraints for the becoming of space and human experience in relation with it (Allen et al., 2020).

In thinking about the school ball as a material-discursive-affective process, school ball talk emerged as a powerful affective force that permeated the material schooling environment, such as classroom spaces and senior common rooms: What are you wearing? Have you got your dress? Are you taking a date? These discussions are entanglements of bodies, discursive expectations, spatial configurations and material objects; for instance, mobile phones were used to peruse websites and share photos of dresses, shoes and hairstyles. This talk generated bodily feelings and reactions such as excitement, boredom and stress; these emotions enter the material-discursive assemblage of 'getting ready':

> *It's quite stressful I find, when people bring it up every conversation though, cause I don't have a lot organised*
> *Mmm I find it quite boring sometimes*
> *Yeah and when you don't have a lot organised and people go on about how they're got everything sorted, it's sort of like, oh my god, like some people have had everything sorted from the first day of this year*
>
> (Year 12, focus group, 2 voices)

> *I remember like, because the ball is in August, people were saying that like MAC make-up was booked out months in advance, and in a way that, because everyone was so prepared that stressed me out a little. Wait, should I be as prepared as these people? Like they were talking about their dresses, and I was not even ... I don't know what's up*
> *I have an internal [assessment] this week, I'm not focussing on make-up!*
> *It's ridiculous, a lot of it is just build up.*
> *Is there as much build up in Year 13 as Year 12?*
> *I think we're more chill about it*
>
> (Year 13, focus group, 3 voices)

These fragments enact the affective relations in between talk, schooling commitments, beauty practices and ball preparations that come to matter in ways that were experienced as *'stressful'* and *'boring'*. As one participant notes, 'I have an internal [assessment] this week, I'm not focussing on make-up!' The expectation to *'make an effort'* was a powerful force circulating within affective relations: making an effort to look different to how they normally look at school; making an effort to have fun on the night. Effort is conceptualized not as something located within or emanating from the human subject, but as an affective force or intensity produced relationally through bodies, physical and emotional labour, discourses of femininity, imaginings and embodied practices. Affect, in the form of effort, is found in the intensities and resonances that circulate and pass in between bodies, both human and nonhuman (Gregg & Seigworth, 2010). The affective force of effort comes to matter through emergent constraints and capacities where power relations traverse bodies of all kinds. Time, emotional and physical labour, a sense of 'build up', feelings of stress and boredom, academic assessment and school responsibilities come together in ways that can both constrain girls' behaviour in the form of expected investment and labour, yet can also produce an affective resistance (Alldred & Fox, 2017) to dominant expectations enabling a *'more chill'* ball-girl.

The affective force of effort is an intrinsic part of the social-material-discursive fabric of the school ball, co-constituting a sense of 'build up'. Build up is itself an affect – a vital force that can make us feel, think and act in different ways. It does not reside in subject or object, but forms part of an affective flow that produces bodies and the social world (Fox, 2015). This 'build up' forms, and is formed by, a multitude of feelings, from anticipation and excitement to boredom, anxiety and worry. These emotions are one element within a broader flow of affect (Ahmed, 2004b; Fox, 2013) that produces the school ball. 'Effort' and 'build up' can be understood as affective forces shaping the becoming of the school ball-girl in particular ways. I argue here that the affective relations of bodies, things and practices are threaded through or flow among multiple spacetimematterings (Juelskjaer, 2013). As such, space and time are understood as always-already affective (Anderson, 2006); affect does not happen after an 'event' but rather enacts space-time. Or, in Baradian terms, affect is part of the intra-activity of spacetimemattering, where components (spatiality, temporality, affect) are produced in one ongoing movement. The next section returns to consider the affective force of effort, how it produced and could be 'felt' in the atmosphere of the school ball.

Continuing to think about school ball preparations as entangled forces in the becoming of the school ball, several girls noted how the lead-up to the ball was *'the fun bit'*:

> *Getting ready was fun, make-up and hair, as I don't normally get an opportunity to do that, pre-ball with friends was fun, but then the actual ball I couldn't really walk, my heels hurt, and like I didn't dance. I sat there and it got really boring towards the end, but having the photos was nice, they looked nice. It was fun, worth it, but the actual event wasn't like this amazing thing, it was kind of boring. Not like you see on American movies when it's like, 'oh my gosh, dancing with my crush' [laughter]*
>
> (Year 13, focus group, 2 voices)

This fragment enacts multiple spatial-temporalities, including *'getting ready'*, the pre-ball and the *'actual event'*. Activities conventionally categorized as 'prior' to the ball, for instance, the styling of hair and make-up, and having photos taken were considered more fun than the 'actual' ball itself; this participant's enjoyment and physical movement at the ball hampered by high heels and sore feet. Rather than being separate to the ball, these 'events' or components are intra-actively entangled in girls' recollections and experiences of the school ball as a whole. Pre-balls were a common part of the ball and occurred just 'prior' to the 'actual' ball. They were informally arranged by groups of friends and usually held at someone's house. Parents were often invited and appeared an integral part of these events:

> *What do you do for pre-balls? Go to someone's house?*
> *Yeah just eat some food and talk to people*
> *It's so much more for the parents' benefit*
> *Yeah*
> *Like my mother was really annoyed that I didn't go to one last year, she was like, 'I wanted to go and see all the people in their dresses Kate, you've let me down'. I'm sorry. Wow ok! [laughter]*
> *Because they go along too?*
> *Yeah [multiple]*
> *It is just for the parents*
> *Yeah, I like prefer the pre-ball to the actual ball, like the food, you get to have whatever food*
>
> (Year 13, focus group, 5 voices)

In addition to foregrounding material elements, photographs convey discursive meanings, ideas and imaginings, perhaps even glimpses of an affective atmosphere (mood and feelings). Photographs create a sense of the overlapping material-affective forces: home, parents, the preparation and sharing of food and drinks, feelings of surprise and enjoyment seeing friends dressed up, meeting friends' dates, cameras and the expectation to stand and smile for photographs. The ball itself involves only students, their dates and school staff, so the pre-ball enabled parents to be part of the festivities. Parental involvement is a further intra-active element in the school ball assemblage encompassing parental idea(l)s and expectations, financial and emotional investment, nostalgia and memories. In the previous fragment, a participant recalls her mother's disappointment she did not attend a pre-ball: *'I wanted to go and see all the people in their dresses Kate'*. Affective dynamics involving parental investment and emotions also emerge in the following fragment:

> *They love it. They love seeing us getting all dressed up and everything*
> *Yeah [multiple]*

My mum loves taking photos, 'Olivia stand over there'
Oh my god, my mother was like crying, so bad, she cries
Parents really love it I think
Yeah it's exciting for them as well, they get involved, due to like the pre-ball and stuff which is nice as well
What do you think they like about it?
Just seeing us, it's kind of like a point in their like, you know, your life when you do, you're finally come to your ball, so I think it's kind of exciting for them, seeing you look all pretty, yeah

(Year 13, focus group, 4 voices)

Participants' recollections of last year's ball enact a flow of affect involving parents' emotions and reactions to seeing them *'look all pretty'* and *'all dressed up'*: taking photos, feelings of pride, excitement and tears. These affective relations are productive in the emergence of school ball space and work to shape

Figure 4.3 Bodies-food-drinks-decorations-home-car-friends-cameras-parents-dates ...

and constrain ball-girl becomings, for instance, parental expectations to attend events such as pre-balls. Blurring the spatial-temporal boundaries of the school ball beyond 'just one night' offers a wider expanse for examining the spatial, material and affective dynamics that collaboratively produce time, girls and the school ball. In doing so, it might enable a perspective that gets closer to the sentiment mentioned earlier: *'it's just one night, but it's one night of the result of everything that's happened'*.

The affective materiality of atmospheric space

The final section of this chapter turns to the school ball 'event' itself – the evening that is the culmination of months of effort, pressure and preparation. The following discussion explores school ball atmosphere as produced through entangled material-discursive-affective relations or multiple spacetimematterings. Affective qualities circulate within the assembling of bodies of all types, human and more-than-human (Deleuze, 1988), offering an understanding of atmosphere that is more than discursive. Various kinds of affective intensities are mobilized or threaded through entangled spacetimematter (Juelskjaer, 2013). I am interested in the affective qualities of the school ball atmosphere and how this atmosphere might exert a force in ball-girl becomings.

The term atmosphere is commonly used to denote mood, feeling, ambience or the tone of a space or place (Anderson, 2009). Atmospheres can be perceived as sensory and emotional experiences – the 'feel' of a place. While atmospheres can be felt or sensed, they are not exclusively personal experiences or states-of-mind; atmospheres are located in-between experiences and environments (Bille et al., 2015). For Böhme (1993), atmospheres cohere in-between subject and object, in that they are not solely attributable to or located in either. Böhme suggests an atmosphere is not free floating but 'something that proceeds from and is created by things, persons, or their constellations' (1993, p. 122). Atmospheres in this sense are relational; they emerge through the intermingling of bodies and matter (Bissell, 2010). As such, the boundaries between object and subject are blurred. In a Baradian sense, we could think of the school ball atmosphere as intra-actively produced; they are not pre-existing, nor are they independent of the relational forces that produce them. This entanglement means atmosphere can also be productive and affective in the becoming of sexuality, gender and the ball-girl, shaping actions and capacities.

The concept of affective atmospheres (Anderson, 2009; Bissell, 2010) highlights the 'affectively charged quality of certain spaces and places' (Healy, 2014, p. 36), perhaps the school ball entrance or the dance floor. Affective atmospheres encapsulate not only the emotional feel of a place, but also what may be possible: 'the store of action-potential, the dispositions, the agencies, potentially enactable in that place' (Duff, 2010, pp. 881–2). Affect in relation to atmosphere is defined more broadly than emotion; it is a force, a capacity to affect and be affected (Deleuze, 1988). The potential for things to act or change is relational (Bissell, 2010). Bissell suggests thinking of an affective atmosphere as 'a *propensity*: a pull or charge that might emerge in a particular space which might (or might not) generate particular events and actions, feelings and emotions' (2010, p. 273, italics in original). Affect flows through the school ball environment in-between bodies and other matter producing particular capacities or possibilities for ball-girl-bodies, such as feelings and actions. Although, these capacities are not fixed or universally experienced as they shift and change depending on other relational forces. A key point here is affective atmospheres actively constitute or produce space (Anderson, 2009); thus we can understand affective atmospheres as exerting a powerful force in the becoming of the school ball-girl.

Understanding affect as relationally constituted means affects do not reside in individual places or bodies, but rather in the dynamic and relational interaction of places and bodies (Massumi, 2002) or rather intra-action (Barad, 2007). Drawing on Deleuze and Guattari, Anderson (2009, p. 80) suggests atmospheres are generated by bodies of multiple types: human, nonhuman, discursive, 'affecting one another as some kind of "envelopment" is produced'. As such, affective atmospheres occur across human and nonhuman materialities and in-between subject/object distinctions (Anderson, 2009). In thinking about the school ball atmosphere as affective and relational, consider the intermingling (intra-action) of things, people and spaces in the following image.

Applying a relational materialist reading to this photograph (Hultman & Lenz Taguchi, 2010), my attention is drawn to matter of all kinds: furniture, lighting, clothing, decorations, architecture and varied bodies. A relational materialist approach attempts to 'flatten' human and more-than-human forces and conceptualize them as 'connecting and overlapping in a relational and horizontal field' (Hultman & Lenz Taguchi, 2010, p. 530). My gaze is drawn to the bright twinkly lines, warm-coloured at the top of the image. I can see clusters of balloons intermingling with the lights that hang like streamers, embellishments to help create a festive occasion, a celebration. I imagine a festive, celebratory

Figure 4.4 Dance floor-balloons-twinkly lights-moving bodies-tables-chairs-seated bodies ...

feeling accentuated by the effort that has been made to decorate the space. There are clusters of furniture – tables and chairs – drawing human bodies together under glowing fairy lights and balloons. I imagine a vibrant energy emanating from these configurations of metal, wood, fabric and flesh.

There is a large space in the middle of the room, a smooth hard surface as opposed to the surrounding soft carpet. There are human bodies gathered on one side of the smooth square space; the shape and form of human bodies vary. I see human flesh/matter, clothing, jewellery, a mobile phone, accessories and corsages intermingling. The lighting is dimmer in this space compared to the rest of the room. The varied bodies encompass feet, legs, arms and heads at differing angles suggesting movement, dancing. I see glimpses of bare feet and can imagine the feel of the hard surface underneath. There are big smiles and hands in the air – these signals fuse with the glittery lights and balloons to further radiate a celebratory feeling. My gaze looks more closely at the clothing in this mobile configuration: long formal dresses, lace and glittery ornamentation. Each dress a unique configuration of style, colour and fabric: when in-relation to a body it covers or exposes arms, back or shoulders. There is one tuxedo. Out of all the human bodies in this cluster there are two, perhaps three that are aware of the camera's existence – they smile and look directly at the camera. The image is a shimmer of the affective atmosphere of the school ball, where affective qualities are produced in the entanglement of things, bodies, energies and spaces.

The ball-girl is not situated in an atmosphere but part of the atmosphere (Bille, 2015) inextricably entwined with an array of material-discursive-affective forces. Earlier in this chapter, I considered 'effort' and 'build up' as intra-active forces in school ball preparations that shape the becoming of the school ball-girl in particular ways. The affective force of effort also permeates the school ball atmosphere as a potential or charge that could be sensed or felt. The following fragment enacts the affective scene of effort, build up and feelings of happiness which produce a collective 'buzz':

I think the good thing about the ball is that it's a nice experience, everyone is dressing up and it's just something you don't do very often, so it's just a nice change
Yeah
And there's also a lot of build up for it as well, like you hear about from Year 6, about this big event
I think my favourite will be just seeing the change actually, just watching everyone kind of like put some effort into it, I know that sounds real materialistic, but it's great to see someone change and like put effort into something that makes them look fantastic and hopefully they will enjoy looking fantastic, so they will be happy to be there, kind of thing
Yeah
So then if they're happy, their happiness will feed onto someone else and eventually everyone will be happy and it'll make for a great time. Hopefully. That is my view
A good buzz going around

(Year 12, focus group, 2 voices)

This 'buzz' can be understood as an affective quality emerging from the assembling of bodies, effort, material-discursive practices and things. It is an affective force registered as a felt intensity – as one voice explains, effort produces the capacity to look fantastic, this produces feelings of happiness, then this happiness will 'feed onto someone else and eventually everyone will be happy'. Another participant elaborates on this collective happiness as 'a good buzz going around'. As an affective atmospheric quality, 'buzz' is a quality felt through sensing bodies, 'something distributed yet palpable, a quality of environmental immersion that registers in and through sensing bodies whilst also remaining diffuse, in the air, ethereal' (McCormack, 2008, p. 413). Affective qualities, such as happiness and a buzz, can be understood as emanating from bodies yet not

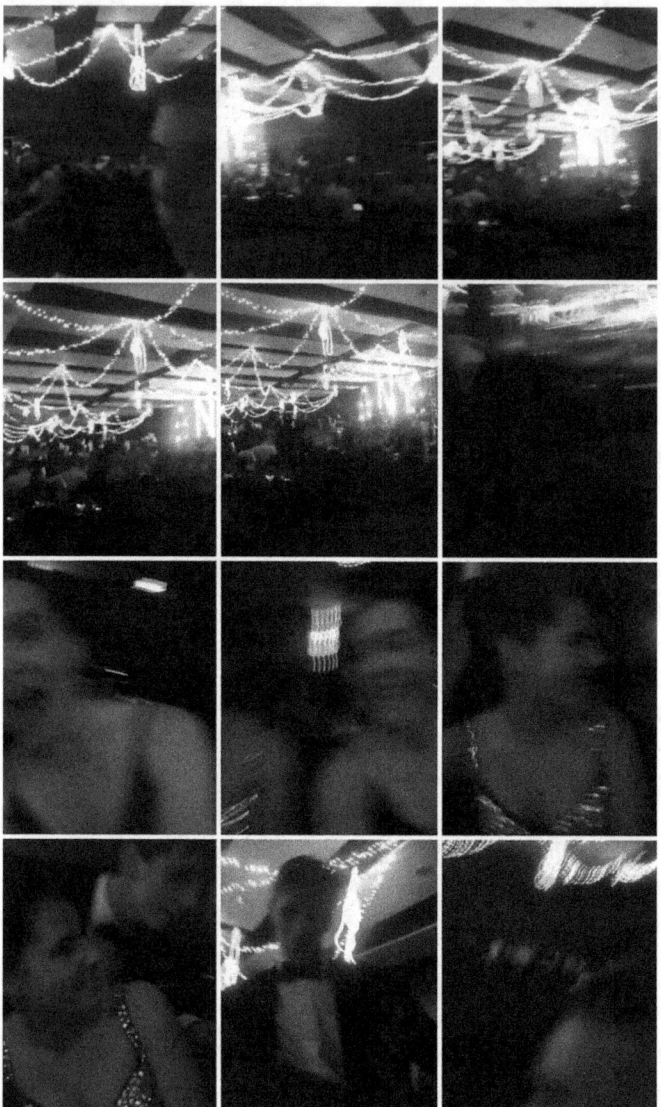

Figure 4.5 Ball video still sequence.

reducible to them (Anderson, 2009); something felt (in individual bodies) yet belongs to a collective space.

This series of images are stills from a video taken by a participant at the school ball. The images capture the physical space of the ball: the dance floor, clusters of bodies, glittering strings of lights, moving bodies, clothing – a tuxedo, a sparkly dress. As they are stills from a video, the images are at times blurred due to the movement of bodies and camera. Listening to the video, I hear music, laughter, the music changes to a new song, there is cheering and singing coming from the dance floor. The camera focuses on two participants laughing, smiling and nodding their heads in time with the music. A male body enters the frame, moves in and looks directly at the camera. These images convey the materiality and 'feel' of the space through the warm twinkly lights, smiling laughing faces and dancing bodies. The collection of forces generates an affective charge – an energy that is intra-actively produced among lighting, bodies, facial expressions, sounds, movement and space.

Earlier, the chapter explored the affective force of effort, where making an effort to look different and have fun on the night circulated as an affective force among and in-between bodies, things and imaginings. *'Seeing the change'* in people was often cited as a favourite part of the ball. While one participant notes, this focus on the aesthetic *'might sound materialistic'*, in a sense it speaks to the very materiality of becoming ball-girl – it is an embodied process involving fleshed, moving, thinking, feeling bodies. Effort is constituted as something you could see and feel, both in individual bodies but also as part of a larger affective 'buzz' circulating in the school ball atmosphere. The affective qualities of an atmosphere can function as a powerful disciplinary force. 'Buzz' is part of an affective flow that produces ball-girl-bodies, shaping expected or desirable behaviour. While atmospheres may be invisible, they are not inert or passive. As Bissell (2010, p. 272) suggests, atmospheres 'are forceful and affect the ways in which we inhabit these spaces'. Girls were expected to not only 'make an effort' in terms of 'looking different' (as I shall discuss in the next chapter), they were also expected to have a good time and not be a *'downer'*:

> *Were there any other expectations for the ball?*
> Be happy I guess, have a good time, yeah
> *And is that expectation from the school or each other?*
> Kind of both
> But if there was one sad friend you'd be like, oh my god, just cheer up
> Yeah that would be frustrating
> It's a ball come on, be happy
> Then the teachers have to deal with it as well, and they don't want to either, it's kind of their night as well, like 'cause it's their girls from their tutor class and stuff like that so, yeah
> *Does it have like a celebratory feel to it as well, like a celebration?*

> *Yeah cause it's our last year, it's special*
> *Kind of sad*
>
> (Year 13, focus group, 3 voices)

Thinking about affect in relation to spaces enables us to consider what the ball-girl *can do* rather than what she is, for instance, the expectation to *'be happy'* and *'have a good time'*. Bissell (2010, p. 284) suggests 'through the movement of affect, dispositions become fostered and bodies become primed to act in different ways'. With this view, we can understand the affective atmosphere of the school ball as both producing and produced by the ball-girl. Being *'sad'* and not having a good time was considered frustrating as it potentially impacted on both student and teacher enjoyment of the ball, therefore, sad bodies become out of place, or 'affect aliens' to use Sara Ahmed's term (2010, p. 30). Ahmed's work opens up understandings of how emotions are distributed and circulate across a social field, playing an important role in the 'surfacing' of individual and collective bodies (2004a). The expectation to *'not bring the mood down'* is echoed in the following fragment:

> *I feel like in some ways, you kind of want to hide, if you're not having a good time you kind of want to hide it, unless all your friends are having a bad time and then you just sit and mope around all together, like sitting around a table, that's fun. But if you're not having as much fun as everyone else and they're all having fun, it's kind of expected, like you expect yourself to not bring the mood down on everyone else. I'm going to write it, you're expected to have fun. You've put all this effort into it so if you're not having fun then there's something wrong with you, or something you brought, or your friends, it's not the actual thing they organised*
>
> (Year 13, focus group, 1 voice)

Mood or feelings do not adhere to the school ball itself, but are produced in the configuration of individuals, friends or *'something you brought'* – perhaps a date – that affects behaviour (see chapter six for this discussion). There is a co-constitutive and entangled relationship among affective intensities, feelings, moods and the affective atmosphere of the school ball. I have already suggested that feelings, things, materialities intra-actively produce spatial-temporalities and the school ball atmosphere; conversely, the affective atmosphere also affects bodies in particular ways, for example, the expectation and individual responsibility to have a good time. As one participant notes, if someone is not having a good time *'you kind of want to hide it'*, an expectation she placed on both herself and others. The atmosphere of the school ball is produced through entangled material-discursive and affective relations that are continually being reconfigured. This atmosphere exerts a force creating shifting conditions of (im)possibility: make an effort to look different, be happy, not sad. The atmosphere does not simply occupy the school ball space; rather, it is intra-actively produced by and produces the school ball-girl.

Concluding–continuing thoughts

During the recruitment stage of the research, I contacted several school principals inviting their school to take part. The response from one principal in particular has remained with me throughout the research. While politely declining the invitation to take part in the research, the principal made the comment that he 'would rather our girls spent more time on their homework and less time thinking about this event that lasts but one evening'. It was not the declining of the research that bothered me; rather, it was the sentiment towards girls that was conveyed in his comment. To me, his comment conveyed ideas about girls' perceived investments in the school ball and their homework responsibilities, along with dominant cultural ideas of the school ball as 'but one evening'. His comment resonates with popular (gendered) constructions of girls and school balls within the media, for instance, the perception that girls are highly invested in the ball, which can lead to excessive and competitive behaviour (Tait, 2014). I was left with the feeling that something was being missed here. Blurring its customary spatial-temporal borders opens up possibilities for reimagining the school ball beyond popular cultural narratives, such as a 'coming of age' milestone or 'rite of passage'. This, in turn, offers a rethinking of the ball-girl beyond linear and developmental logic. Becoming ball-girl does not occur *in* space and time; rather, ball-girl becomings are continually reconfigured *with* space, time and matter.

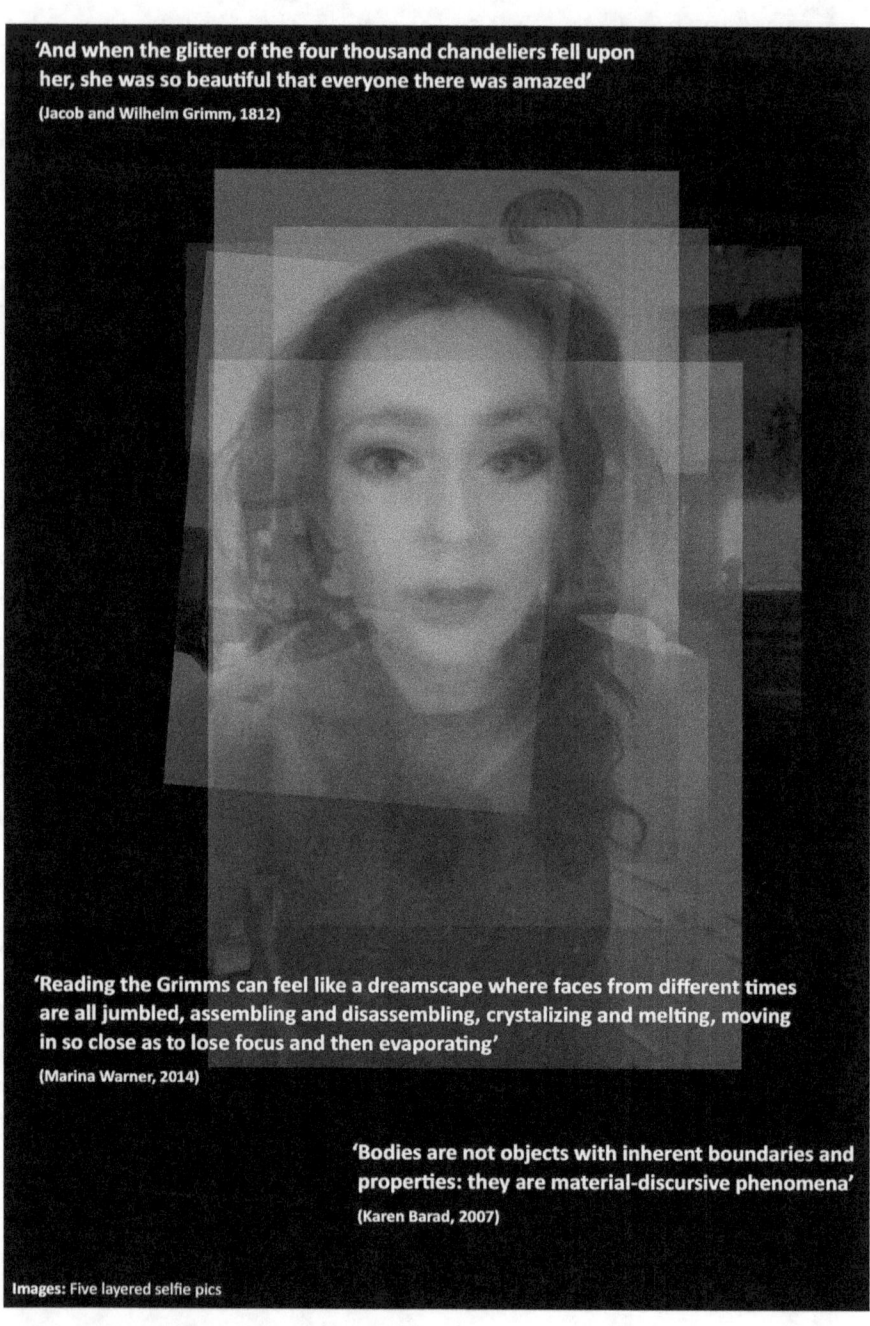

Figure 5.1 Becoming ball-girl-bodies.

5

Becoming ball-girl-bodies

Human bodies are dense lively networks of muscles, skin, blood and bone. They are also fleshy clusters of more-than-human matter, ideas and feelings – some conscious, some not. The coming chapter explores entanglements that produce the ball-girl-body. Previously, school balls and proms have been theorized as a space where girls are able to 'solidify and display their feminine identities' (Best, 2000, p. 35): an approach premised on an understanding of bodies as produced or materialized through particular norms of femininity. Employing a feminist new materialist approach to bodies (Barad, 2007), the following discussion considers the materiality of the body and other matter as active forces in the becoming of ball-girl-bodies. In this framing, discursive practices associated with beauty and the feminine body are not prior or pre-determining; instead, discourses are understood as intra-actively entangled with material forces to produce (or enact) the ball-girl-body. I am interested in how this approach opens a space for understanding ball-girl-bodies differently, where bodies are not wholly reduced to social scripts and bodily capacities are never fixed. With a focus on beauty-body practices, the chapter considers how relations limit and/or extend the capacities of ball-girl-bodies: What can a ball-girl-body do? What might a ball-girl-body become? (Alldred & Fox, 2015; Allen, 2013b; Blaise, 2013; Coleman, 2009). This approach draws attention to the way beauty and 'feeling pretty' emerges as an affective feeling rather than a discursive positioning. Affective forces (feelings, sensations) are not simply a product of beauty-body practices; rather, they form part of the affective flow that produces both beauty-body practices and the ball-girl-body.

The agential ball-girl-body

Feminist research has paid significant attention to the ways dominant discourses shape how female bodies are understood, experienced and regulated (see Bartky, 1990; Bordo, 1993). This important work has shown how discourses create a powerful range of meanings, structuring how we think and speak about bodies. Bodies are disciplined in accordance with social and cultural ideas of beauty and femininity, and these regulatory discourses constitute bodies as intelligible or non-intelligible. It is through this lens that language and discourse are seen to have material effects, in that the materiality of the body is understood and shaped through discursive practices and meanings. While examining the discursive has been immensely productive for feminist research, the body and other matter are often constructed as passive products of discursive practices, in that it is only through discursive practices bodies and matter are constituted as intelligible. While this approach draws attention to the ways norms, power relations and language produce or materialize girls' bodies and material objects, the potential agency of matter and the material world can be overlooked.

Feminist new materialisms offer a different approach by considering the materiality of the body (and other matter) as active forces in the process of materialization (Alaimo & Hekman, 2008; Barad, 2007; Coole & Frost, 2010). Following Barad's (2007) posthumanist performative account of the production of material bodies, neither the discursive nor the material is privileged in the materialization of the body; instead, meaning and matter are in a relationship of mutual entailment. As Alaimo and Hekman suggest, the body can be an 'active, sometimes recalcitrant force' (2008, p. 4); rather than a linear model of causation where power relations produce the body in particular ways, the material-discursive relationship is reciprocal and multi-directional (Barad, 2007). Employing a Baradian account of the materialization of bodies, ball-girl-bodies are conceptualized as 'material-discursive phenomena' (Barad, 2003, p. 815). The body of the ball-girl is not a pre-existing object with clearly defined boundaries and properties; rather, ball-girl-bodies are known and experienced (or become) through intra-active relations of multiple elements and forces. The coming discussion focuses on beauty-body practices as intra-active forces in the becoming of ball-girl-bodies. In doing so, corporeal practices involving hair, make-up and shoes are examined not as something the ball-girl does, but as material-discursive intra-activity.

Conceiving beauty-body practices as intra-active processes offers a rethinking of the relationship between discursive practices (of beauty and femininity) and the material ball-girl-body. Bodies are the result of intra-action; therefore, the material and discursive are ontologically inseparable. Conceptualizing the ball-girl-body as becoming (or agential) enables understandings of bodies that exceed discourse, opening up new ways of thinking about what might be possible for ball-girl-bodies. Analytic attention turns to 'matters of practices, doings and actions' (Barad, 2007, p. 135). These dynamic nonlinear processes open up ways of understanding what the ball-girl-body can do, where bodily capacities do not derive from, nor constitute, human intention and action: as evident in analyses where agency is located in girls' capacity to resist or challenge dominant discourses of femininity. A feminist new materialist approach reconfigures how we think about bodies and notions of agency. In a Baradian sense, agency is a force emerging in-between elements such as material and discursive (matter and meaning). In a similar vein, agency can be understood to emerge via assemblages that are made up of all manner of material-discursive relations (Bennett, 2005; Deleuze & Guattari, 1987). These approaches posit an understanding of agency that is not located in or ascribed to the individual (i.e. the ball-girl) but is an emergent force or *becoming*.

In exploring the becoming of ball-girl-bodies, attention is drawn to affective relations (Ahmed, 2004a; Deleuze, 1988) threaded through agential processes of mattering. Examining affective relations is argued to raise new questions for feminist research (Coleman, 2009), moving analysis beyond the understanding that certain things or practices have negative effects on bodies. Instead, relations are theorized as productive of particular affects. These affects, perhaps feelings or actions, can limit or extend the becoming of ball-girl-bodies. Affective forces are intra-actively entangled with corporeal practices, things, bodies, cultural norms and expectations to produce or constrain ball-girl-bodies in varied ways, for instance, structuring the ways bodies might look, how they move and what they can do. In thinking about the agential ball-girl-body, consider the intra-active material-discursive and affective relations in the following fragment: dresses, dancing, make-up, friends, feelings of enjoyment and surprise.

> *What are you looking forward to … the good things about the ball?*
> *Um, the dancing is fun*
> *Dancing*
> *I do enjoy a good dance*
> *Looking pretty*
> *Yeah, I just like dressing up real nice*
> *Taking good photos*
> *Cause you never get the chance to dress up like that fancy, for anything else, so you can just get dressed up and 'I feel so pretty' [laughter]*
> *Seeing everyone is actually a highlight because everyone looks good*
> *Especially because like people like us who don't wear heaps of make-up to school, or people you only see in your sport teams, you don't usually see them dressed up real nice, and then you see them at the ball and you're like …*

Whoa! (in unison)
Damn! Is that the same person?
Some people it's actually hard to recognise, like wow! Wowee
(Year 13, focus group, 4 voices)

This fragment enacts aspects of the ball participants are looking forward to, such as dancing, *'looking pretty', 'dressing up real nice', 'taking good photos'* and their enjoyment and surprise in seeing both themselves and their peers looking different. These 'highlights' can be understood as material-discursive practices entangled in the production of ball-girl-bodies. Entanglements involve evening dresses, make-up, beauty practices, body work, their own bodies, bodies of friends, everyday bodies at school, sporty bodies, looking and feeling pretty, discourses of femininity, beauty ideals, photos, seeing others and being seen. Comments such as *'Whoa!' 'Damn'* and *'Wow!'* create a sense of the affective forces – feelings, emotions and sensations. These material-discursive and affective components form dynamic shifting assemblages that co-constitute and enact ball-girl-bodies as material-discursive phenomena.

Ball-girl-bodies are inseparable from material things, practices and discourses: they form an interdependent relationship, always affecting and being affected by one another (Barad, 2007; Lenz Taguchi, 2012). As a result, ball-girl-bodies are unstable, emergent phenomena continually (re)assembling at any given moment. We can think about these matterings as productive, producing capacities for what the ball-girl-body can do or become in particular moments. This on-going process means there is no authentic or 'real' ball-girl-body and it is impossible to know in advance what a ball-girl-body might do or become. For feminist researchers interested in the relations in-between gender, sexuality and the body, it reorients the questions we might ask of data: 'We ask not "why" but "how" gender happens and consider not what was intended (a working of possessive agency) but on what was experienced, as agency flows through bodies' (Lyttleton-Smith & Robinson, 2019, p. 74). Importantly, these intensities and flows are not constrained to conventional boundaries of the human body.

The following data snap is created through the layering of four selfie photographs: each photograph of a different participant. By adjusting the opacity of the photographs, the images fuse and meld into one another – boundaries are blurred. The data snap preceding this chapter is another example of this idea. By changing the opacity levels and the order in which the photographs are layered, a new image is created – a new mattering. This mattering does not resemble a fixed 'real' ball-girl-body; instead, the ball-girl-body continually becomes anew with each adjustment, each layer.

Images: Four layered selfie pics

Figure 5.2 Ghost selfie.

Beauty-body practices

Like the agential body, beauty-body practices are dynamic, fluid and unstable. Understood as material-discursive intra-activity, they are open-ended processes of mattering emerging through messy webs of human and more-than-human relations and flows of affect: things, ideas, feelings and physical sensations. In this chapter, 'data' (photos, verbal fragments) perform agential cuts to produce or enact the material-discursive embodied practices participants engaged in. Understanding beauty-body practices intra-actively attends to the productive entanglement of more-than-human materialities, including the relational forces of 'things' such as false eyelashes, clothing and high-heeled shoes. The following images enact a sense of the materiality of hair, make-up and beauty work by bringing material objects, both human and more-than-human to the fore (Allen, 2015b):

Figure 5.3 Beauty products-home-make-up artist-gender norms-nails-polish-jeans-leg-sofa-pink-head-hair-text …

Human bodies in these images are in a state of inseparableness with matter such as beauty products, nail polish, camera, spatial-temporalities and photographs. These materialities are entangled in material-discursive assemblages that include other overlapping forces, such as feelings of excitement and anticipation, beauty ideals, gender norms, physical labour, the beauty industry and advertising, environmental implications of beauty product production and packaging. The image (top-left) depicts an array of make-up products and implements nestled together in opened cases: plastic bottles, tubes and containers of foundation of varying shades, several clear plastic packets of false eyelashes, other smaller containers of make-up, brushes and tissues. Light streams in from a window of one of the girl's homes; there is partial body – a make-up artist – arm, hand and torso. I can recall the participant who shared this image talking about the excitement of getting ready, the enjoyment of having a professional do her make-up and the physical sensation of wearing false eyelashes.

Another image (top-right) shows bright pink painted nails – possibly false – a hand, fingers, partial leg, denim jeans and sofa. The glossy pink of the nails draws my attention; the intensity of pink sparks 'sensations of' pinkness (Springgay, 2016, p. 77): ideas of femininity, prettiness and the gendering of colour. The shiny pinkness accentuates the length of the nails, elongating the hand. The lower half shows a photographic collage made by a participant. It includes four smaller photographs depicting various head-hair configurations: the bottom two images are of a participant; the human body in the top images is unknown. The participant has added the text: *'Hair inspiration' 'Ball day!'* to the collage. This collage enacts a sense of the planning and labour that are entangled in beauty-body practices. I am reminded of participants' talk about ball preparations: deciding what to wear, ideas for hair and make-up, the expectation to make an effort to look different, the financial investment and labour this entails. These photographs can be understood as specific agential matterings or material-discursive configurations that exist in a particular given moment.

Viewing these photographs through a relational materialist perspective (Hultman & Lenz Taguchi, 2010), attention is given to all kinds of matter, including the more-than-human forces that co-constitute beauty-body practices. This 'different style of seeing and thinking' expands the possibilities of understanding the ball-girl-body as 'emergent in a relational field' (Hultman & Lenz Taguchi, 2010, p. 527): the 'relational field', in this instance, is the material-discursive intra-activity of beauty-body practices within the school ball assemblage. The focus is not what beauty-body practices *do* to ball-girl-bodies;

rather, attention turns to how bodies, things and practices form reciprocal co-constitutive relationships. There is a reconfiguring of the relationship between cultural norms and the body beyond a linear, one-way process (i.e. cultural norms producing or materializing the ball-girl-body), to a relational emergent process that is multi-directional and co-constitutional.

This perspective has implications for how we think about the human 'subject' and subjectivity. Hultman and Lenz Taguchi explain how rather than an autonomous and independent humanist subject, 'we have the subject as an effect of an event on a relational field: an *assemblage* of overlapping and intra-acting forces. In the *event* the subject can no longer be understood as a fixed being, but rather a "way of being" – a verb rather than a noun' (2010, pp. 531–2, italics in original). There is a shift to thinking about human bodies as 'multiply entangled and ethically enfolded with(in) other bodies, forces and materialities' (Niccolini & Ringrose, 2019, p. 4). This includes wider ethical and political entanglements concerning the lucrative beauty industry and manufacturing processes, labour and pollution: Where are they made? Who by and under what conditions? What are the environmental implications of the production, transportation and disposal of these products? These material dimensions are deeply entangled with the production and consumption of beauty-body products and practices.

High heels and the body: Rethinking the subject/object divide

The high-heeled shoe is a potent and enduring symbol of femininity (Gamman, 2001; Jeffreys, 2005). From Cinderella and her glass slipper to Lady Gaga's extensive high-heeled shoe collection, high heels are inextricably linked with Western cultural ideas of female beauty, desirability and sexuality. The relations between high heels and female sexuality have been examined across a broad range of disciplines and theoretical paradigms. This literature is often premised on a clear separation between women's bodies as subjects and high heels as objects. For instance, biomedical research has examined the effects of wearing high heels on female gait and perceptions of attractiveness (Morris et al., 2013); anthropology and evolutionary studies have explored the function of high heels in attracting mating partners (Fisher, 2005; Smith, 1999); and psychoanalysts have examined high heels as an object of fetishism (Freud, 1927). High-heeled shoes have also been a source of debate within feminist scholarship amid enduring questions of whether high heels oppress or empower women (Jeffreys, 2005; Walter, 1999).

Feminist new materialisms offer a rethinking of the subject/object divide in relation to female bodies and high-heeled shoes. Rather than conceptualizing bodies and shoes as separate entities, ball-girl-bodies emerge through, and as a part of, entangled intra-actions with high heels, other bodies, discursive practices and the school ball environment. It is an approach that recognizes high-heeled shoes as vital forces (Bennett, 2004) in the becoming of ball-girl-bodies.

At the time of the research, high platform heels were popular and worn by many girls attending the school ball. The photograph below (Figure 5.4) was taken by a participant when ball shoe shopping. The image conveys a sense of the materiality of high-heeled shoes – the style, structure and curve of the arch, colour, textile and length of the heel. It helps create a sense of the materiality, or indeed the *vitality* (Bennett, 2010) of high-heeled shoes. Understanding the practice of wearing high heels intra-actively, we might think about how high heels intra-acting with a ball-girl-body have the capacity to affect the body in multiple ways: movement and gait, (in)ability to walk and dance, bodily

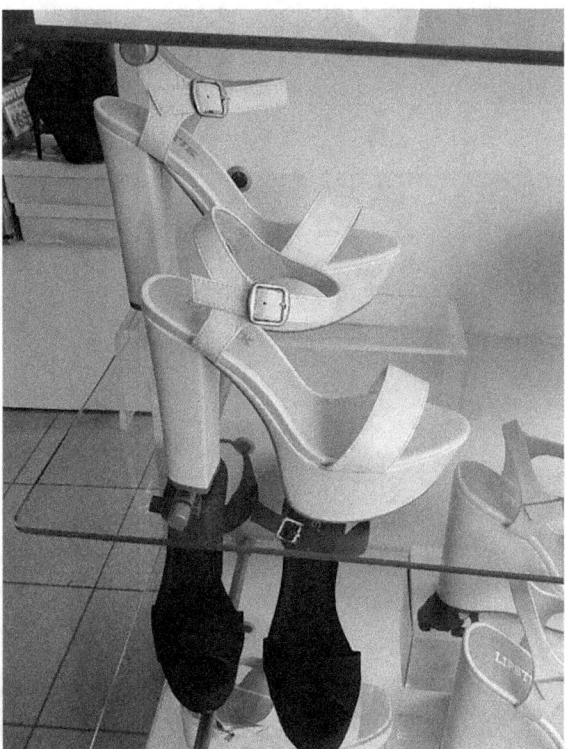

Figure 5.4 Shoe-shopping-camera.

composition and posture, increased height, physical sensations and affective embodied responses (i.e. feeling confident, desirable, uncomfortable). The capacities produced are dependent upon the intra-active relations within high heel-ball-girl-body assemblages: for example, a girl's existing height, whether she is taking a date, whether that date is male or female, gender and heterosexual norms and ideas of feminine respectability. Relations within assemblages produce affects in the ball-girl-body; for instance, increased height was novel and appealing for some girls, yet for others it produced feelings of anxiety about being taller when in-relation with a male date (see chapter six for this discussion). This anxiety did not emerge in relation to dates in general, but only for girls taking a male date signalling the regulatory heterosexual discourses at play in certain assemblages.

In an attempt to offer a material and affective reading of the practice of wearing high heels, consider the entanglement of human and more-than-human matter in the following photograph. Applying a traditional anthropocentric gaze to this photo, I might notice the lower half of girls' bodies (the subjects) wearing and displaying for the camera a range of high-heeled shoes (objects). From this perspective, girls are constituted as the active agent and the high heels passive; therefore, agency lies with the girl who manipulates the high heels. This style of seeing is premised upon the subject/object binary. In contrast,

Figure 5.5 High heels-dresses-legs-feet-nail polish-rug-jewellery-floor ...

working with a relational materialist approach to visual images (Hultman & Lenz Taguchi, 2010), attention is drawn to the more-than-human aspects in the image. There are high-heeled shoes of varying styles, colours and shapes; the high heels converge towards the centre of the image, drawing my gaze in. Each shoe is made from different materials: smooth or textured to the touch; glittered, black, white; buckles, thin straps, thick straps, large wide heels, stiletto heels, platform heels. The high-heeled shoes intra-act with bodies; we see partial glimpses of flesh, feet, ankles and legs. One bare foot peeps through at the upper centre of the image. Layers of fabric, textures (organza, satin), pattern and colour (cream, blue, black, white, fluorescent green) gather and drape at various angles. Some toenails are painted: red, white. There is carpet – a mat of multi-coloured fibres with fringed edging – touching polished wooden floorboards. Some high heels touch the surface of the carpet – others do not.

Elements in this image can be thought of as performative mutually intra-active agents (Barad, 2007; Lenz Taguchi, 2010): the high-heeled shoes, bodily matter, fabric, carpet, flooring are in a state of inseparableness as overlapping forces in the becoming of ball-girl-bodies. As a result, the traditional hierarchy between 'subject' and 'object' becomes flattened: we could say the high-heeled shoe wears the girl as much as the girl wears the high-heeled shoe. Conceptualizing the wearing of high heels as material-discursive intra-activity, the 'wearing' is not something the ball-girl does, rather it is produced relationally and takes place in-between the high heels, the girl and other entangled forces, including discourses of femininity and heterosexuality, the fashion industry, consumerism, beauty ideals and expectations. If wearing high heels is understood as material-discursive intra-activity, and it is through intra-active relations the ball-girl-body as phenomena materializes, then how might these entanglements limit and extend the capacities of ball-girl-bodies?

High heel-ball-girl entanglements

As high heels, dresses and bodies overlap and relate to each other, they are doing something to one another simultaneously (Hultman & Lenz Taguchi, 2010); or, as Barad (2007) would suggest, it is a case of matter making itself intelligible to other matter. In a Deleuzian sense, we can think about how they have the capacity to affect and be affected by each other. The high heels, girls, dresses all become different as a result of the intra-action. The high heels in the previous photograph (Figure 5.5) would evoke a different look if worn with a short tight dress as opposed to a long flowing gown. High-heeled shoes modify the matter in which they come into contact. The body is taller; posture is altered. The lower back and chest are pushed forward and the centre of gravity shifts. Corporeal movement – walking, dancing and standing – will feel and look different. We get a sense here of what Bennett (2010) might mean when she suggests 'things' are able to perform actions, produce effects and alter situations. Consider, as an example, the a/effects produced in the following fragment:

> *Are you wearing heels?*
> *Yeah, and cause I dislocated my knee a few weeks ago, I probably shouldn't, I mean, like I'm fine to wear heels if I strap my knee and that's fine because I'm wearing a long dress, but I guess I was thinking, why do I have to wear heels? Why can't I just wear flat shoes? But then, I guess I want to feel tall for the night, like when I wear them I think wow, everything looks so different. I was wearing them in the house and like the fridge looked so different when I went to look in it, and like gee, and I'm like as tall as my dad and I'm thinking this is what things look like at your height, this is so weird.*
>
> (Year 13, individual interview, 2 voices)

Thinking about high heels as a performative agent (Barad, 2007; Hultman & Lenz Taguchi, 2010) or an actant (Bennett, 2010), we can understand how in the mutual entanglement the girl-body is produced differently, in comparison with wearing flat shoes for instance. In this fragment, a participant discusses the decision to wear high heels to the ball and appears keenly aware of the effect high heels have upon her body: for example, the stress they put on her injured knee and the ability to be taller. While this participant did not normally wear high heels as she considered them impractical, she was planning to do so on this occasion. This fragment enacts the potential to *'feel tall for the night'* as particularly alluring and indeed provides a new perspective of the surrounding world. In wearing high heels around the house, the participant explains how she saw her home, for instance, the contents of her fridge, from a whole new perspective – one that she seemed to find both novel and *'weird'*. In this sense, we can see how 'things' can alter our thinking (Lenz Taguchi, 2010); in this case, high heels offer a glimpse of her world from her Dad's perspective.

As the participant considers her decision to wear high heels to the ball, she wonders *'why do I have to wear heels?'* This question can be read through discursive practices of femininity and sexuality that configure in the high heel-ball-girl-body assemblage. Discursive practices such as dominant understandings of 'appropriate' or 'desirable' femininity enter the assemblage influencing how high heels and girls come into connection. Discursive practices can be easily traced through the girls' comments around high-heeled shoes. The following conversation is a typical example of the gendered norms that were enacted in girls' discussions:

> *Everyone is expected to wear heels*
> *Yup [several girls in unison]*
> *I remember Josie last year was going to wear flats and everyone was like …*
> *hmmm*
> *Oh, Caroline wore flats but only because she's really tall, but they were like sandals so …*
> *It's sort of the not wanting to be taller than your date thing for …*
> *Oh yeah, that's an issue for the tall girls*
> *I just wanted to be a bit taller so I was happy to wear them*
> *I just wanted an excuse to buy a pair of shoes [laughter]*
>   (Year 13, focus group, 4 voices)

Here, both possibilities and tensions are produced in the mutual entanglement of girls' bodies, high heels, discursive practices and the school ball. While the wearing of high heels produces possibilities, such as being *'a bit taller'* and the buying of new shoes, there were clear limitations: notably the expectation to wear high heels at the same time as being expected to be shorter than their (male) date. These expectations articulate with dominant gender discourses and social norms of femininity. Discursive practices intra-act with high heels, bodies and the school ball to define what counts as meaningful. We can see this enacted in the example of Josie and the collective *'hmmm'* she received upon stating she was going to wear flats to the ball. Following Barad's (2007) concept of posthumanist performativity, material phenomena and discourses are not separate from one another. As Lenz Taguchi (2010, p. 5) points out, if 'intra-actions are simultaneously material and discursive in an intertwined relation', it therefore 'matters what notions and beliefs are at work in our intra-activities with the material world'. Discursive practices in relation to femininity, masculinity, sexuality and high heels are implicated in the becoming of the ball-girl-body; however, rather than being privileged or prior, they are considered co-constitutive of ball-girl-bodies as material-discursive phenomena. This approach prompts new questions: what happens when we also think about the materiality of the shoe or the materiality of the body? How might material forces potentially rework or sustain discursive norms?

Figure 5.6 Walking video still sequence.

This video still sequence (Figure 5.6) shows a hallway, bookshelf and front door, light streaming in through the windows, reflections of light on the polished floor. It is the morning of the ball; a participant practises walking in high heels; she walks down the hallway, turns and walks back towards her friend (another participant) holding the camera. I can hear a 'clunk clunk' sound as the high heels and floorboards meet. The participant holding the camera speaks: *'We're practising walking, to just make sure we don't fall over when we actually go to the ball'*. They swap roles: the second participant walks down the hallway while the other films. The participant walking comments, *'I think it should be ok, but I think though, if I fell over I'd be ridiculously embarrassed, and that wouldn't be good'*. Together, they laugh.

A discursive reading of the video footage would offer discourses associated with the embodiment of feminine norms, beauty ideals and the preparations and labour these practices require. A new materialist approach urges us to consider the material and sensory aspects of fashion where materiality is active and productive (Smelik, 2018): fabric and flesh, the height and structure of the high-heeled shoe, modifications in bodily posture and movement, a sense of instability and threat of potential embarrassment. This perspective helps shift debates about high heels and the female body from dichotomous positionings of good/bad or oppressive/empowering, towards what gets produced in the entanglements. Jen Lyttleton-Smith and Kerry Robinson describe this shift in relation to their work with childhood, gender and clothing as a 'focus on material effects in the (re)configuring of the world, rather than discursive lineage, and on consequences rather than causes' (2019, p. 75). High-heel-foot entanglements include the rubbing of flesh, fibre and sweat to create sensations of discomfort and pain, prompting the removal of high-heeled shoes at the ball. It was not unusual to see shoes (without feet) under tables and feet (without shoes) on the dance floor and in photographs. Recalling the earlier photograph of shoes, bodies, dresses and floor (Figure 5.5), I remember the bare foot peeping through. In the following fragment, a participant explains how she removed her shoes frequently throughout the ball:

Yeah, I did, soon as I got in there pretty much, then I kept putting them back on and off. For the photos I had them on, and sometimes when I went and danced I had them on, but most of the time I had them off

(Year 12, focus group, 1 voice)

The materiality of the body in-relation with high heels affects the ability to be able to walk and dance comfortably. The physical discomfort produces varied feelings (affective responses) including a dislike for high heels, relief upon taking them off and pride at being able to keep them on. While many girls removed their high heels in order to move freely, other girls enacted a sense of achievement in being able to keep their high heels on all night:

Your feet get ruined [groan in agreement]
Yeah they're like so sore
Yeah but I didn't take mine off all night
Yeah neither, I was so proud of myself
Yeah that was my goal
When I took them off, that was like the best feeling of my life
Mmm [multiple]
Yeah everyone like takes them off at the ball

> *Yeah [multiple]*
> *But not me, I refused to do that*
> *Yeah that's not a good look*

(Year 13, focus group, 4 voices)

In this fragment, there is the enactment of 'appropriate' femininity and 'classiness' in girls' determination to keep high heels on all night. While these participants noted it was common for girls to take their shoes off at the ball, and indeed shared in the commiseration of *'sore'* and *'ruined'* feet, they were determined not to take their shoes off. Enmeshed in this 'goal' are ideas about feminine respectability; for these girls, taking shoes off was *'not a good look'*, these ideas articulating with classed and gendered discourses of 'being a lady' and being 'classy'. The idea of classiness and being 'ladylike' was frequently cited in girls' brainstorms of what they felt were expected of girls attending the ball. The 'lady' discourse has deep historical roots and still has an enduring and powerful presence in the lives of girls today (Allan, 2009). Taking high heels off, or the determination to keep them on, are material-discursive embodied practices that enable and constrain ball-girl-bodies in particular ways. Taking heels off potentially breached rules of feminine respectability (in some girls' eyes) yet enabled the ball-girl-body to move around the room and dance more freely. Sore feet restricted girls' bodily movements and often resulted in more time spent sitting down, as opposed to dancing or walking around. The following fragment further highlights these entangled affective forces as girls wrestle with the desire to be comfortable and a sense of achievement in being able to keep high heels on all night:

> *Yeah, you can dance so much better without them*
> *At the Kalsey ball I couldn't jump or do anything, and ... just bopping up and down, My friend Hannah and I, we took off our shoes and just went and danced, and then when they said last song, we ran back and put them on, and Caro [her date] said, why did you do that? Cause I wanted to feel like I lasted [laughter]*
> *So, you just had a little intermission break?*
> *Yeah for like half the night [laughter]*

(Year 12, focus group, 3 voices)

The physical discomfort produced by high heels impinged upon dancing, restricting movement to *'just bopping up and down'*. Laughing, she retells how they ran back and put them on for the last song so she could *'feel like I lasted'*.

Here, the materiality of the body and shoes are active forces in the becoming of the ball-girl-body and high-heeled shoes. It is not simply an accommodation or rejection of discursive expectations to wear high heels; there is more at play. Thinking about the practice of wearing high heels as material-discursive intra-activity helps account for (some of) the *more* here, for instance: the school ball environment and dance floor, the desire to have fun and dance, flesh, sweat, the shape and material of high heels, the rubbing of fibre and skin, physical sensations of discomfort and freedom, the expectation to be 'respectable', feelings of pride, frustration and satisfaction.

Blurring material-discursive 'boundaries'

Conceptualizing beauty-body practices intra-actively has significant implications for how we think about bodies and notions of causality and agency. It is not simply a matter of saying material things have individual agency; rather, agency is an emergent quality produced through entanglements of human and more-than-human forces, including high heels, bodies, physical sensations and other forces. One emergent quality is the 'on and off' wearing of heels/girl at the ball; another, is a refusal to wear them at all:

> *I'm not wearing them, I refuse to wear them. I'm very anti high heels. I can't walk in them, I can't do anything in them, so I'm just wearing like …*
> *Chucks*
> *Yeah I'm not kidding, I'm either wearing my black Chucks or my black Vans*
> (Year 12, focus group, 2 voices)

This fragment enacts an adamant dislike of high heels, the participant declaring they plan to wear Chucks or Vans to the ball instead (popular sneaker style shoes). This participant did indeed wear Chucks to the ball, buying a new pair for the occasion. I recall her coming up to me on the evening of the ball; with a big smile on her face she proudly lifted the bottom of her dress to show me her Chucks. I recall laughing and asking if her feet were comfy; she responded with a resounding '*yes!*'. In a post-ball chat, she noted:

> *It was really nice, like everyone would be like, 'let's go take off our shoes', I'd be like 'okay', so it was really nice, and people would be like 'are you wearing Chucks?' and I was like yeah and I'd lift up my dress. Cause no one knew and they were like 'why aren't your feet sore?' Cause I'm not wearing high heels!*
> (Year 12, focus group, 1 voice)

Wearing Chucks instead of high heels increased bodily comfort and freedom of movement throughout the ball. Sore feet were avoided and the ball-girl-body was not encumbered by having to sit down or take shoes on and off. While easily undetected due to a long dress, the wearing of Chucks evoked both envy and surprise from her peers:

> *Heaps of people were like 'I wish I wore Chucks', and I was like 'why didn't you?'*
> *And you kind of had the people who were like, 'why are you wearing Chucks?' But it was all right*
> *What did you say to them?*
> *I was like, 'you go home and have sore feet' [laughing]*
> (Year 12, focus group, 2 voices)

Brushing off any negative comments this participant was so pleased with her decision she planned on wearing Chucks again the following year. These fragments enact ball-girl-bodies in ways that do not strictly cohere to dominant expectations of girls attending the ball and traditional norms of femininity (i.e. expectation to wear high heels). Here, there is a reworking of gendered discourses. This capacity emerges through multiple forces: the materiality of shoes, bodily sensations and movement, previous experience wearing high heels, emotions, confidence, clothing and the school ball space. Agency does not reside in the individual but emerges in the high heel-ball-girl-body assemblage (Bennett, 2004). These material-discursive and affective forces are intimately connected to what the ball-girl-body can become, and importantly what a ball-girl-body can and cannot do.

Choosing not to wear high heels to the ball might be conceived as 'resisting young bodies': 'resisting' being an 'affective movement' rather than individual agency (Fox & Alldred, 2016, p. 125). The new materialist approach to power and resistance posited by Fox and Alldred suggests the capacity for 'resisting' emerges through material forces and intensities within various assemblages. The affective movement is not stable, it flows and shifts as relations assemble and reassemble in new open-ended matterings. It is not simply that discursive forces produce wearing of high heels as normal and expected (although that is definitely apparent), and these discursive ideas affect bodies in a one-way direction; it also works the other way around. The materiality of the shoes and the body, sensations, (dis)comfort and emotions are entangled in both the becoming of the ball-girl-body *and* the material-discursive practice of wearing high heels. Therefore, it is impossible to think of high heels as an object that either empowers or oppresses the human 'subject', as this would suggest a linear model of causation and a subject/object binary. Instead, high heels and bodies are entangled, both affecting and being affected by each other.

Body-matter entanglements are productive. The force or vitality of matter (Bennett, 2010) continually (re)configures beauty-body practices and how they are understood and experienced. In the following fragment, two participants reflect upon the beauty-body practices they engaged in for the school ball and what they would do differently next time:

Not wear fake eyelashes
Yeah
Ooh they feel horrible [face screwed up]
And then they start to fall off
During the night I wanted to like [rip sound and motion] take them off
As soon as I got home, I ripped them off. I couldn't handle it anymore
Yip so next time no fake eyelashes for me
Yip no thanks, it's so much better to just have, I'd rather have lots of mascara on than these things that feel weird and weigh down your eye. That was not fun.
(Year 12, video diary, 2 voices)

Discussing the experience of wearing fake eyelashes to the ball, these participants enact the false eyelashes-ball-girl-body encounter as 'weird' and 'horrible'. The human intention behind false eyelashes is their ability to augment or enhance the human body (i.e. to lengthen eyelashes and enlarge eyes); however, the effects of this false eyelashes-ball-girl-body encounter exceed human intention. This particular mattering includes, but is not limited to, the weight and materiality of false eyelashes, the heat and movement of the body, glue, eyelid, the school ball environment, temperature, sensations and feelings in that particular moment. The weight and feel of false eyelashes make an impression through bodily sensations, while simultaneously the body orients and affects the false lashes. When attached to the body, false eyelashes move differently, they come into contact with glue, skin, heat and moisture, producing different affects. As the false eyelashes '*start to fall off*', this detachment from the human body suggests a certain efficacy that defies human will and intention (Bennett, 2010). The force and vitality of false eyelashes (and the body) renders matter productive and unpredictable in the becoming of beauty-body practices. As a result, beauty-body practices are open-ended and cannot be understood or known in advance.

As material-discursive phenomena, ball-girl-bodies are not contained to an individual human body and the boundaries of living flesh and skin. Instead, ball-girl-bodies are made up of lively matter of all forms – some human, some not. False eyelashes are one example of entangled more-than-human matter; silicone/gel breast enhancers are another:

> I got those stick-on bra things [...] like yeah [laughing]. By the end of the night, cause I was like sweating and stuff, they had fallen off. My boobs had disappeared. I looked like I was flat cause they were down here ... but yeah, my Dad picked me up in the car and I got in and I was like 'ugh' I just took it off and oh it was such a relief, it was pretty much falling off anyway
>
> I don't think I'll ever really be using them again, they're sitting up on my bookshelf, and you and Georgia came around the other day and you were like 'oh nice boobs'. Like they're just up there, I don't know what to do with them. You can't put them anywhere, or fold them because they stick to each other
>
> (Year 12, focus group, 1 voice)

In these fragments, a participant recalls the 'stick-on bra things' she wore to the school ball. Rather than a traditional bra that goes around the body, she is referring to a backless self-adhesive bra that covers the breasts (also commonly referred to as 'chicken fillets'). The participant explains how after an evening of dancing, sweating and moving 'they had fallen off, my boobs disappeared'. Laughing, she re-enacts the feeling of taking them off as soon as she got in the car. They currently sit on the bookshelf in her bedroom, which raises the question of what are they now? Are they simply an inert material collection of gel, plastic and worn adhesive substance? Or are they more? They do not appear passive; their unruly sticky qualities means the participant does not know what to do with them – hence being on the shelf. Do they need to be attached to a human body to be ball-girl-boobs? The comment from her friend 'oh nice boobs' might suggest not. These body-matter entanglements involving shoes, fake eyelashes and stick-on bras blur the conventional 'boundaries' of ball-girl-bodies. They are not wholly constrained by regulatory gendered discourses or contained within a physical human body. This theorizing fosters attentiveness towards the multiplicity and open-ended potential of ball-girl-body becomings, not in the sense that everything and anything is always possible, rather how boundaries are continually reconfigured via on-going relations.

'Feeling pretty': Beauty as an affective process

This final section explores beauty as an embodied affective process (Coleman & Moreno Figueroa, 2010). It is interested in the way beauty emerges as a feeling (Colebrook, 2006) where the concept of 'pretty' is more than simply a discursive positioning. *Becoming-pretty* is argued to be an intra-active affective process where 'feeling pretty' is an entangled element in the becoming of ball-girl-bodies. In Coleman and Moreno Figueroa's (2010, p. 358) analysis of beauty *as hope*, they propose affect as a productive way of examining beauty as it 'emphasises not only content but also *process*'. By this they mean that in addition to examining specific beauty practices, 'it is also important to see beauty as an embodied social, cultural and economic process' (2010, p. 358). This approach supports Colebrook's (2006) assertion that feminist politics would benefit from a pragmatic approach to beauty, moving beyond questions of whether beauty is 'good' or 'bad' for women. These familiar questions often confine feminist politics to dualistic framings and cause and effect logic, where beauty is conceived as solely oppressive or problematic. Conceptualizing beauty as an affective-material process provides a way to think about the complex, nuanced and often contradictory relations in-between beauty and the ball-girl-body.

Thinking about the ball-girl and the concept of beauty, the expectation and desire to 'look good' is central. This process involves an array of material-discursive embodied practices that intra-actively produce ball-girl-bodies in particular ways, for instance, wearing make-up, false eyelashes, the styling of nails and hair. The following fragment draws attention to the ways girls enact 'looking good' or 'pretty' as a felt quality:

What are the positives about the ball?
Finding a dress that looks nice
Getting to like, feel like you're looking good
I feel pretty [singing]
Having an opportunity to get your make-up done and like expressing yourself, cause like at school you have to wear a uniform and no one really knows like what sort of stuff you're into, so you can choose, if you go to the ball you can show what your opinions are
And like seeing all your friends dressed up as well, it's really nice, it's like you normally see them in school uniform or sweaty sports gear, so it's nice
Getting nice photos to keep, not that mine were nice but
Yeah I think like a fun night with your friends is always exciting
(Year 13, focus group, 5 voices)

In this discussion, girls enact *'getting to like feel like you're looking good'* as a positive aspect of the school ball. A participant supports this comment by singing '*I feel pretty*' from the musical *West Side Story*. This idea of 'feeling pretty' resonates with the opening conversation in this chapter, where girls share their thoughts on what they like about the ball: they state *'cause you never get the* chance to dress up like that fancy, for anything else. So, you can just get dressed up and "I feel so pretty"!' The utterance 'I feel so pretty' was expressed in a light-hearted jovial singing voice, not dissimilar to the cheery enactment of the song. In these fragments, the concept of 'pretty' appears to be expressed as a feeling rather than a fixed attribute associated with someone's identity.

'Feeling pretty' is an affect produced in the intra-activity of various matter – where things affect and are affected by other matter. The intra-action of bodies, beauty-body practices such as wearing make-up, the labour and cost of having make-up professionally done by a make-up artist, the styling of hair, long formal ball dresses, corsages, painted nails, along with discursive beauty ideals associated with femininity, produce the affective response of 'feeling pretty'. Pretty in this sense, is associated with dominant understandings of femininity and beauty, including wearing make-up, painted nails and a dress. The ways girls enacted 'feeling pretty' through their cheery light-hearted utterances, such as singing West Side Story's 'I feel pretty', evoked a sense of playfulness and 'dress up', perhaps even a sense of artificiality. This sense of playfulness resonates in the following fragment:

> So yeah, I think most girls are just like 'oh yeah, I want to look my best, this is my one occasion a year where I get to like go all out and be the most ridiculous', but it's nice, it's nice. You get to feel like a princess, if that's what you're into [...] so yes, don't know how I feel about that one, but yeah, I'll get to dance with all the princesses so that'll be fun [laughter]
>
> *(Year 13, individual interview, 1 voice)*

In this fragment, the embodied beauty practices associated with the school ball produce the affective responses of 'feeling pretty' and feeling '*like a princess, if that's what you're into*'. As mentioned, previous studies have highlighted how 'princess femininity' – a socially constructed femininity that accentuates particular beauty ideals – is an unattainable goal for girls; therefore they are continually destined to fail (Shannon, 2015). An agential realist framework reorients feeling 'like a princess' to be a relational force in the becoming of school ball-girl, this force includes childhood memories and fairy-tale (as seen in the previous chapter), traditional feminine norms, consumerism and beauty-body practices. Within an intra-active frame, feeling 'like a princess' is a force that shifts and changes depending on other relations, which means it does not circulate within beauty-ball-girl-body assemblages in the same way. In this sense, intra-actions can be constraining but not determining. The desire to *'feel like a princess*' did not personally resonate with this participant: laughing, she notes, *'don't know how I feel about that one, but yeah, I'll get to dance with all the princesses so that'll be fun'*.

'Feeling pretty' becomes one component within a broader flow of affect (Fox, 2015) that constitutes beauty and the ball-girl-body. There is a sense of whimsy and temporality to the enactment of 'feeling pretty'; it is not a permanent state, nor does it reveal an 'authentic' feminine self. Rather, it is an affect produced via particular spacetimematterings, similar to the idea of effort as an affective force that was proposed in the previous chapter. 'Feeling pretty' as an affective relation works to limit or expand the becoming of ball-girl-bodies. The affects of 'feeling pretty' function to direct ball-girl-bodies towards certain objects and practices. Here, affect is what 'sticks' or sustains the connection between particular ideas, values and things (Ahmed, 2010): in this instance, beauty practices and things associated with gendered beauty norms. This connection is evident in the expectation that girls would wear make-up to the ball and the embarrassment or shame someone might experience if they did not:

> *I think people would laugh at you if you didn't wear make-up*
> *Mmm [in agreement]*
> *What about someone who isn't into make-up?*
> *You wear make-up; if you're not into make-up, you don't go to the ball*
> (Year 13, focus group, 3 voices)

In this fragment, dominant discourses of femininity circulate as powerful co-constitutive forces in the becoming of beauty and the ball-girl-body. This affective flow (or mattering) produces boundaries enacting what bodies 'fit' and what bodies do not: as one participant notes, *'if you're not into make-up, you don't go to the ball'*. Another participant echoes this sentiment: *'it's not really an option, everyone does it, no one thinks about not doing it'*. The 'decision' to wear make-up is not located in the individual human subject. Rather, as Barad suggests, 'intentionality might better be understood as attributable to a complex network of human and nonhuman agents, including historically specific sets of material conditions' (2007, p. 23). The network of relations, in this instance, includes the enduring discursive expectation to wear make-up and a perceived threat (affective force) of being laughed at if someone did not. These relations produce a powerful exclusionary affective force: *'if you're not into make-up, you don't go to the ball'*.

The material-discursive practice of wearing make-up is an integral element in girls' enactments of 'feeling pretty' and the capacity to 'look different'. Pondering what was 'good' about the ball, a participant noted the following:

Um, I guess it gives you the opportunity to try looking different, cause I know especially for me and quite a few of my friends we don't really, I don't really know how to apply make-up that well. I'll put mascara on or a bit of foundation but never so like nicely as at the ball. So like last ball was the first time I had ever seen myself with full-on make-up, so that was quite nice to try something new. Um, yeah I don't know really, I guess it's just you get to try looking different to how you usually do

(Year 13, individual interview, 1 voice)

Conceptualized as an enactment, *'looking different to how you usually do'* is produced through material-discursive relations of bodies, make-up, 'usual' beauty-body practices, and the feeling of trying something new. One participant talks about how she usually wears only a small amount of foundation and mascara; therefore, seeing herself with *'full-on make-up'* was novel and different. 'Looking different' is not an attribute of a particular body, for example, a body that changes from one state to another; rather, it is an enactment produced through particular configurations. The enactment of 'looking different' involves multiple temporalities and bodies, such as a girl's 'usual' everyday-body, school-girl-body and the ball-girl-body. One body is not prior to the other; instead they are inseparable and mutually dependent on one another. Neither body is fixed or stable; they are continually reconfigured depending on affective relations.

'Looking different' is a specific form of embodiment (or enactment) co-constituted through boundary-making practices that distinguish the ball-girl-body from the everyday-body and school-girl-body (Barad, 2007). For another participant, having make-up applied by a professional, not having *'fluffy hair'* and wearing fake eyelashes are material-discursive practices that collaboratively enact the ball-girl-body as 'looking different'. These productive practices are entangled with, and produced through, affective forces such as 'making an effort' and 'feeling pretty'. As mentioned, these affects are intimately connected with, and shaped by, dominant discourses of feminine beauty and the beauty industry: for instance, the expectation that girls would wear make-up and style their hair for the occasion, and the economic implications of this labour. While pervasive, expectations and beauty norms are one element within a broader flow of affect that produces beauty-body practices and the ball-girl-body. Consider the affective dynamics in the following discussion:

> *There's a huge expectation to make an improvement to yourself*
> *Oh yeah, hard, like everyone is like 'oh I need to look better than what I do normally'*
> *[scoff] Screw that, I always look good*
> *[group laughter]*
> *In terms of making that effort and looking better, you mentioned make up …*
> *Your hair and even your dress*
> *Losing weight*
> *Oh my gosh, so many people are talking about that*
> *Everyone is fasting for the ball*
> *I'm not*
> *Hell no*
>
> (Year 12, focus group, 4 voices)

This fragment details various expectations surrounding the becoming of ball-girl-bodies: the expectation to wear make-up, to *'make an improvement to yourself'* and *'look better than what I do normally'*. These expectations form part of the affective process that also includes material-discursive relations of hair, make-up, dresses, beauty norms, dieting, body image and body satisfaction, affective bodily responses such as a scoff, laughter and feelings of indignation. Conceptualizing bodies as becoming, ball-girl-bodies are produced through but not determined by their relations with other things (Coleman, 2009). Capacities and constraints are contingent and situated: for instance, while some girls may feel pressure to lose weight and fast before the ball, others may not, as evident with dismissal of dieting and refusal to lose weight in this fragment. This 'resistance' is an 'affective movement' or process (Fox & Alldred, 2016) within a particular ball-girl-body-beauty assemblage. Agency is a quality or capacity that emerges 'in-between' wider relations including the material (Barad, 2007; Bennett, 2004). In the intra-action of bodies, corporeal practices, feelings, ideas, values, body image and confidence, the ball-girl-body materializes in ways that may destabilize beauty norms and expectations, for instance, rejecting the idea the female body needs improvement through make-up and dieting.

Becoming-pretty and 'looking different' are intra-active affective processes comprising materialities, gender norms, feelings and corporeal practices. It is through these dynamic configurations that ball-girl-bodies materialize as 'looking good'. More than simply how a body looks, these enactments involve bodily feelings and sensations. Indeed, becoming-pretty and 'looking good' are felt intensities; these *feelings* are powerful affective forces in the becoming of ball-girl-bodies. Ball-girl-bodies are multiple and become in connection with other girl-bodies, such as everyday-bodies, sport-girl-bodies and school-girl-bodies. There is no essential girl-body; rather, bodies are material-discursive phenomena continually becoming through dynamic affective relations. This means bodily capacities are also unfixed; possibilities and constraints are continually (re)configured through material-discursive and affective entanglements.

Concluding–continuing thoughts

By exploring beauty-body practices as material-discursive intra-activity, this chapter has mapped the ways discursive practices are entangled with material bodies, things, corporeal practices and affects to collaboratively enact the ball-girl-body. This approach extends feminist post-structural thought to think not only about how girls' bodies are produced through discursive forces, but to pay attention to the force of materiality in these becomings. Approaching beauty-body practices as material-discursive entanglements establishes them as relational practices. They are not uni-linear processes where something is simply done *to* bodies; rather, they emerge as multi-linear and affective matterings involving human and more-than-human forces. Inspired by Barad, we can think of the ball-girl-body not as a 'fully formed, pre-existing' subject, but rather as 'intra-actively co-constituted through the material-discursive practices they engage in' (2007, p. 168). As such, bodies are inseparable from the practices, spaces and materialities that produce them.

A feminist new material framework offers a way of thinking about beauty-body practices and ball-girl-bodies as *becoming-with* one another. These entangled and mutual becomings extend relations between girls' bodies and materialities, such as high-heeled shoes, beyond the subject/object divide. Understanding boundaries between material objects (things, bodies) as porous helps dismantle one-way linear cause-and-effect logic. Instead, entanglements of bodies, things, practices, ideas and affects are understood to limit and/or extend ball-girl-body becomings in specific ways. Affective flows within assemblages may sustain connections in-between bodies, traditional feminine norms and beauty ideals, yet at other times may emerge as 'resistance' – an affective movement (Fox &

Alldred, 2016) that can destabilize gendered bodily norms and open up new becomings for ball-girl-bodies. Conceptualizing ball-girl-bodies as becoming means they are open-ended, never complete or closed. They become multiple and messy. Becoming ball-girl is a making and unmaking of bodies, through an entanglement of material things, affective forces, discursive practices, histories and imaginings.

Figure 6.1 Ball-girl-date affections.

6

Ball-girl-date affections

Themes of romance permeate cultural imaginaries of a ball or prom (Best, 2000; Mazzarella, 1999; Smith, 2014). These enduring cultural meanings have firm historical literary roots: Cinderella, of course, met her handsome prince at the ball (Disney, 1950; Perrault, 1697), as did Lizzie and Mr Darcy in *Pride and Prejudice* (Austen, 1813). In many a Jane Austen novel, balls are portrayed as lavish affairs brimming with potential suitors. This magical connection between a ball and romance remains a popular trope in contemporary literature (Downing, 2014; Eulberg, 2011) and movies. High school love stories often cohere around, or culminate in, the night of the prom: *Never Been Kissed* (1999), *Prom* (2011), *Pretty in Pink* (1986), *Footloose* (1984, 2011), *10 Things I Hate about You* (1999) and *Twilight* (2008) are just a few examples. The portrayal of the ball in teen magazines is similarly infused with themes of romance (Mazzarella, 1999; Zlatunich, 2009): these portrayals primarily adhere to heterosexual and gender norms, such as boy asks girl, romantic gestures and slow dances.

Such themes construct having or being a date as a signifier of 'appropriate' femininity in the social space of the ball. In Best's analysis of the American prom, she argues there was considerable pressure to have a prom date: for girls, having a date was 'internalized as a means to both measuring feminine self-worth and to solidifying their heterosexual identities' (2000, p. 68). Best's analysis associates having a date with the expression or 'solidification' of a feminine ideal constituted through dominant discourses of femininity and heterosexuality. As Best (2000, p. 10) succinctly notes, 'proms champion heterosexuality'; these events contributing to the broader heteronormative landscape of schooling (Allen, 2006; Ferfolja, 2007; Pascoe, 2007; Quinlivan & Town, 1999; Rasmussen, 2004; Smith, 2014). Dominant discourses of heterosexuality and femininity constitute particular positionings for girls, including a presumed investment in having and/or being someone's date.

Instead of thinking about ball-girl and date dynamics as solely positioned within discursive forces, this chapter examines ball-girl-date relations 'as encounters between ontologically diverse actants, some human, some not, though all thoroughly material' (Bennett, 2010, p. xiv). Ball-girl-date encounters are conceptualized as more than a relationship between two people as individually determinate entities; instead, they can be thought of as posthuman encounters (Braidotti, 2013) or 'more than' encounters (Springgay, 2016: p. 77) comprising an array of human and more-than-human relations. Employing a new materialist ontology of sexuality, the discussion explores ball-girl-date encounters as sexuality-assemblages (Allen, 2013b; Fox & Alldred, 2013), opening up understandings of ball-girl sexualities as emergent rather than an attribute of individual bodies. I consider how this approach offers a broader expanse for understanding who or what plays a role in the becoming of sexuality, that includes but is not limited to the human or discourse. Importantly, I consider the productive potential this offers for rethinking ball-girl-date dynamics beyond popular cultural and romantic constructions.

A feminist new materialist approach marks a shift away from an anthropocentric frame of reference, where sexuality derives from or is an attribute of the human body. Instead, aspects of sexuality – desires, attractions, bodily capacities, sexual codes, customs and conduct – emerge through flows of affect within sexuality assemblages (Fox & Alldred, 2013). Hence, Fox and Alldred argue within a new materialist frame 'how sexuality manifests has little do with personal preferences or dispositions, and everything to do with how bodies, things, ideas and social institutions assemble' (2017, p. 102). The focus of the chapter is not simply what forms sexuality-assemblages (i.e. bodies, things, school ball spaces and ideas), but how affective relational dynamics within ball-girl-date assemblages create conditions of possibility for ball-girl-bodies to act, feel and desire (Fox & Alldred, 2013). Here, affect is a force or intensity that flows through and in-between bodies and things, enhancing or diminishing capacities to act (Ringrose & Coleman, 2013). As such, the notion of sexuality-as-assemblage provides a different starting point for conceptualizing sexual capacities and agency, including (un)romantic expectations, desire and the 'decision' to take a date (or not) to the ball.

The chapter begins by conceptualizing the importance of a date as an affective-material process, produced through relational forces such as friends, expectations and imaginings. I consider the vitality of school ball photographs: not just what a photograph shows, but how the taking-sharing-viewing of photographs are productive forces in ball-girl-date encounters. Photographs are both a product of affect and also productive of ball-girl capacities (feelings and actions). Within sexuality-assemblages, flows of affect produce ball-girl capacities, including but not limited to emotions. Following Fox (2015), emotions are understood to form part of a broader affective flow, in-between bodies, other entities (human and more-than-human) and the social. A relational approach to emotions is useful in thinking about how emotions (including those conventionally classified as sexual and not) play a part in producing the school ball-girl. The focus is not on what emotions *are* but what they *do* (Ahmed, 2004b), in that emotions are not simply bodily responses to particular events, but have a capacity to affect (Fox, 2015): for example, emotions and feelings may propel a ball-girl to do something (e.g. take a date), which may then produce further affects within the assemblage (e.g. restricted freedom, frustration and annoyance).

Exploring assemblages of girls, male dates, high heels and heterosexual discursive practices, I consider how the flow of affect delineates particular bodies (i.e. tall-girl-bodies in relation to short-boy-bodies): how feelings of anxiety and sympathy 'stick' (Ahmed, 2004a) to certain bodies generating particular capacities and constraints. This discussion highlights how certain constraints emerge specifically within heterosexual date assemblages and were not an issue for girls taking female dates. In these scenarios, the date is identified as male. This does not ascribe a heterosexual identity to the ball-girl; rather, it is an attempt to explore some of the emergent capacities and constraints within date dynamics. The final section in the chapter examines spatial-material arrangements, what I call 'hot spots' such as the school ball entrance and dance floor, and how these relations restrict or generate particular actions, movement and feelings for the ball-girl. I consider how these spatial-material dynamics provide openings for reconfiguring popular notions of the ball as a romantic space.

The becoming of ball-date (un)importance

At both participating schools, ball dates were optional and could include female and male dates from inside or outside of school. Dates ranged from boyfriends and girlfriends, to close female and male friends, ball swaps and set-up dates. Ball swaps are a reciprocal arrangement where two students from different schools attend each other's ball. Set-up dates were often arranged through friends and the students may or may not have known each other. These varied date arrangements reflect recent changes to school ball rules and policies in Aotearoa. As mentioned earlier, student complaints have drawn media attention to unjust and heteronormative practices such as the banning of same-gender dates (Shuttleworth, 2012; Wade, 2011), prompting many schools to reconsider their regulations regarding school ball partners (Tait, 2013). Participants from both schools were able to bring same or opposite-gender dates to the ball, helping to destabilize the heteronormativity long associated with these events. There were also participants who chose not to take a date and attend the ball with a group of friends instead. Contrary to popular romantic constructions, the importance of a date is not fixed or (discursively) presumed. Instead, the importance of a ball date can be conceptualized as a material-affective process produced through multiple forces, including friends, imaginings, photographs, relationship status, expectations and historical legacies associated with the ball. The following fragment introduces some of these affective relations, including expectations, friends and feelings:

So, is it a big deal – taking partners?
I think it depends on who you talk to
Yeah
It also depends on what your expectation is, cause like it's not like if you didn't have a partner everyone would be like 'oh my gosh, you're so lame'. But lots of people want to have a partner, cause like the whole prom thing, they want to have a date and be like 'oh my gosh, let's go together'
And like some people I talk to and I'm like 'oh yeah I'm not going with anyone' and they're like 'oh my gosh we need to find you a ball date' and I actually don't really care. Going by myself is fine, but yeah, some people like have this idea in their head that it's a ball, you have to go with someone, but nah
Just go in groups, groups are more fun
Yeah
And like people even though they're in couples they will all go together, there will be couples and there will be people on their own

(Year 12, focus group, 4 voices)

In this discussion, the ball-date becomes (un)important via an array of forces: prom culture portrayed through movies; girls' imaginings and expectations of the ball; friendship group dynamics, *'oh my gosh, we need to find you a date'*; and feelings of ambivalence, *'I actually don't really care'*. These entangled forces generate a sense of ball-dates as important for some girls and not for others. This varied importance is a material-affective process or intensity that shifts and changes depending on particular forces and affects. One example is the way affective relations in-between girls and their friends could increase or diminish the desire to take a date. If most people in a friendship group were going with or without a date, these collective dynamics could produce a sense of pressure or expectation for girls to follow suit:

Is there pressure to take a partner or it feels fine?
I feel like there is in some aspects, um, like when all your friends are taking one and you're the only one not taking one. We had one of our friends last year not take someone and she got ... I feel like she didn't get crap about it, but she got 'oh you're not taking anyone? Ok' kind of thing

(Year 13, focus group, 2 voices)

I know a couple of girls, a girl group, and one of the girls does want to take a date, but everyone else in the group isn't taking a date, so she's getting pressure not to take one
Yeah
She wants to take one but all her friends aren't taking one, so she feels like her date will be uncomfortable and all her friends aren't taking dates and they're making her feel uncomfortable because she is ...
They're like 'oh we want it to be just friends'

(Year 12, focus group, 2 voices)

These fragments enact a sense of pressure or expectation in relation to what the majority of the friendship group were doing: that is, taking dates or not. Affective connections in-between ball-girls, dates and friendship group dynamics include peer judgment, uniformity, pressure to conform to the group, feeling conflicted or uncomfortable. These affects circulate in-between bodies, spaces, ideas and social relations as a collective force that produce ball-girl capacities and desires: in this instance, the desire to take a date or not. Desire is understood here as an affect (Deleuze & Guattari, 1984) rather than an essential quality of a body; as affect it 'produces specific capacities to act or feel in a body or bodies, be it arousal, attraction, sexual activity, rejection' (Alldred & Fox, 2015, p. 4), in this instance, the desire to take a date or not. This theorization of desire shifts sexual desiring from a 'yearning for an "object of desire" ... into a productive force capable of transforming bodies, social formations and ideas' (Fox & Alldred, 2017, p. 101). Rather than being pre-determined or discursively produced, the importance of a ball-date becomes fluid and contingent.

In these ball-girl-date-friend assemblages, the 'decision' to take a date shifts away from the notion of an autonomous agentic ball-girl, to flows of affect within assemblages comprising multiple forces. Ball-girl-date encounters draw together not just two people, but personal and cultural contexts, norms of conduct, aspects of the setting, including practices like having your photo taken:

> *Why do you think it was a bigger deal last year to take a date than this year?*
> *I guess the image of having a guy to take probably, and the photos. I don't know though, I don't know what it was for me. It was probably just that my friends, like one of my friends had a boyfriend so she was taking him, and you know I guess that was kind of a pressure for me, to be like the only one in the photos who didn't have someone standing beside them, that was a stress for me*
> (Year 13, individual interview, 2 voices)

This fragment enacts a sexuality-assemblage comprising ball-dates, friends, photographs, feelings of pressure and stress, *'the image of having a guy to take'* and not wanting to appear other or the odd one out. The notion of 'image' in this fragment (i.e. *'the image of having a guy to take'*) is understood as a projected or perceived persona, itself an affect. It is an impression or perception produced through varied relations: materiality of a ball-date, discourses of heterosexuality and femininity, and girls' imaginings. Within a sexuality-assemblage, human and more-than-human relations affect (and are affected by) each other to produce material e/affects (Alldred & Fox, 2015). For this participant, the desire to take a date was intensified in relation to school ball photographs: the thought of being *'the only one in the photos who didn't have someone standing beside them'* created a *'kind of pressure … a stress'*. In this ball-girl-date-photo assemblage, the photograph can be understood as an object that amplifies affective forces (Niccolini & Pindyck, 2015), specifically the desire to take a date. The following snap captures a material, and in this instance gendered, configuration: bodies are positioned next to other bodies; one arm from each body wrapped around their date. It is a fragmented photograph: a filter obscures the finer details, preventing the gaze from being drawn to clothing and facial expressions. Yet an impression remains; or rather, emerges through the configuration of bodies, heterosexual and gendered historical legacies of the ball and our perception and memories as the viewer.

The physical arrangement where bodies are positioned as (heterosexual) couples plays an affective role in the intensity of the ball-girl-date-photo encounter. In this sense, the positionings of bodies captured by a photograph are not simply positioned *in* space and time but *of* spacetime in a specific affective spacetimemattering (Barad, 2007). The prospect of standing in a photo and being the only one without a date is an 'affective moment' (Mulcahy, 2012, p. 16) that triggered feelings of pressure and not wanting to feel different; these affective feelings generate a desire or motivation to have a date. As a

Figure 6.2 Ball-girl-date mattering.

material-discursive object, the (male) ball-date holds symbolic (discursive) value in the projection of a particular ball-girl persona as heterosexually desired–desiring. This persona is intimately connected with enduring cultural understandings that construct the ball as a space for heterosexual couplings in particular (Allen, 2006; Best, 2000). The ways girls and dates get imagined in these constructions is constrained by dominant structural forces, such as discourses of heterosexualized femininity, where the projection of heterosexual identity is considered the 'normal and natural sexual expression of healthy growing girls' (Aapola, Gonick & Harris, 2005, p. 148). The type of femininity that emerges within this ball-girl persona (i.e. as part of a heterosexual couple) is produced via the material-discursive practice of having someone standing beside you for photos, the sharing and viewing of these photographs by friends and family, in-relation with heteronormative romantic expectations associated with the school ball. Within the sexuality-assemblage, material forces are inseparable from dominant discursive norms in the mattering ball-date importance.

While the material presence of a date can be a powerful intra-active force in the production of a particular persona or the enactment of a particular femininity, it is not entirely fixed. The following fragment reworks ideas of femininity typically constituted through ball-girl and date relations:

> *Are you taking a partner?*
> *Well I took one last year, but um, this one is a bit complicated for me because I want to take a date but then I'm kind of like, I'm head girl, do I want to have that image? Or do I want to be the strong independent woman, you know like. I'm still trying to figure out if I want to take one or not*
>
> *(Year 13, individual interview, 2 voices)*

In this fragment, a participant considers whether she wants to take a date and have *'that image'* (i.e. being part of a couple), or whether she wants to go on her own and be *'the strong independent woman'*. The participant was Head Girl, and ideas of image in relation with her leadership role are entangled in this ball-girl-date assemblage. In contrast to going with a date which enacts dominant forms of desirable femininity, going solo enacts a sense of independence, pride and strength. In one way, this could be understood through Best's (2000) approach as expressing a particular feminine identity; however, it is not one produced through taking a date. Indeed, it is the opposite. In this fragment, what is enacted as a feminine 'ideal' is reimagined as *'the strong independent woman'*. A feminist post-structuralist reading of this scenario might highlight the participant's negotiation of two competing discourses of girlhood, for example, desirable femininity versus ideas of independence and strength that resonate with discourses of girl power (Aapola et al., 2005). This negotiation would be located in an agentic individual girl subject and their accommodation and/or resistance of dominant discourses. A feminist new materialist approach broadens the frame to think about the material-discursive relations in this scenario: the leadership position of Head Girl, physical responsibilities during the evening of the ball, freedom of movement, affective forces related to a perceived/projected 'image', relationships with fellow students and staff. These varied relational forces collaboratively produce ball-date (un)importance.

A key point here is if the importance of a ball-date is an affect that emerges via intra-active relations, then it remains open to change. For example, on several occasions participants at All-Girls High commented that taking a date held greater importance the previous year; this year, there was less stress about ball-dates and more girls were going on their own:

Well last year, everyone was like I want to take a date, but this year, less people are, like, more people are just 'ah nah, I'll go by myself'
I think it's, if you don't have someone that you will really feel comfortable with and enjoy it, then there's no point in taking them
Yeah [multiple]
I think last year lots of people took dates that they weren't, like …
They got set up
Yeah and they sort of have to look after them and it put a dampener on the night
If they don't have any friends or whatever

(Year 13, focus group, 3 voices)

Having to 'look after' a date could hamper girls' enjoyment of the ball and restrict their freedom to move around and spend time with their friends. Girls in Year 13 were particularly cognizant of how ball-girl-date dynamics could *'put a dampener on the night'*: this awareness often a product of their experiences at last year's ball and feelings of frustration, annoyance and ambivalence. Remembered feelings of discomfort and the responsibility to *'look after'* or *'baby-sit'* someone enact ball-dates as problematic or a hindrance. These feelings appeared heightened if they did not know the ball-date well, or if the date did not know many people at the ball.

Entangled in ball-girl-date encounters is the expectation and responsibility to be a 'good date'. This expectation resonates with an idealized form of femininity where attributes of kindness and being nice are highly valued (Paechter, 2006). Feminist scholars have long drawn critical attention to the restrictive and negative implications of 'nice girl' discourses (Brown, 1998; Reay, 2001): for instance, how niceness is positioned in opposition to being assertive or bossy (Hey, 1997) and can require girls to play down their intelligence and academic success (Renold & Allan, 2006). As another participant explained, *'you kind of have to baby-sit them a bit, like you don't want to make them feel too lonely, but you don't want to like bring them everywhere with you, you still want to see your own friends'*. This sense of responsibility can work to contain girls' bodies, in particular their movement and freedom within the school ball space. This constraint was not fixed but shifted depending on other relations in the ball-girl-date assemblage: for example, the pressure of feeling like you had to *'baby-sit'* a date was reduced if the date had friends at the ball who they could spend time with. This new configuration afforded the ball-girl more freedom to spend time with their own friends. Several participants also chose to take a close female friend to the ball. In this fragment, a participant explains how rather than attending the ball with a set-up (male) date, she chose to take her a close (female) cousin/friend instead:

> *I had this friend who was like 'oh you could take him, or you could take him'. I was like 'oh yeah I guess I could' and now she's like 'oh I'll ask him', but you know if I am doubting myself, I realised I didn't want to take someone if I'm doubting myself, especially because I'm on running of the night. I can't have someone who needs babysitting or someone that doesn't know anyone else or is just annoying. I'm not the type of person to just take a good looking guy to just have photos with him, and at the end of the day I'm taking one of my close cousins, we're like best friends, so now I know I'm going to have fun and we're just going to have such a great night, it's going to be special to us cause like we're so close.*
>
> (Year 12, focus group, 1 voice)

While initially considering going with a set-up date, the participant enacts a sense of reluctance, which she experienced bodily as self-doubt. Noting *'I didn't want to take someone if I'm doubting myself'*, she decided to take her female cousin/best friend which alleviated issues of having to baby-sit or put up with an *'annoying'* date. The affective relations within ball-girl-date assemblages can be experienced as both positive and negative. While they may constrain girls to dominant school ball norms (i.e. attending with a date), they may also enable girls to go on their own, be *'the strong independent woman'* and have *'more fun'* with a group of friends. Hence, the importance of a ball date is not fixed or discursively presumed. Thinking about ball-girl-date encounters as material-affective (sexuality) assemblages, the focus is not simply on whether dates are important in the phenomenon of the school ball-girl, but *how* dates become (un)important in the entanglements with material things, ideas, spaces and affects.

The affective-materiality of the school ball photo

School ball photographs are conceptualized as material-discursive phenomena, intra-actively produced in connection with material forces (i.e. bodies, camera, spatial elements), gendered discourses and traditional ideas associated with the ball, the photographer, viewer and mode of dissemination (i.e. internet and social media). We can conceptualize these relations as a sexuality-assemblage that 'accrues around an event' (Alldred & Fox, 2015, p. 4), in this instance, the photograph. Material elements include: clothing – a formal gown, suit and tie; a wrist corsage; two human bodies that are positioned closely to one

Figure 6.3 Ball-girl-date-dress-suit-corsage-gendered discourses-photographer-viewer ...

another, an arm from each body is wrapped around the other body, smiling faces looking directly at the camera; glittered gold backdrop; soft diffused lighting which simultaneously creates shadow, sparkly highlights and shape. These material elements (i.e. things I can see) overlap with discourses and cultural understandings associated with the school ball, such as romance and heterosexual couplings; the camera, photographer and school ball space; the viewer and our memories and feelings. There is a 'thing power' (Bennett, 2010) or vitality to photographs that far exceeds representation, that is, what the photograph simply shows. Imagine, for instance, what the two bodies in the above photograph might see and hear: the click of the camera, flicker of the flash, the photographer and comments they might make, the crowd of people waiting to have their photograph taken.

The sharing and viewing of school ball photographs are inextricably entangled in ball-girl-date-photo encounters. A flow of affect emerges in the following discussion when a participant connects the importance of a date with parents and the sharing of photographs with wider family:

> *Do you think it's like, the whole thing about the date, it's so much just so our parents can see the photos of you, and 'oh look a date', so they can send it to my family?*
> *Oh my gosh, my mum took so many photos of me last year*
> *I know*
> *I got messages like 'you looked gorgeous at your ball' and I was, 'how did you know?'*
> *Because your Mum was sending them all out?*
> *So embarrassing*
> *[sighs and laughter]*
>
> (Year 13, focus group, 4 voices)

This fragment connects ball-girls and dates with parents taking and sharing photographs with family, gendered norms and emotions. Here, photographs emerge as lively and mobile; they do something. The taking, sharing and 'movement' of ball photographs elicit an array of affective forces including parental pride *'oh my gosh, my mum took so many photos of me last year'*, participant embarrassment and laughter. School ball photos evoke responses from family, such as *'oh look a date'* and *'you looked gorgeous'*, these comments enact beauty ideals and traditional norms of femininity. This 'viewing' of photographs is a productive force in the becoming of both the photo and ball-girl (Allen, 2015b; Hultman & Lenz Taguchi, 2010).

There is a public nature to ball photos that cannot be overlooked: this includes the sharing of photos by ball-girls and parents, but also the public online sharing of professional photographs taken at the ball. At all three balls I attended, the digital photographs taken by a professional photography company are shared with students via a website where anyone, including me, could access, view and download the photographs. Students had no control over the photos uploaded, nor did they have the power to edit or remove images they did not like. One photography company also had a live feed uploading ball photos to the company's Facebook page throughout the evening of the ball. Recent feminist scholarship draws on new materialist thought to highlight the material and affective entanglements of socially mediated digital images (see Warfield, 2016; 2018), opening up understandings of online sharing and viewing of photos beyond representational framings (i.e. simply what the image shows). Affective intensities and inequalities are produced through social media and the gendered material-discursive relations within the schooling environment (Charteris & Gregory, 2021): in the context of the school ball, this includes the gendered surveillance and critique of girls' bodies in accordance with traditional norms of femininity and heterosexuality. For some girls, the lack of privacy and control over ball photographs generated feelings of discomfort. As one participant explained, *'this random can see your photo before you do and that makes me uncomfortable'*: these feelings form part of the affective flow within the affective-material event of a photograph. For another participant, these feelings were intensified in relation with the photographer prompting *'uncomfortable poses'*:

> *Last year, the photographers, one of them was really unusual and he wanted us to do all these really weird like uncomfortable poses, like 'make it look awkward', 'I want an awkward family photo', and it was just really weird. I didn't want that to be put on the internet. And then he made us do these really weird poses and stuff, and it was so weird the pictures that we got out. And you never got to see what the pictures looked like before they put it up, and that kind of stressed me out*
>
> (Year 13, individual interview, 1 voice)

Photographs – how they are taken and shared – materialize as a source of stress and potential embarrassment. These feelings are affective intensities – a product of a particular configuration of an *'unusual'* photographer, his prompts for *'really weird poses'*, digital photography and modes of online dissemination, and the participant's lack of control over images that are shared via the internet. Of course, photographers are just one force in the becoming of a photograph, students also move and choose poses of their own volition. They wore bare feet, lay on the floor, stuck out their tongues, pulled faces, looked surly and turned their backs to the camera: these subversive actions further contributing to the material-affective event of the photograph.

Figure 6.4 Ball-girl-bodies-friends-dresses-decorations-camera …

A key point is a ball photo is not simply reducible to what it shows (i.e. two girls in long dresses with their backs to the camera), nor is it a mere snapshot capturing an isolated moment or space in time. There is far more at work here. Photographs are both a product of affect and productive of ball-girl affective capacities, including feelings and actions that generate a sense of resistance. Photographs are woven through many of the ball-girl-date encounters discussed in this chapter. In the previous discussion, photographs were an affective force in the desire to take a date. The next section revisits high heels and their productive entanglements with photographs, ball-girls, dates and the becoming of gendered bodies.

High heels, gendered bodies and 'sticky' affects

Ball-girl-date encounters involving a male date draw girls into a broader assemblage of gendered norms, in particular heterosexual bodily gendered ideals. From a relational materialist standpoint, gender is no longer taken for granted or a fixed given; instead, gender becomes 'naturalized in the entanglements' (Bodén, 2013, p. 1125). A prevalent gender norm within ball-girl-date encounters was the expectation that girls would be shorter than a male date; this regulatory expectation a non-issue for girls taking female dates. The expectation to be shorter than a male date was intensified when entangled in assemblages with high-heeled shoes and photographs. While the possibility of increased height was enticing for some girls, for other girls (and some boys) this capacity induced feelings of anxiety and embarrassment:

> *Oh yeah be shorter than your date*
> *Everyone is freaking out about that, like you can only wear this [much] higher heel because like then you'll be taller*
> *Yeah some people are like 'oh I'm going to have to wear flats'*
> *Yeah like um this guy is going with this girl as friends, and he's like 'oh my god she's already taller than me, now she's wearing heels, I'm so embarrassed' blah blah blah*
> *Oh, so the guys have said it too?*
> *Yeah [multiple]*
> *Yeah, they think they're less masculine if the girl is more whatever*
> (Year 12 girls, focus group, 4 voices)

This conversation enacts an array of affective forces: *'freaking out'* about being taller than a male date, embarrassment and boys feeling *'less masculine'*. These affective feelings are not individually produced; instead, they emerge via particular configurations of high heels, bodies, the social setting, (hetero) sexual codes and customs, gendered masculine and feminine ideals. As an actant (Bennett, 2010), high heels produce a taller body, and this altered ball-girl-body has the capacity to affect and be affected by other bodies, in particular a male-date-body (Deleuze & Guattari, 1987). It is not that high heels have negative effects on the bodies of girls (or boys for that matter), as within a feminist new materialist ontology there are no clear lines of division between bodies and high-heeled shoes. Rather, it is via the affective relations within assemblages of bodies, high heels, heterosexual norms, discursive practices and the school ball setting that particular ball-girl capacities or constraints emerge.

Thinking about how bodies become gendered through the expansion and limitation of affective capacities (Coleman, 2009) enables an understanding of the ways affect can participate in the regulation of social and gender norms (Ahmed, 2004a). As affect, feelings of anxiety over being taller than a male date contain some bodies and secure femininity within gendered norms. These norms are constituted in a binary with masculinity. There is a gendered (and heterosexual) expectation of how a girl/boy couple should look, and this appears particularly intensified when bodies are in-relation with the school ball and photographs. This intensification is entangled with historical and traditional ideas surrounding the space, imaginings and the expectation of achieving 'the right look' for the heterosexual couple, the sharing and viewing of photographs by family and friends. The following fragments enact these entangled forces including social gender norms, imaginings and photographs:

Well you see couples and you just assume that the guy is supposed to be a decent amount taller than the girl and it's just like how the projected couple is supposed to be, you know, so it's weird if you see them like the same height or the girl taller
(Year 13, focus group, 1 voice)
Why do you think it's an issue if the girl is taller?
Because you want to look good
Like you want to complete the look, if you look taller than your date then your whole look doesn't matter as much 'cause people will look at the photo and go 'oh look, she's a head taller than him'.
(Year 12, focus group, 3 voices)

Figure 6.5 Sticky affects.

In these enactments, being taller than a male date diminishes or threatens a girl's ability to *'look good'*. Looking the way *'the projected couple is supposed to be'* refers to what a body can do or might become. The 'right' look is an intensity that 'hooks' girls (Niccolini, 2016, p. 231) into gendered norms, placing restrictions around what a body can do in this particular spatial-temporal moment. Achieving this 'right' look is relational. A taller girl-body is only problematic when in relation with a male date-body and discursive norms of femininity as this was not an issue or anxiety for girls who were attending the ball with female dates or going on their own. A body can be understood as becoming through connections it makes with multiple and different bodies (Coleman, 2009) (see also chapter 5); therefore, it is not that a taller girl-body is problematic on its own, but it is in the intra-activity of a tall-girl-body, short-boy-body, high heels, photos, discourses of femininity and masculinity, school ball imaginings and affective intensities (e.g. embarrassment, shame, emasculation), that the tall-girl-body becomes problematic. These entangled relations constrain ball-girl becomings in particular ways: in this instance, the production of girls' bodies as 'acceptable' in ways that conform to and shore up gender and heterosexual norms.

Feelings of anxiety over being taller than a male date involve an entanglement of multiple temporalities. Following Massumi (2005), affect can be understood to draw the future into the present through the entanglement of fear and threat. For example, the threat of emasculation or embarrassment causes fear in the present, more specifically an anxiety over potentially being taller than a male date. Massumi suggests that without the presence of fearful feelings, or anxious feelings in this instance, the threat (e.g. of emasculation and embarrassment) would have no hold on the present. Threat in the future and anxiety in the present are 'indissociable dimensions of the same event' (Massumi, 2005, p. 36). As such, the event is 'a matter of multiple time-spaces' (Clough, 2009, p. 49). In a Baradian sense, this can be conceptualized as a spacetimemattering, where not only the present and future are inextricably entangled, but also the past. As girls discussed the anxiety over being taller than a male date, they drew my attention to historic gendered ideas of masculinity and femininity they felt regulated male and female bodies in this space:

> *Going back to girls and the whole height thing, what do you think that's about?*
> *Like wanting the guy to be taller?*
> *Um wanting them to be like … they want to be superior, have the power*
> *It's the whole sexist thing that goes way back*
> *For girls, it's just this expectation, idea about that's how it should be*

That the boys are tall and muscly and protect you and stuff like that
[groan] oh my gosh, I'll protect myself
And it's an aesthetic thing as well, like if you take the pictures and then the girl is taller than the guy, then like I don't know it's just weird for both parties. It's ingrained in the culture I guess
You just pick them up
Just lie on the floor [laughter]

(Year 12, focus group, 4 voices)

This fragment enacts the entangled relations of high heels, bodies, photos, gender discourses and the flow of affect that links them: cultural and social gender norms, expectations, feelings of unfairness and mockery of these ideas. The 'past surfaces affectively' in girls' talk (Ivinson & Renold, 2013, p. 1) as they trace the historical roots of these gendered power relations: *'it's the whole sexist thing that goes way back'*. Here, the 'past' and the 'future' are entangled forces in producing the 'present' moment. The affective capacities of the ball-girl-body become organized and produced in socially and culturally recognizable ways (i.e. girl-body shorter than male date); these gendered becomings emerge in assemblages that contain vestiges of the past (Ivinson & Renold, 2013). Discussing the gendered historical expectation that *'boys are tall and muscly and protect you and stuff'*, affect registers bodily (MacLure, 2010; Mulcahy, 2012) through a participant's groan and exclamation of *'oh my gosh, I'll protect myself'*. The tone of voice, facial expressions (rolling of eyes) and use of humour *'you just pick them up … just lie on the floor'* produces a subsequent flow of laughter. These affective responses (indignation, mockery, humour) entangled with human bodily matter and other materials (high heels) bring 'an *affective assemblage* into effect' (Mulcahy, 2012, p. 18, italics in original). One effect in this assemblage, even if momentarily, is the unsettling of traditional gendered discourses where males should be taller and females are in need of protection.

Affect works to delineate particular bodies (Ahmed, 2004a), in this instance, tall-girl-bodies in relation to short-boy-bodies. The anxiety that circulates does not reside in bodies; rather, it 'sticks' to bodies within the flow of affect. Thinking about affect as 'sticky' offers a way of understanding elements as 'bound together'; some forms of stickiness can create blockages to movement; however, this 'transference of affect' (Ahmed, 2014, p. 91) can also give rise to new capacities for thinking and doing (Mulcahy, 2016). In one-way, this affect *fixes* (Ahmed, 2004b) and problematizes tall-girl-bodies, particularly in relation to gender norms; however, affect is productive, in that it can orient and incite bodies towards specific actions. Affect also travels. Through Ahmed's notion of *affective economy* (2004a, p. 120), she proposes an understanding of emotions (as affect) that not only 'stick' but also 'slide'. In what she calls the rippling effect of emotions, feelings of anxiety or tension (over being taller than a male date) move sideways onto boys' bodies. Consider the shift of affect in the following fragment:

> *Yip I've heard a lot of people say that 'oh he's a bit short', like one of my friends Tyler, he wanted to come, and everyone is like 'oh I don't want to take Tyler because I'm already taller than Tyler, then I can't wear heels'. So, it's a big thing for a few of the girls [laughing]. I do feel bad for short boys in ball season*
>
> (Year 12, focus group, 1 voice)

Here, short-boy-bodies become sites of social tension: their bodies are read as a threat to girls' 'freedom' to wear high heels. There is a sense that short-boy-bodies can take something away from girl bodies (Ahmed, 2004a) and vice versa (i.e. threat of emasculation). This is an affect that delineates particular bodies from other bodies. For some girls, especially those who were arranging ball dates through friends or ball swaps, a tall partner enabled them to wear shoes of their 'choosing'. A taller date created a different scenario than one created by a short date – different intra-activity. The capacities for what a body can do changes. Within this flow of affect, the date is potentially problematic and therefore altered, rather than the shoes. Put another way, the anxiety or affect clings and attaches to particular bodies not high heels. A discursive reading of this example might suggest girls are conforming to gendered norms (i.e. wearing high heels) and shoring up hegemonic masculinity (tall males as desirable); however, how might thinking about this scenario through concepts of affect show us something more in this high heels-ball-girl-date encounter?

Within a sexuality-assemblage, human and more-than-human relations produce sexual capacities and desires: attraction, sexual activity, rejection and so forth (Fox & Alldred, 2013). In this framing, desirability and what is perceived as attractive is relational. A different assemblage can alter what might be considered desirable in a male date: for instance, if the male and female were in a relationship, then as one participant stated *'it wouldn't be the end of the world'* if the male date was shorter; however, if it was ball-swap situation, which involved girls 'choosing' their date, then most girls would choose not to be taller. Similarly, the anxiety over height seemed to be intensified when in-relation with the school ball and its unavoidable photos: a different space and setting might not produce the same affects at the same intensity. We get a sense of what Fox and Alldred (2017) might refer to when they say the manifestation of sexuality has little to do with personal preference, and everything to do with *how* relations assemble. The meanings associated with tall-girl-bodies and short-boy-bodies are emergent in relation with things (i.e. high heels, photos), space and affect. This framing shifts the notion of inherent properties of material bodies, to bodies that *become* intra-actively.

In thinking about 'sticky' affects, a feeling of sympathy also attached itself to male bodies. In the previous fragment, a participant concludes by light-heartedly expressing *'I feel bad for short boys during ball season'*. The enactment of sympathy works to situate short-boy-bodies as other. A sense of sympathy also emerged when another participant discusses how she chose to compromise her shoe choice in order to spare her partner's ego:

> Oh, he's only a tiny bit taller than me, so I was like, I can't really do that to him, be taller, 'cause it happened at another ball with a couple of friends, the girl was this tall ... So I spared his ego. Next year I'm going to go solo and going to go really high [laughing]
>
> (Year 12, focus group, 1 voice)

Here, the expression of sympathy in the form of *'sparing his ego'* was used as justification for not wearing *'really high'* shoes to the ball. Laughing, the participant proposes that next year she would forego the date enabling her to *'go really high'*. This brings us back to the allure and 'thing power' of high heels. Rather than being an inert object, high heels are an agentic force in this ball-girl-date encounter producing particular affective capacities. These capacities can undermine or reconfigure discursive understandings of the school ball, for instance, the idea that a ball date is an important or intrinsic part of the school ball experience. Meanings associated with ball-dates shift and change depending on the sexuality assemblage, for instance, the ball-date can become desirable, problematic or an object of sympathy.

Affective-spatial encounters

More than a mere backdrop to ball-girl-date relations, spatial arrangements and practices, such as the school ball entrance and dance floor, can intensify or produce particular affects within ball-girl-date assemblages. I conceptualize these carefully staged spaces as affective-material 'hot spots' where affects circulate around and through bodies, school ball spatial configurations and practices. Within these sexuality-assemblages, specific material affects for bodies emerge, which restrict and generate particular actions, movement and feelings. The following fragment introduces a few of these affective dynamics:

> *Some people think it would be embarrassing walking in without a date, like I definitely think that doesn't even matter, no one would care but some girls would feel …*
> *I feel like it would be awkward, like unless you were in a relationship with them or friends with them, it would be awkward*
> *Yeah [multiple]*
> *Like pressure to have to dance with them and have photos, I can't be bothered with that*
> *Yeah, you were friends with Matt so it was all good*
> *If random people asked you, and I don't know how to spend a whole evening with you. That totally happens*
> *I remember last year Luke asked me and I just had to be like, nooo. Like I didn't have an excuse but I had to say no*
> *It was sad when one of our friends said yes to a friend and then ditched him the entire night, and he was kind of like left 'oh I wanted to have a dance with my date, she said yes but she's just kind of ditched me' so that gets kind of sad*
>
> (Year 13, focus group, 4 voices)

This fragment enacts multiple affective relations within ball-girl-date encounters: embarrassment at walking in on your own, (un)comfortable conversations, feeling awkward if you do not know your date well, sympathy for dates left sitting on their own, pressure to have photos and dance together. One participant recalls being asked to last year's ball, to which she declined, '*I didn't have an excuse but I had to say no*'. There is an affective force here that registers as a feeling or intensity that exceeds language (Massumi, 2002). It registered bodily as '*I had to say no*' – perhaps a gut feeling – it was a force that propelled this participant to act (say no), even though she did not have (or need) a specific reason. Ball-girl-date encounters can produce certain expectations and responsibilities, for instance, having to dance and have photos together. These expectations could be enjoyable or potentially awkward.

In this fragment, a participant notes that some girls might think it embarrassing walking in without a date. At all three balls I observed, entering the ball was a

Figure 6.6 Girl-date-ball-entrance-photographer-decorations-camera-lighting-carpet-queue of students-people watching …

slow and highly visible process. Students formed a line, were greeted by and shook hands with the principal and head pupils. Teachers were positioned around the entrance collecting tickets and welcoming students: this role also functioned to observe and identify students who may be intoxicated. At two of the three balls I attended, there was a photographer stationed at the entrance capturing people as they entered the ball, as evident in the above photograph of a participant arriving with her female date.

This image depicts the entrance to the ball adorned with dragon figurines: it is well lit with overhead lighting and spotlights. A black strip of carpet leads attendees into the school ball space. In the background there is a queue of people, they are shaking hands and being greeted by the welcoming party. Behind the photographer is a large ballroom filling up with students, dates and teachers. As the participant and her date walk into the ball, they are asked to pause, and a photo is taken. At another ball, after being greeted by the principal and head students, ball attendees entered the ball via an escalator descending into the middle of the ballroom. As ball attendees came down the escalator, bubbles floated down from the ceiling, and a photographer waited at the bottom to capture the 'moment' of their arrival. In both these examples, the photographs were uploaded to the photo-sharing website for all students to view and access.

The school ball entrance is not something simply situated *in* space but is a spacetimemattering that constitutes the making or marking of space and time itself (Barad, 2007). Spatial-material 'hot spots' reorient the human as becoming *with* space, time and matter in the becoming of gender and sexuality, which means spatial configurations are not simply a backdrop or stage for human activity but do powerful and subtle work. From a new materialist perspective, space is relational and actively shapes how humans experience it (Allen et al., 2020): for example, entering the ball is an affective-material event involving multiple bodies (entering, greeting, watching and waiting), spatial-material objects (open doors, entrance carpet, stairs, escalators, decorations, a camera), atmosphere (lighting, bubbles, music), bodily sensations and impressions. As a spatial-material 'hot spot', the school ball entrance can produce an array of intensities and affects: for instance, embarrassment of showing up without a date may be intensified in this particular moment due to the dynamic forces producing this event – photographer, public sharing of photographs, queue of people waiting to enter the ball, the greeting party and those who have already arrived observing people entering the ball.

Like the school ball entrance, the dance floor can intensify or produce particular affects within sexuality-assemblages. The dance floor is a spatial-material arrangement that brings human bodies together with other bodies, music and lighting, practices such as 'romantic' slow dances and expectations (e.g. to dance with a date). At all three balls, the dance floor was centrally located in the school ball space. Music was primarily popular music played by a DJ or a live band, with only a couple of slow dances during the evening. The dance floor is not simply a physical space that bodies inhabit; rather, it is a spatial relation that materializes through the dynamics of intra-activity or the process of *spacetimemattering* (Barad, 2007). As such, bodies, the dance floor and time emerge in the 'moment' of coming together. Dancing was often cited as a fun part of the evening, yet the dance floor also emerged as a complex space in relation with ball-dates and slow dances. Traditionally associated with imaginings of couples and romance, slow dances are an intrinsic part of popular movies that portray the ball as a romantic space. While there were only a few slow dances, they emerged as an affective-material practice that sparked a complex range of affects and feelings: from awkwardness and panic to a (re)configuring of the romantic couple slow dance:

I think they played one slow song last year
And we danced as a group [laughter]
That was when I got a bit panicked, I was like oh ok, everyone has got their ball partners
I wasn't going to slow dance with my date. There were some awkward slow dances last year
Yeah when people who didn't really go out, then got asked to slow dance and it was really awkward. I mean people ask you to slow dance to fast songs and you're like no, stop
(Year 13, focus group, 4 voices)
Apparently at slow dances there's always that big group of people just swaying around, hugging each other, a slow dance is not necessarily just two people, with their dates, having the moment of their lives, it's so overrated
(Year 12, focus group, 1 voice)

These comments open up the meaning of slow dances beyond notions of couples and romance. As one voice suggests, a slow dance is not necessarily *'just two people … having the moment of their lives'*. Slow dances, at least in the traditional sense, could be *'awkward'*, or, as evident in the first fragment, could induce feelings of panic if everyone else has ball partners. Feelings of awkwardness in relation with slow dances are intensities or affects that traverse bodies, circulating in-between bodies on the dance floor. The change in music creates a shift in the air, sparking an affective force. These affects generate further affects and new capacities. In this example, the affective-spatial arrangement of the dance floor enables a particular form of collective activity that reconfigures the material-discursive practice of a slow dance. Here, the dance floor, bodies, music, slow dances and atmosphere come together in ways that disrupt ideas of the ball as a romantic space. In contrast to the countless teen movies that feature the prom in all its romantic glory – grand gestures, first kisses and slow dances – the majority of participants in this research did not construct the ball as a romantic event:

Oh my god, balls are the most unromantic thing ever
Yes
Like I don't see how?
Yeah the music they play, like they play party music, they don't play even remotely romantic music, like the majority of the time. They play like one or two slow dances

It's what you'd play at a normal party, like just on the weekend. So I guess that takes away the awkwardness of having a lot of slow dances, but there are still some. And like I remember noticing a lot of girls walked off with their dates when the slow songs came on, but our friends just stayed

(Year 13, focus group, 2 voices)

The dance floor, party music and the small number of slow dances, come together to enact the school ball as *'the most unromantic thing ever'*. This resonates with Smith's (2012) research that found girls rarely constituted the ball as a site of romance. In this fragment, ideas of romance (or lack thereof) were connected to the style of music, that is *'party music'* as opposed to *'romantic music'*, and very few slow dances. The school ball dance floor is not fixed as a romantic or non-romantic space, nor do I want to suggest this space is devoid of sexual intimacy and touch. Rather, the dance floor is an affective-material 'hot spot' where flows of affect generate particular actions, movement and feelings. Consider the affective forces in the following fragment where participants discuss couples *'getting frisky'* on the dance floor:

Ugh, couples at the ball, ugh
Sorry
Oh no you were fine but oh my gosh, on the dance floor, some couples ...
Oh wow!
Oh, getting frisky
They were getting very close and personal on dance floor. And I just found it kind of awkward
I felt slightly disturbed
Like if you do that there's nothing wrong with you, but it was just very ... open and in view
Yes
And I think a lot of people weren't like 'oh I wish I had a date like that', it was more like 'oh that's really awkward, what are those people doing?'

(Year 12, post-ball video diary, 2 voices)

This enactment can be conceptualized as an affective moment (Mulcahy, 2012) where affect flows through and in-between bodies and the spatial-materiality of the dance floor. Observing couples *'getting frisky'* on the dance floor elicits affective responses of feeling *'kind of awkward'* and *'slightly disturbed'*. Dance floors are a complex and contradictory scene – while they can present an opportunity for bodies to get *'very close and personal'*, they are also a space that engenders a rethinking or destabilizing of the popular constructions of the ball as a romantic space for couples. Keeping in mind, bodies are not simply situated in time and space (Barad, 2007), but are part of the very making and marking of space and time; as such, meanings associated with the ball, dates and slow dances are continually reconfigured. Rather than constructing the school ball as a predominantly romantic space that some students may accommodate or resist, school ball spaces are messy and contradictory. Like the ball-girl, school ball spaces are always coming into being – never fixed or finished. This indeterminacy provides openings for reimagining ball-girl-date encounters in ways that attend to (un)predictable affects and capacities.

Concluding–continuing thoughts

A feminist new materialist approach to sexuality destabilizes conventional boundaries of sexuality as linked to identity and the human body. Crucially, this offers a relational framework for reconfiguring sexual subjectivity 'not as involving a fully formed subject but as the conditions of emergence' (Allen, 2018, p. 130). There is an inherent indeterminacy where (im)possibilities are contingent upon assembled relations. At times, capacities and constraints may be recognizable within prevailing discursive norms, however, when 'conditions of emergence' are open-ended, so too are (im)possibilities. For instance, the desire to take a date is not (discursively) presumed, nor is it simply a matter of personal preference; rather, dates become (un)important through shifting entanglements of material things, ideas, spaces and affects. Understanding girlhood sexualities as emergent also has potential to rework enduring binaries that cohere around girls and sexuality, for instance, virgin/slut, good/bad, straight/gay (Aapola et al., 2005). These dichotomous positionings entail powerful normalizing/exclusionary effects and have long been the source of feminist analysis and critique.

Ball-girl-date relations are affective-material encounters – multi-body, affect-laden affairs encompassing material things, spaces, bodies, ideas and feelings. Exploring these encounters as sexuality-assemblages highlights forces that might conventionally be considered background or peripheral: more-than-human forces, spatial-material configurations and practices. Material things such as high-heeled shoes and school ball photographs, affective-spatial 'hot spots' like the dance floor and school ball entrance, are considered vital co-producers in sexuality-assemblages, and it is through flows of affect that ball-girl (sexual and other) capacities for action, feeling and desire emerge. Attending to affective forces within ball-girl-date encounters has enabled a focus on affective moments – the entanglements that produce gut feelings, pleasures, annoyances, niggles, attraction, awkwardness, desires and anxieties: capacities that might conventionally be described as 'sexual', yet also those not necessarily considered sexual at all (Fox & Alldred, 2017). This approach draws attention to the 'micropolitics' of the sexuality-assemblage (Alldred & Fox, 2016), the textures and nuance within ball-girl-date encounters of which humans are just one part.

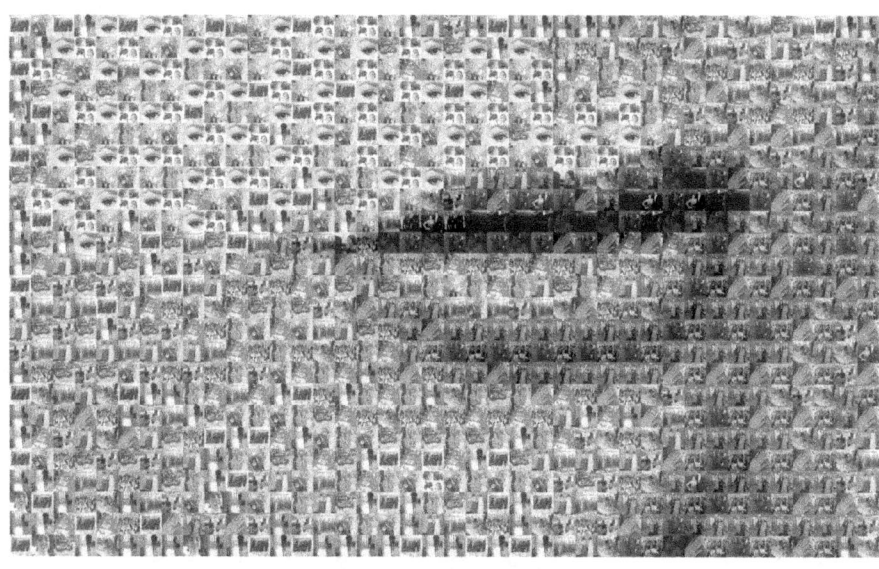

Figure 7.1 Becoming school ball-girl.

7

Ever after ... an ending of sorts

This final chapter opens with a data snap that cuts together visual images from the research. The participant photographs are arranged in such a way that a mosaic photographic image is formed. By bringing together images in this fashion, it becomes difficult to perceive the girl (and original photo) as a separate or individual entity. For me, the 'new' image gets to the very heart of the book – the idea that the ball-girl emerges through, and as part of, entangled intra-actions with school ball things, spaces, practices, ideas and affects. Neither the school ball nor the girl are distinct entities that precede one another; instead, they emerge through their mutual engagement. In Maggie MacLure's eloquent words: 'We are all produced from intensities and flows that far exceed and fall short of the contours of our bodies' (2017, p. 50); thus *becoming ball-girl* encompasses far more than an individual human body, a subject position, identity or discourse.

Recalling the newspaper articles in the introductory chapter, girls are often constructed as highly invested in the school ball, competitive and excessive. These portrayals are produced through and reproduce discursive norms of femininity and beauty. Dominant constructions are primarily underpinned by an understanding of the girl as an ontologically distinct entity engaging or interacting with the school ball event. In this frame, there is a clear subject/object divide, where 'things' or cultural practices are seen to produce material bodies in a one-way fashion. A new materialist ontology steps outside of these arguments as bodies and practices are no longer ontologically distinct. The relationship between cultural norms and the body becomes a relational emergent process that is multi-directional and co-constitutive. A reorientation towards entangled becomings compels feminist researchers to think of causation differently and to consider anew the location and potential for agency. In relation to the ball-girl, a material-discursive focus recognizes the numerous ways (im)possibilities materialize, helping destabilize reductive arguments based on simple cause and effect logic and a clear subject/object divide.

What has become of particular interest in this book is *how* entanglements limit and extend ball-girl capacities, and what this might offer for (re)thinking gender, sexualities and schooling. In the opening chapter, I described this book as an attempt towards curiosity and experimentation; an openness towards different questions and new ways of conceptualizing the becoming of bodies, femininities and sexuality. In a traditional sense, this chapter does the work of a concluding chapter by bringing together key ideas and arguments. Yet at the same time, in keeping with the study's ontological foundations, this chapter is not an ending in a finite sense. A feminist new materialist ontology entails an open and unknown potential of the school ball-girl. As such, this chapter is both a conclusion and an opening to new possibilities and ongoing questions.

Conceptualizing the 'new'

A conclusion often entails answers derived from questions like 'what does all this mean?' 'What do we now know about girls and the school ball that we did not know before?' These questions become redundant within a feminist new materialist onto-epistemology, as they are premised on a separation between 'the knower' and 'object to be known' (Allen, 2016b). An agential realist framework posits knowing and being as occurring in the same moment; therefore, there is no ontological distance between the knower (the feminist researcher) and the known (girls and the school ball). As the researcher, I am entangled in the becoming of the research. Therefore, I cannot stand back, look upon the data and give meaning to it – this is something a traditional representational account might offer, yet is impossible within a feminist new materialist approach. As Allen (2018, p. 125) succinctly notes: 'Within a new materialist framework, failure to end is an onto-epistemological inevitability'. This unending and unknown potential may sit uncomfortably with some readers and the conventional expectations of a conclusion; however, it is this open-ended potential that forms part of the 'new' that a feminist new materialist approach opens up (Allen, 2016a). In Barad's words, 'the "new" is the trace of what is yet to become' (2007, p. 383). This 'newness' is not nameable or representable because feminist new materialism 'renders it indeterminate'; instead, we might think of this 'newness' as creating '*a space where something new can emerge*' (Allen, 2016a, p. 8, italics in original): an invitation or an opening perhaps.

Methodologically, a feminist new materialist framework generates an alternative perspective to a representational reading of the school ball. Posthumanist and new materialist thought invites a way of understanding participant photographs and voice, where the human is conceived relationally. It has also opened a space for me to engage creatively with data, pushing the methodological boundaries of what it is and can be. This endeavour contributes to a growing body of work challenging the often taken-for-granted ideas about what data is, its role in research, and our relationship to it as researcher (Allen, 2016b; Benozzo et al., 2013; Brkich & Barko, 2013; Holmes & Jones, 2013; Koro-Ljungberg & MacLure, 2013; Koro-Ljungberg, 2013; Osgood & Giugni, 2015; Otterstad & Waterhouse, 2016; Springgay & Zaliwska, 2015). Data snaps (my own variations of data) are data-researcher (thinking-doing) encounters that constitute a move away from a representational reading, disrupting the idea that I have the ability to capture what data 'is' or what it means. A data snap does not capture a 'truth'; rather, it is a mattering – the researcher-data-methodology coming into being at the same moment. These data-researcher encounters demonstrate a lack of ontological separation between 'being' and 'knowing' (Barad, 2007). The lack of separation can also be applied to the subject of the book – the school ball-girl – and the book itself. The ball-girl and this book do not exist as individual distinct elements; they are inextricably entwined.

Barad's ethico-onto-epistemology offers generative potential for childhood and educational research as 'it forces us to pay attention to which kinds of matter, human and non-human, matters' (Taylor & Ivinson, 2013, p. 667); and in doing so, entails a sense of ethical response-ability (Haraway, 2008; Barad, 2007). For Hultman and Lenz Taguchi, attending to 'things and matter, usually perceived of as passive and immutable, ... can be understood as promoting a more ethical practice' (2010, p. 540). Within educational research, this might entail an increased 'attentiveness' to students' relations with things and schooling spaces, not as separate entities, but rather to what 'emerges in-between' (Hultman & Lenz Taguchi, 2010, p. 540). This book is an example of increased attentiveness to the relations in-between girls and the things, practices and spaces that co-constitute the school ball. Rather than conceiving girls as separate to these material objects and practices, the ball-girl is understood as emergent in the *in-between*. Hence, ball-girl-bodies are not contained to an individual human body and the boundaries of living flesh and skin. This framing shifts the human 'subject' from a central or privileged position to one where human and more-than-human matter are conceptualized relationally. Agency is reconceptualized as no longer tied to the human subject or the workings of discourse, disrupting an anthropocentric focus where humans reign supreme. Instead, agency becomes an emergent quality produced through an array of forces, opening up a multiplicity of (im)possibilities.

Conceptualizing the school ball-girl as intra-actively becoming takes into account material dimensions, material constraints and material possibilities. This framing shifts the ball-girl from discursive subject positionings and understandings of femininity, to a conceptualization of ball-girl femininities as materializing through the productive entanglements of human and more-than-human matter, embodied practices, ideas and affects. We can think about these matterings as productive, producing shifting ball-girl capacities, feelings and desires. The ball-girl becomes unstable, emergent phenomena continually (re)assembling at any given moment. This does not mean anything or everything is always possible; rather, (im)possibilities are continually reconfigured with the assembled relations. The dynamics of intra-activity (and possibility) are neither a matter of strict determinism nor unconstrained freedom; rather, the liveliness of matter(ing) ensures 'the future is radically open at every turn' (Barad, 2007, p. 235).

Thinking-doing research and the production of knowledge

The school ball as phenomena and the methodologies for researching the school ball are always entangled. They can only be distinguished from one another through provisional or temporary cuts. This book constitutes an agential cut (Barad, 2007) in the on-going reconfiguration of the school ball: it is the cut that enables me to write about the phenomena of the school ball-girl. Different agential cuts produce different phenomena, and this situatedness entails an ethical responsibility. Hultman and Lenz Taguchi remind us 'what we do as researchers *intervenes* with the world and creates new possibilities but also evokes responsibilities' (2010, p. 540, italics in original). For Barad, ethics is entangled with knowing and being, 'ethics is about accounting for our part of the entangled webs we weave' (2007, p. 384). Or, as Taylor and Ivinson (2013, p. 666) put it, ethics involves taking seriously 'our own messy, implicated, connected, embodied involvement in knowledge production'. As feminist researchers, being ethically responsible entails an awareness of how realities are produced, what has been cut in or out of emergent phenomena.

In relation to this project, the research assemblage has produced the school ball-girl in a specific way. What has been cut in or cut out of the phenomenon has been shaped by the research aim and questions, theory, the data that reached out to grasp me (MacLure, 2013b) and the reciprocal, co-constitutive relationship that have formed my encounters with this data. If reality is never independent from how it is researched, these forces contribute to what matters and what is excluded from mattering. In a sense, these forces contribute to what conventionally might be described as 'limitations of the research': there are boundaries that have been enacted. For example, as feminist post-structuralist thought shaped the 'beginnings' of the research, the research methods employed are conventionally humanist and qualitative (i.e. participant-generated photographs and video, group and individual conversations and observation). While I have attempted to conceptualize data within a posthumanist framework, these methods cohere around and are generated by the human. As such, the humans (participant/researcher) have decided what is worth speaking about and what is worth taking photos of; thus, shaping and placing limits on, what has come to matter in the research. I use the word 'beginnings' above tentatively; in a diffractive sense, there are no clear beginnings or endings to this research project. Nor is it a clear shift from one theoretical approach to another, where the 'old' is left behind; they are inextricably entangled.

The research has been an attempt to think about girls, sexuality and the school ball as emergent via material-discursive entanglements, and in doing so, account for some of the multiple forces at play. In part, it is an attempt to destabilize the centrality of the human: a post-anthropocentric aim within posthumanist and new materialist approaches. Yet, I am mindful of not overextending this claim. As Lenz Taguchi (2020) questions: to what extent is the human really decentred? Reflecting on her relational materialist approach to visual data developed with Karin Hultman (2010) – which I have engaged with in this book – Lenz Taguchi (2020, p. 39) suspects this approach might appeal to researchers because it can show how other actors 'are important in the construction of experiences and knowledge of the child, but also because the child remains the main interest of this research'. Indeed, the everyday lives of girls remain central to this project and its feminist politics. While working with new materialisms offers a more expansive frame for reimagining girls, sexuality and the school ball, these possibilities emerge alongside challenges, tensions and unresolved questions. I do not conceptualize new materialisms to be a magic wand that will solve all that ails feminist scholarship – there is no fairy godmother in this scenario. What feminist new materialisms have offered is a way to shift the emphasis from the ball-girl as a pre-existing entity towards the relations from which they emerge. This idea resonates with Casey Myers's (2020, p. 105) sentiment that 'a better way of framing this is not "decentering" but rather "making room" methodologically … I'd rather understand the center as expanding'.

A central aim of the book has been to (re)conceptualize the school ball as intra-active entanglements of materialities, ideas, practices and affects, expanding the scope of who and what *matters* in this schooling practice (Barad, 2007): material things (clothing, shoes, photographs), multiple human bodies (friends, dates, family, hair and make-up professionals), spaces (homes, shopping malls, beauty salons, school, online spaces), discursive practices (feminine beauty ideals and expectations) and affects (intensities, sensations and feelings) are all implicated in the becoming of the school ball. This expansive reframing opens up possibilities for (re)conceptualizing what the school ball can be and become, where meanings are not reducible to language or discourse, nor are humans and human meaning-making considered the sole constitutive force in how we come to understand the school ball (Hultman & Lenz Taguchi, 2010). Instead, a more 'flattened' landscape destabilizes human/nonhuman, material/discursive and subject/object divides and conventional spatial-temporal boundaries become blurred. To return to Myers's (2020) phrasing: the centre is expanding.

Agential realism offers a dynamic reworking of the materialization of the ball-girl-body in all its material-discursive fullness and messiness. This wider frame recognizes broader aspects of phenomena, for instance, the material-affective force of a high heel shoe or false eyelashes, a photograph as more than simply what it shows, the spatial-materiality of the school ball entrance and dance floor, the affective force of the atmosphere. These objects and spaces are not fixed or pre-determined, in that they too are in a process of becoming. Bargetz (2019, p. 188) explains there is an 'un/ruliness of materiality that the new materialist emphasis on posthumanist agency seeks to reveal – one that harbours indeterminacy, excess and obstinacy. In this vein, materialities embody moments of surprise and of the unforeseen'. I admit, as a fan of the unruly, this potential is quite appealing. Yet, I am also cautious of the limits of language; Lenz Taguchi makes an important point that while striving for a post-anthropocentric and non-representational research practice, 'the body and matter comes to matter merely in the way *we*—as humans—seem to be able to discursively describe it and thus articulate it or (re)present it. In this way anthropocentrism stares right back at us' (2020, p. 37, italics original emphasis). This is a difficult conundrum.

New materialist ontologies seek to deprivilege the centrality of language in how we come to understand the world. One strategy for grappling issues of language and representation is to attend to the materiality of language: 'its material force and its entanglements in bodies and matter' (MacLure, 2013a, p. 658). Although, productive gains have been made in the 'demotion of language and discourse', MacLure (2017, p. 53) wonders whether we have gone far enough:

> We are often left unclear about just how language tangles with matter; how words, bodies, signs, minds, and discourses intra-act and entangle. And the materiality of language itself is often not addressed – the fact that speech is formed from noises, breath, grimaces, and silences, and shot through with prelinguistic pulses of affect, while still being animated by something immaterial that somehow transforms it into a passage for meaning and ideas.
>
> (p. 53)

A challenge for researchers is being able to attend to, and importantly recognize, these material forces in the becoming of data. This connects to questions around method, but also wider issues in relation to language and representation that are difficult to shake. MacLure contends part of the difficulty is 'we continue to underestimate the sheer difficulty of shedding the anthropocentrism that is built into our world-views and our language habits. We find it hard to *practice* critique and analysis on terms other than mastery' (2017, p. 56, italics in original). Part of the difficulty in 'shedding the anthropocentrism' that infiltrates our research practices could stem from humanist (and feminist) concerns in relation to social justice. Reflecting upon new materialist thinking in relation to sexuality education, Allen (2018, p. 143) notes the tension between social justice and politics as 'a deeply human project' and the decentring of human agency that new materialisms inaugurates:

> How can we pursue social justice with a theory which is humanly represented (by those thinking with it) and yet which occludes in its very viability the possibility of human agency and centrality? We might then want to give up our pursuit of social justice as pointless and impossible. But who wants to live without ethics, even if they are flawed?
>
> (p. 143)

These are important and unresolved questions. This is not to suggest justice is not integral to Barad's agential realist framework. Rather, as MacLure (2017, p. 56) points out, if 'our new materialist work is framed and legitimated by familiar narratives of empowerment, emancipation, or social justice, ... we need to acknowledge that this is likely also to reinstall humanist notions of self'. How then, might we (feminist researchers) proceed? Allen (2018, p. 143) suggests 'we are compelled to find some way of perceiving ourselves as <u>not</u> leading in research and life. This might entail a "losing" of ourselves, at least for a while, and in turn an openness and vulnerability that requires an unravelling of human identity and ego'. For me, feminist new materialisms provide space for such an endeavour; an invitation towards challenging habitual ways of undertaking research, questioning what counts as data and researcher relationship to it. Allen further suggests it might also involve 'a loss of trust in the practices of "thinking" and "language" upon which we have relied to know ourselves and the world' (2018, p. 143). Although as Allen notes, whether this is humanly possible remains unseen.

Openness, vulnerability and a loss of trust in the practices of 'thinking' and 'language' entail a step into the unknown – a step which requires us to let go of familiar ways of thinking-doing research. Although, the accessibility of this step may vary within the tiers of academia, for instance, the affordances given to an experienced and established researcher, compared to a doctoral candidate bound within the confines of academic policies and conventions that regulate what is deemed success or failure (Ingram, 2021). MacLure posits 'perhaps it is a matter of learning to ask better questions: learning how to tap into the problematic structure of events, so that we can learn to be less guided by what we already think we know is important' (2017, p. 56). I find this an interesting proposition when thinking about critiques, questions and assumptions that often underpin judgements of what constitutes 'good' or 'bad' feminist scholarship. What we think we know as important often underpins these judgements. Brownyn Davies points out '*to bring about lasting change is an extraordinarily complex thing to do because of this tendency for it to go back into the already known, and because of the way the new actually depends on, is inter-woven with, the already known*' (cited in Osgood & Robinson, 2019, p. 55, italics in original). In relation to this project, the already known includes the heteronormativity of school ball spaces, the regulatory norms of femininity that structure schoolgirl bodies, the negative construction of girls in the media; these ideas are foundational to the project and inseparable from the spacetimemattering that constitutes the research itself. The aim of this project has been to take a step further, to explore feminist new materialisms' possibilities for expanding the *more* or *what else* we might (un)know.

To the unknown

A feminist new materialist approach alters not only how we come to understand sexuality but the becoming of sexualities research (Allen, 2018). As Renold and Ringrose (2017b, p. 548) note, 'finding new ways to capture the ruptures, ripples and regulations of contemporary young sexualities is no simple task, and demands ever inventive ways of doing research and being a researcher'. This book is concerned with girls, sexuality and the school ball, but also the very *doing* of gender and sexualities research. New materialist approaches do not produce 'better' or 'truer' ways of knowing the world; rather, as Lenz Taguchi suggests, they enable us to 'produce knowledge in a *different* way. A way which we think can help us—collaboratively and with the agents the research concerns—do as best we possibly can in the socio-historical and material context we are in' (2020, p. 34, italics in original). This book offers a particular perspective of the school ball – a particular mattering. While the girl remains a core interest, it has been an attempt to understand the ball-girl and sexuality as emerging through intricate material-discursive entanglements. The aim has been to generate a perspective premised on a relational ontology – a collaborative production of knowledge that is open-ended and uncertain, and where the researcher is inextricably entangled.

Becoming ball-girl is a matter of entanglement; as such, each intra-action matters. And what matters, is inextricably linked to questions of ethics. All bodies, including but not limited to human bodies, come to matter through the dynamics of intra-activity. This has significant implications for notions of responsibility and accountability. Intra-activity determines what is 'real' and what is possible; possibilities are opened up and others are foreclosed. With each intra-action, the entangled relations are reconfigured. As a result, Barad suggests 'there are no singular causes. And there are no individual agents of change. Responsibility is not ours alone' (2007, p. 394). Accountability and responsibility are rethought in terms of what matters and what is excluded from mattering. As Davies (2016, p. 9) explains, ethics 'is a matter of questioning what is being made to matter and how that mattering affects what is possible to do and to think'. Ethics, in this sense, is about mattering. It is about entanglement. It is not simply what or who has come to matter in the research, but *how* each intra-action matters in the continual becoming of the school ball-girl.

Lenz Taguchi reminds us 'productions of knowledge are also productions of reality that will always have specific material consequences' (2012, p. 278). What are the political and material consequences for rethinking the ontological foundations of girls, sexuality and the school ball? Where sexualities are not connected to identity, the human body or the human individual? Where the school ball is a more-than-human phenomenon and the ball-girl-body is temporary and fleeting, continually reassembling at any given moment? A feminist new materialist ontology disrupts what we might conventionally understand the school ball to be. When thought through Baradian concepts of intra-action and spacetimemattering, the school ball is no longer confined to the physical space or evening of the school ball. How might this rendering reimagine the role of the school ball in the becoming of sexuality at school? What implications might there be for conceptualizations of sexuality education, where 'sex ed is not, nor has it ever been, confined to a teacher standing in front of a room of students, talking about sex' (McClelland & Fine, 2017, p. 212). Within a new materialist framing, sexuality education is not limited to the 'official' space of the classroom or curriculum; rather, 'the world is in a perpetual state of be(com)ing the sexuality education "classroom"' (Allen, 2017, p. 162). As such, we might ask how the school ball is implicated in this becoming and with what e/affects?

A feminist new materialist approach not only asks new questions, but it also demands new ways of asking them. With this potential, existing language may be inadequate. A new vocabulary is required (Braidotti, 2013). As Jones and Hoskins (2016, p. 82) point out, 'current debates demand new language in order to produce or find *something else*': terms like *thing-power* (Bennett, 2010) and *intra-action* (Barad, 2003) are examples of new terminology created by theorists 'to encounter a material world quite different from that assumed in dominant western epistemologies' (Jones & Hoskins, 2016, p. 82). These terms are more than mere words; they are conceptual creativity that opens spaces for *something new* to emerge. Bennett (2010, p. 108) argues 'we need not only to invent and reinvoke concepts ... but also to devise new procedures, technologies, and regimes of perception that enable us to consult nonhumans more closely'. How might we do this?

For Jones and Hoskins, it requires we 'reach towards *something* that exceeds language: an *attitude*, a sympathy, a feeling, an openness' (2016, p. 83, italics in original). For me, this 'openness' is a shift from a 'hard reductive gaze' on the individual girl 'to a softer and widened attentive gaze that includes that which takes place in the spaces in-between' (Lenz Taguchi, 2010, p. 58). This has not always been an easy task – resisting an anthropocentric gaze can be difficult, as can avoiding the seductive tendency to slip into a representational account and say what this all means. As a researcher, my encounters with data have shifted significantly throughout the study. It has been an intriguing, challenging, yet ultimately exciting methodological becoming, and one by its very ontological 'nature' is not finished. There is an excess that cannot be written and 'captured' by words. This excess circulates in-between you the reader, me the researcher, the participants, data and theory – an endless lively configuration of things, ideas and sensations. And it is this very excess – this liveliness – that conveys the possibility of the ball-girl's endless becoming.

References

Aapola, S., Gonick, M., & Harris, A. (2005). *Young femininity: Girlhood, power and social change*. Palgrave Macmillan.

Ahmed, S. (2004a). Affective economies. *Social text, 79*, 22(2), 117–39.

Ahmed, S. (2004b). *The cultural politics of emotion*. Edinburgh University Press.

Ahmed, S. (2008). Imaginary Prohibitions: Some preliminary remarks on the founding gestures of the 'New Materialism'. *European journal of women's studies*, 15(1), 23–39. https://doi.org/10.1177/1350506807084854

Ahmed, S. (2010). Happy objects. In M. Gregg, & G. Seigworth (Eds.), *The affect theory reader* (pp. 29–51). Duke University Press.

Ahmed, S. (2012). *On being included: Racism and diversity in institutional life*. Duke University Press.

Ahmed, S. (2014). *The cultural politics of emotion* (Second ed.). Edinburgh University Press.

Alaimo, S., & Hekman, S. (Eds.). (2008). *Material feminisms*. Indiana University Press.

Allan, A. (2009). The importance of being a 'lady': Hyper-femininity and heterosexuality in the private, single-sex primary school. *Gender and education*, 21(2), 145–58.

Alldred, P., & David, M. (2007). *Get real about sex: The politics and practice of sex education*. Open University Press.

Alldred, P., & Fox, N. J. (2015). The sexuality-assemblages of young men: A new materialist analysis. *Sexualities*, 18(8), 905–20. https://doi.org/10.1177/1363460715579132

Alldred, P., & Fox, N. J. (2017). Materialism and micropolitics of sexualities education research. In L. Allen, & M. Rasmussen (Eds.), *The Palgrave handbook of sexuality education* (pp. 655–72). Palgrave Macmillan.

Allen, L. (2005). *Sexual subjects: Young people, sexuality and education*. Palgrave Macmillan.

Allen, L. (2006). Keeping students on the straight and narrow: Heteronormalising practices in New Zealand secondary schools. *New Zealand journal of educational studies*, 41(2), 311–32.

Allen, L. (2007). Denying the sexual subject: Schools' regulation of student sexuality. *British educational research journal*, 33(2), 221–34.

Allen, L. (2013a). Behind the bike sheds: Sexual geographies of schooling. *British journal of sociology of education*, 34(1), 56–75. https://doi.org/10.1080/01425692.2012.704719

Allen, L. (2013b). Sexual assemblages: Mobile phones/young people/school. *Discourse: Studies in the cultural politics of education*, 36(1), 120–32. https://doi.org/10.1080/01596306.2013.846901

Allen, L. (2015a). Picturing queer at school. *Journal of LGBT youth*, 12(4), 367–84. https://doi.org/10.1080/19361653.2015.1077766

Allen, L. (2015b). The power of things! A 'new' ontology of sexuality at school. *Sexualities*, 18(8), 941–58. https://doi.org/10.1177/1363460714550920

Allen, L. (2016a). Learning about sexuality 'between' home and school: A new materialist reading. In S. Dagkas, & L. Burrow (Eds.), *Families, young people, physical activity and health: Critical perspectives* (pp. 29–40). Routledge.

Allen, L. (2016b). Photos of (no)thing: The *becoming* of data about sexuality at school. *Reconceptualising educational research methodology*, 7(1), 1–15.

Allen, L. (2017). *Schooling sexual cultures: Visual research and sexuality education*. Routledge.

Allen, L. (2018). *Sexuality education and new materialism: Queer things*. Palgrave Macmillan.

Allen, L., & Ingram, T. (2015). 'Bieber Fever': Girls, desire and the negotiation of girlhood sexualities. In E. Renold, J. Ringrose, & R. D. Egan (Eds.), *Children, sexuality and sexualization* (pp. 141–58). Palgrave Macmillan.

Allen, L., & Rasmussen, M. (Eds.). (2017). *The Palgrave handbook of sexuality education*. Palgrave Macmillan.

Allen, L., Fenaughty, J., & Cowie, L. (2020). Thinking with new materialism about 'safe-un-safe' campus space for LGBTTIQA+ students. *Social and cultural geography*. https://doi.org/10.1080/14649365.2020.1809012

Allhutter, D., Bargetz, B., Meißner, H., & Thiele, K. (2020). Materiality-critique-transformation: Challenging the political in feminist new materialisms. *Feminist theory*, 21(4), 403–11.

Anderson, A. (2012). *High school prom: Marketing, morals and the American teen*. McFarland & Company, Incorporated Publishers.

Anderson, B. (2006). Becoming and being hopeful: Towards a theory of affect. *Environment and planning D: Society and space*, 24, 733–52. https://doi.org/10.1068/d393t

Anderson, B. (2009). Affective atmospheres. *Emotion, space and society*, 2, 77–81. https://doi.org/10.1016/j.emospa.2009.08.005

Åsberg, C., Koobak, R., & Johnson, E. (2011). Post-humanities is a feminist issue. *NORA - Nordic journal of feminist and gender research*, 19(4), 213–16. https://doi.org/10.1080/08038740.2011.625369

Atwood, M. (1969). *The edible woman*. McClelland and Stewart.

Austen, J. (1813). *Pride and prejudice* (First ed.). T. Egerton.

Bahou, O., & Orenstein, H. (2016, April 29). *These 9 girls were kicked out of school dances for their outfits*. http://www.cosmopolitan.com/style-beauty/fashion/news/a40441/banned-from-prom/

Barad, K. (2001). Re(con)figuring space, time, matter. In M. DeKoven (Ed.), *Feminist locations: Global and local, theory and practice* (pp. 75–109). Rutgers University Press.

Barad, K. (2003). Posthumanist performativity: Toward an understanding of how matter comes to matter. *Signs: Journal of women in culture and society*, 28, 801–31.

Barad, K. (2007). *Meeting the universe halfway: Quantum physics and the entanglement of matter and meaning*. Duke University Press.

Barad, K. (2008). Posthumanist performativity: Toward an understanding of how matter comes to matter. In S. Alaimo, & S. Hekman (Eds.), *Material feminisms* (pp. 120–56). Indiana University Press.

Barad, K. (2010). Quantum entanglements and hauntological relations of inheritance: Dis/continuities, spacetime enfoldings and justice-to-come. *Derrida today*, 3(2), 240–68. https://doi.org/10.3366/E1754850010000813

Barad, K. (2012a). 'Matter feels, converses, suffers, desires, yearns and remembers'. Interview with Karen Barad. In R. Dolphijn, & I. van der Tuin (Eds.), *New materialism: Interviews & cartographies* (pp. 48–70). Open Humanities Press.

Barad, K. (2012b). Intra-actions. Interview of Karen Barad by Adam Kleinman. *Mousse*, 34, 76–81.

Barad, K. (2014). Diffracting diffraction: Cutting together-apart. *Parallax*, 20(3), 168–87. https://doi.org/10.1080/13534645.2014.927623

Barad, K., & Gandorfer, D. (2021). Political desirings: Yearnings for mattering (,) differently.

Bargetz, B. (2019). Longing for agency: New materialisms' wrestling with despair. *European journal of women's studies*, 26(2), 181–94.

Bargetz, B., & Sanos, S. (2020). Feminist matters, critique and the future of the political. *Feminist theory*, 21(4), 501–16.

Bartky, S. (1990). *Femininity and domination: Studies in the phenomenology of oppression*. Routledge.

Basile, G. (1634–36). *Cunto de li Cunti*. Ottavio Beltrano (Days 1, 2, 5) and Lazzaro Scoriggio (Days 3, 4).

Bennett, J. (2004). The force of things: Steps towards an ecology of matter. *Political theory*, 32, 347–72. https://doi.org/10.1177/0090591703260853

Bennett, J. (2005). The agency of assemblages and the North American blackout. *Public culture*, 17(3), 445–65.

Bennett, J. (2010). *Vibrant matter: A political ecology of things*. Duke University Press.

Benozzo, A., Bell, H., & Koro-Ljungberg, M. (2013). Moving between nuisance, secrets, and splinters as data. *Cultural studies – Critical methodologies*, 13(4), 309–15. https://doi.org/10.1177/1532708613487878

Best, A. (2000). *Prom night: Youth, schools and popular culture*. Routledge.

Best, A. (2005). The production of heterosexuality at the high school prom. In C. Ingraham (Ed.), *Thinking straight: The power, the promise and the paradox of heterosexuality* (pp. 193–214). Routledge.

Bilby, L., & Gaffaney, C. (2016, May 25). Catholic girls' school's strict ball rules: No cleavage, no backless dresses, no taking off shoes and your date must be serious. *The New Zealand Herald*.

Bille, M. (2015). Lighting up cosy atmospheres in Denmark. *Emotion, space and society*, 15, 56–63. https://doi.org/org/10.1016/j.emospa.2013.12.008

Bille, M., Bjerregaard, P., & Sørensen, T. F. (2015). Staging atmospheres: Materiality, culture, and the texture of the in-between. *Emotion, space and society*, 15, 31–8. https://doi.org/10.1016/j.emospa.2014.11.002

Bissell, D. (2010). Passenger mobilities: Affective atmospheres and the sociality of public transport. *Environment and planning: Society and space*, 28, 270–89.

Blackman, L., & Venn, C. (2010). Affect. *Body & society*, 16(1), 7–28.

Blaise, M. (2005). *Playing it straight: Uncovering gender discourses in the early childhood classroom*. Routledge.

Blaise, M. (2013). Activating micropolitical practices in the early years: (Re)assembling bodies and participant observations. In R. Coleman, & J. Ringrose (Eds.), *Deleuze and research methodologies* (pp. 184–200). Edinburgh University Press.

Blaise, M., & Pacini-Ketchabaw, V. (2019). Enacting feminist materialist movement pedagogies in the early years. In J. Osgood, & K. Robinson (Eds.), *Feminists researching gendered childhoods: Generative entanglements* (pp. 109–20). Bloomsbury.

Bodén, L. (2013). Seeing red? The agency of computer software in the production and management of students' school absences. *International journal of qualitative studies in education*, 26(9), 1117–31. https://doi.org/10.1080/09518398.2013.816887

Bodén, L. (2015). The presence of school absenteeism: Exploring methodologies for researching the material-discursive practice of school absence registration. *Cultural studies critical methodologies*, 14(3), 192–202. https://doi.org/10.1177/1532708614557325

Bodén, L. (2016). *Present absences: Exploring the posthumanist entanglements of school absenteeism*. [Doctoral thesis, Linköping University]. https://www.diva-portal.org/smash/get/diva2:951239/FULLTEXT01.pdf

Böhme, G. (1993). Atmosphere as the fundamental concept of a new aesthetics. *Thesis eleven*, 36, 113–26.

Bordo, S. (1993). *Unbearable weight: Feminism, western culture and the body*. University of California Press.

Bottigheimer, R. (2016). Cinderella: The people's princess. In M. Hennard Duthiel de la Rochère, G. Lathey, M. Wozniak, C. Bacchilega, R. Bottigheimer, & K. Hoffmann (Eds.), *Cinderella across cultures: New directions and interdisciplinary perspectives* (pp. 27–51). Wayne State University Press.

Braidotti, R. (2013). *The posthuman*. Polity.

Brkich, C., & Barko, T. (2013). Fictive reality: Troubling our notions of truth and data in Iambic pentameter. *Cultural studies – Critical methodologies*, 13(4), 246–51. https://doi.org/10.1177/1532708613487869

Brown, L.M. (1998). *Raising their voices: The politics of girls' anger*. Harvard University Press.
Budgeon, S. (2003). Identity as an embodied event. *Body and society*, 9(1), 35–55.
Butler, J. (1990). *Gender Trouble: Feminism and the subversion of identity*. Routledge.
Butler, J. (1993). *Bodies that matter: On the discursive limits of sex*. Routledge.
Charteris, J., & Gregory, S. (2021). Snapchat and affective inequalities: Affective flows in a schooling assemblage. *International journal of qualitative studies in education*. https://doi.org/10.1080/09518398.2021.2003886
Childers, S. M. (2013). The materiality of fieldwork: An ontology of feminist becoming. *International journal of qualitative studies in education*, 26(5), 599–609. https://doi.org/10.1080/09518398.2013.786845
Clough, P. T. (2009). The new empiricism: Affect and sociological method. *European journal of social theory*, 12(1), 43–61.
Coffey, J. (2013). Bodies, body work and gender: Exploring a Deleuzian approach. *Journal of gender studies*, 22(1), 3–16. https://doi.org/10.1080/09589236.2012.714076
Cole, B. (1987). *Prince cinders*. Puffin Books.
Colebrook, C. (2006). Introduction. *Feminist theory*, 7(2), 131–42.
Colebrook, C. (2017). What is this thing called education? *Qualitative inquiry*, 23(9), 649–55. https://doi.org/10.1177/1077800417725357
Coleman, R. (2008). The becoming of bodies. *Feminist media studies*, 8(2), 163–79. https://doi.org/10.1080/14680770801980547
Coleman, R. (2009). *The becoming of bodies: Girls, images, experience*. Manchester University Press.
Coleman, R., & Moreno Figueroa, M. (2010). Past and future perfect? Beauty, affect and hope. *Journal for cultural research*, 14(4), 357–73. https://doi.org/10.1080/14797581003765317
Coole, D. (2005). Rethinking agency: A phenomenological approach to embodiment and agentic capacities. *Political studies*, 53, 124–42.
Coole, D. (2013). Agentic capacities and capacious historical materialism: Thinking with new materialisms in the political sciences. *Millennium – Journal of international studies*, 41(3), 451–69. https://doi.org/10.1177/0305829813481006
Coole, D., & Frost, S. (Eds.). (2010). *New materialisms: Ontology, agency and politics*. Duke University Press.
Cowie, C., & Lees, S. (1981). Slags or drags. *Feminist review*, 9, 17–31.
Davies, B. (1989). *Frogs, snails and feminist tales: Preschool children and gender*. Allen and Unwin.
Davies, B. (2016). Ethics and the new materialism: A brief genealogy of the 'post' philosophies in the social sciences. *Discourse: Studies in the cultural politics of education*.
Davies, B. (2020). An interview with Bronwyn Davies. In C. Diaz-Diaz, & P. Semenec (Eds.), *Posthumanist and new materialist methodologies: Research after the child* (pp. 21–32). Springer Nature.

Davis, N. (2009). New materialism and feminism's anti-biologism: A Response to Sarah Ahmed. *European journal of women's studies*, 16(1), 67–80. https://doi.org/10.1177/1350506808098535

De Landa, M. (2002). *Intensive science and virtual philosophy*. Continuum.

Deleuze, G. (1988). *Spinoza: Practical philosophy*. City Lights.

Deleuze, G. (1990). *The logic of sense* (M. Lester Trans.). Columbia University Press.

Deleuze, G. (1992). Ethology: Spinoza and us. In J. Crary, & S. Kwinter (Eds.), *Incorporations* (pp. 625–33). Zone.

Deleuze, G., & Guattari, F. (1984). *Anti-Oedipus: Capitalism and schizophrenia*. Athlone.

Deleuze, G., & Guattari, F. (1987). *A thousand plateaus: Capitalism and schizophrenia* (B. Massumi Trans.). University of Minneapolis Press.

Disney, W. (1950). *Cinderella* (First ed.). Dean.

Disney, W. (1998). *Cinderella*. Golden Books: Random House.

Disney, W. (Producer), & Geronimi, C., Jackson, W. and Luske, H. (Directors). (1950). *Cinderella*. [Motion Picture] USA: Disney.

Dolphijn, R., & van der Tuin, I. (2012). *New materialism: Interviews & cartographies*. Open Humanities Press.

Donoghue, E. (1997). *Kissing the witch*. Penguin.

Downing, E. (2014). *Prom crashers (The romantic comedies)*. Simon Pulse.

Duff, C. (2010). On the role of affect and practice in the production of place. *Environment and planning D: Society and space*, 28, 881–95. https://doi.org/10.1068/d16209

Dundes, A. (Ed.). (1988). *Cinderella: A casebook* (Second ed.). University of Wisconsin Press.

Dworkin, A. (1974). *Women hating*. Dutton.

Edwards, R., & Fenwick, T. (2014). Critique and Politics: A sociomaterialist intervention. *Educational philosophy and theory*, 1–20. https://doi.org/10.1080/00131857.2014.930681

Egan, R. D., & Hawkes, G. (2008). Imperiled and perilous: Exploring the history of childhood sexuality. *Journal of historical sociology*, 21(4), 355–67.

Epstein, D., & Johnson, R. (1998). *Schooling sexualities*. Open University Press.

Epstein, D., O'Flynn, S., & Telford, D. (2003). *Silenced sexualities in schools and universities*. Trentham Books.

Eriksen, A. (2012, June 16). Frock horror as ball girls turn up in same dress. *The New Zealand Herald*.

Eulberg, E. (2011). *Prom and prejudice*. Point. Scholastic Incorporated.

Ferfolja, T. (2007). Schooling cultures: Institutionalizing heternormativity and heterosexism. *International journal of inclusive education*, 11(2), 147–62.

Fisher, H. (2005). *Why we love: The nature and chemistry of romantic love*. Henry Holt and Co.

Foucault, M. (1976). *The history of sexuality, Volume 1* (R. Hurley Trans.). Penguin.

Foucault, M. (1977). *Discipline and punish*. Penguin.

Foucault, M. (1980). *Power/knowledge: Selected interviews and other writings 1972–1977*. Pantheon Books.

Foucault, M. (1983). Afterword: The subject and power. In D. Hubert, & P. Rabinow (Eds.), *Michel Foucault: Beyond structuralism and hermeneutics*. The University of Chicago Press.

Fox, N. J. (2012). *The body: Key themes in health and social care*. Polity Press.

Fox, N. J. (2013). Flows of affect in the olympic stadium and beyond. *Sociological research online*, 18(2), 2.

Fox, N. J. (2015). Emotions, affects and the production of social life. *The British journal of sociology*, 66(2), 301–18.

Fox, N. J., & Alldred, P. (2013). The sexuality-assemblage: Desire, affect, anti-humanism. *The sociological review*, 61, 769–89. https://doi.org/10.1111/1467-954X.12075

Fox, N. J., & Alldred, P. (2014). New materialist social inquiry: Designs, methods and the research-assemblage. *International journal of social research methodology*, 18(4), 399–414. https://doi.org/10.1080/13645579.2014.921458

Fox, N. J., & Alldred, P. (2016). The resisting young body. In J. Coffey, S. Budgeon, & H. Cahill (Eds.), *Learning bodies: The body in youth and childhood studies* (pp. 125–40). Springer.

Fox, N. J., & Alldred, P. (2017). *Sociology and the new materialism: Theory, research, action*. Sage Publications.

Freud, S. (1927). Fetishism. *Standard edition*, 21, 152–9.

Frost, S. (2011). The implications of the new materialisms for feminist epistemology. In H. E. Grasswick (Ed.), *Feminist epistemology and philosophy of science: Power in knowledge* (pp. 69–83). Springer Science+Business Media. https://doi.org/10.1007/978-1-4020-6835-5_4

Gamman, L. (2001). Self-fashioning, gender display, and sexy girl shoes: What's at stake – Female fetishism or narcissism? In S. Benstock, & S. Ferriss (Eds.), *Footnotes: On shoes* (pp. 93–115). Rutgers University Press.

Garland-Levett, S. (2020). Knowing-in-being: Traversing the mind/body dualism to dissolve sexuality education's 'knowledge/practice' gap. *Gender & education*, 32(6), 691–714. https://doi.org/10.1080/09540253.2018.1482414

Gonick, M. (2003). *Between femininities: Ambivalence, identity and the education of girls*. SUNY Press.

Gorrell Anstiss, C. (2012, April 22). Bills pile up for ball belles. *The New Zealand Herald*.

Gregg, M., & Seigworth, G. (Eds.). (2010). *The affect theory reader*. Duke University Press.

Grimm, J., & Grimm, W. (1857). *Kinder- und Hausmärchen*. Dieterische Buchhandlung.

Grosz, E. (1994). *Volatile bodies: Toward a corporeal feminism*. Indiana University Press.

Grosz, E. (2010). Feminism, materialism, and freedom. In D. Coole, & S. Frost (Eds.), *New materialisms: Ontology, agency and politics* (pp. 139–57). Duke University Press.

Haase, D. (Ed.). (2004). *Fairy tales and feminism: New approaches*. Wayne State University Press.

Hackett, A. (2022). *More-than-human literacies in early childhood*. Bloomsbury.

Hames-Garcia, M. (2008). How real is race? In S. Alaimo, & S. Hekman (Eds.), *Material Feminisms* (pp. 308–39). Indiana University Press.

Happel, A. (2013). Ritualized girling: School uniforms and compulsory performance of gender. *Journal of gender studies*, 22(1), 92–6. https://doi.org/10.1080/09589236.2012.745680

Haraway, D. (1997). *Modest_witness@_millennium.FemaleManß_meets_OncoMouseTM: Feminism and Technoscience*. Routledge.

Haraway, D. (2008). *When species meet*. University of Minnesota Press.

Haraway, D. (2016). *Staying with the trouble: Making kin in the Chthulucene*. Duke University Press.

Harris, A. (Ed.). (2004). *All about the girl: Culture, power and identity*. Routledge.

Hauge, M. (2009). Bodily practices and discourses of hetero-femininity: Girls' constitution of subjectivities in their social transition between childhood and adolescence. *Gender and education*, 21(3), 293–307.

Healy, S. (2014). Atmospheres of consumption: Shopping an involuntary vulnerability. *Emotion, space and society*, 10, 35–43. https://doi.org/org/10.1016/j.emospa.2012.10.003

Hein, S. (2016). The new materialism in qualitative inquiry: How compatible are the philosophies of Barad and Deleuze? *Cultural studies – Critical methodologies*, 16(2), 132–40. https://doi.org/10.1177/1532708616634732

Hennard Duthiel de la Rochère, M., Lathey, G., Wozniak, M., Bacchilega, C., Bottigheimer, R., & Hoffman, K. (Eds.). (2016). *Cinderella across cultures: New directions and interdisciplinary perspectives*. Wayne State University Press.

Hennessy, R., & Ingraham, C. (Eds.). (1997). *Materialist feminism: A reader in class, difference, and women's lives*. Routledge.

Hey, V. (1997). *The company she keeps: An ethnography of girls' friendships*. Open University Press.

Hickey-Moody, A., Palmer, H., & Sayers, E. (2016). Diffractive pedagogies: Dancing across new materialist imaginaries. *Gender and education*, 28(2), 213–29. https://doi.org/10.1080/09540253.2016.1140723

Hinton, P., & Liu, X. (2015). The im/possibility of abandonment in new materialist ontologies. *Australian feminist studies*, 30(84), 128–45.

Hinton, P., & van der Tuin, I. (2014). 'Preface': Special issue 'Feminist Matters: The Politics of New Materialism'. *Women: A cultural review*, 15(1), 1–8.

Hinton, P., Mehrabi, T., & Barla, J. (2015). New materialism/New colonialisms. https://newmaterialism.eu/content/5-working-groups/2-working-group-2/position-papers/subgroup-position-paper-_-new-materialisms_new-colonialisms.pdf

Hird, M. J. (2009). Feminist engagements with matter. *Feminist studies*, 35(2), 329–46.

Hohti, R. (2015). Now – and now – and now: Time, space and the material entanglements of the classroom. *Children & society*. https://doi.org/10.1111/chso.12135.

Holford, N., Renold, E., & Huuki, T. (2013). What (else) can a kiss do? Theorizing the power plays in young children's sexual cultures. *Sexualities*, 16(5/6), 710–29. https://doi.org/10.1117/1363460713487300

Holmes, D., O'Byrne, P., & Murray, S. J. (2010). Faceless sex: Glory holes and sexual assemblages. *Nursing philosophy*, 11, 250–9.

Holmes, R., & Jones, L. (2013). Flesh, wax, horse skin, and hair: The many intensities of data. *Cultural studies – Critical methodologies*, 13(4), 357–73. https://doi.org/10.1177/1532708613487869.

Hultman, K., & Lenz Taguchi, H. (2010). Challenging anthropocentric analysis of visual data: A relational materialist methodological approach to educational research. *International journal of qualitative studies in education*, 23(5), 525–42. https://doi.org/10.1080/09518398.2010.500628

Ingram, T. (2021). The curious predicament of an (un)comfortable thesis conclusion: Writing with new materialisms. In C. Badenhorst, B. Amell, & J. Burford (Eds.), *Re-imagining doctoral writing*. WAC Clearinghouse. https://doi.org/10.37514/INT-B.2021.1343.2.12

Irni, S. (2013). The politics of materiality: Affective encounters in a transdisciplinary debate. *European journal of women's studies*, 20(4), 347–60. https://doi.org/10.1177/1350506812472669

Ivinson, G., & Renold, E. (2013). Valleys' girls: Re-theorising bodies and agency in a semi-rural post-industrial locale. *Gender and education*, 25(6), 704–21. https://doi.org/10.1080/09540253.2013.827372

Jackson, A. Y. (2017). Thinking without method. *Qualitative inquiry*, 23(9), 666–74. https://doi.org/10.1177/1077800417725355

Jackson, A. Y., & Mazzei, L. A. (2012). *Thinking with theory in qualitative research: Viewing data across multiple perspectives*. Routledge.

Jackson, A. Y., & Mazzei, L. A. (2013). Plugging one text into another: Thinking with theory in qualitative research. *Qualitative inquiry*, 19(4), 261–71. https://doi.org/10.1177/1077800412471510

Jackson, A. Y., & Mazzei, L. A. (2016). Thinking with an agentic assemblage in posthuman inquiry. In C. A. Taylor, & C. Hughes (Eds.), *Posthuman research practices in education* (pp. 93–107). Palgrave Macmillan.

Jacobs, J. (1916). *The Cinder-Maid*. https://fairytalez.com/cinder-maid-joseph-jacobs-version-cinderella/

Jeffreys, S. (2005). *Beauty and misogyny: Harmful cultural practices in the West*. Routledge.

Jones, A., & Hoskins, T. K. (2016). A mark on paper: The matter of indigenous-settler history. In C. A. Taylor, & C. Hughes (Eds.), *Posthuman research practices in education* (pp. 75–92). Palgrave Macmillan.

Jones, N. (2013, July 16). Parents face up to school-ball sting. *The New Zealand Herald*.

Jones, N. (2014, May 27). Must-have accessory this ball season: Lots of cash. *The New Zealand Herald*.

Joosen, V. (2011). *Critical and creative perspectives on fairy tales*. Wayne State University Press.
Juelskjaer, M. (2013). Gendered subjectivities of spacetimematter. *Gender and education*, 25(6), 754–68. https://doi.org/10.1080/09540253.2013.831812
Juelskjaer, M., & Schwennesen, N. (2012). Intra-active entanglements: An interview with Karen Barad. *Kvinder, Køn & Forskning NR*, 1(2), 10–23.
Kehily, M. J. (2002). *Sexuality, gender and schooling: Shifting agendas in social learning*. RoutledgeFalmer.
Kelly, D., Pomerantz, S., & Currie, D. (2005). Skater girlhood and emphasized femininity: 'You can't land an ollie properly in heels'. *Gender and education*, 17(3), 129–45.
Kirby, V. (2006). *Judith Butler: Live theory*. Continuum.
Kirby, V., & Wilson, E. (2011). Feminist conversations with Vicki Kirby and Elizabeth A. Wilson. *Feminist theory*, 12(2), 227–34. https://doi.org/10.1177/1464700111404289
Koro-Ljungberg, M. (2012). Researchers of the world, create! *Qualitative inquiry*, 18(9), 808–18. https://doi.org/10.1177/1077800412453014
Koro-Ljungberg, M. (2013). 'Data' as vital illusion. *Cultural studies – Critical methodologies*, 13(4), 274–8. https://doi.org/10.1177/1532708613487873
Koro-Ljungberg, M. (2016). *Reconceptualizing qualitative research: Methodologies without methodology*. Sage Publications.
Koro-Ljungberg, M., & MacLure, M. (2013). Provocations, re-un-visions, death, and other possibilities of 'data'. *Cultural studies – Critical methodologies*, 13(4), 219–22. https://doi.org/10.1177/1532708613487861
Kristeva, J. (1981). Women's time. *Signs*, 7(1).
Kuntz, M. A., & Presnall, M. M. (2012). Wandering the tactical: From interview to intraview. *Qualitative inquiry*, 18, 732–44.
Lambevski, S. A. (2005). Bodies, schizo vibes and hallucinatory desires – Sexualities in movement. *Sexualities*, 8(5), 570–86. https://doi.org/10.1177/1363460705058394
Lane, L., & Haun, E. (2020). *Cinderella and the glass ceiling: And other feminist fairy tales*. Seal Press.
Lather, P., & St. Pierre, E. A. (2013). Post-qualitative research. *International journal of qualitative studies in education*, 26(6), 629–33. https://doi.org/10.1080/09518398.2013.788752
Latour, B. (2004). Why has critique run out of steam? *Critical inquiry*, 30, 225–48.
Leiberman, M. (1972). Some day my prince will come: Female acculturation through the fairy tale. *College english*, 34, 383–95.
Lenz Taguchi, H. (2010). *Going beyond the theory/practice divide in early childhood education: Introducing an intra-active pedagogy*. Routledge.
Lenz Taguchi, H. (2012). A diffractive and Deleuzian approach to analysing interview data. *Feminist theory*, 13(3), 265–81.
Lenz Taguchi, H. (2013). Images of thinking in feminist materialisms: Ontological divergences and the production of researcher subjectivities. *International journal of qualitative studies in education*, 26(6), 706–16.

Lenz Taguchi, H. (2017). 'The concept as method': Tracing-and-mapping the problem of the neuro(n) in the field of education. *Cultural studies – Critical methodologies*, 16(2), 213–23. https://doi.org/10.1177/1532708616634726

Lenz Taguchi, H. (2020). Interview with Hellevi Lenz Taguchi. In C. Diaz-Diaz, & P. Semenec (Eds.), *Posthumanist and new materialist methodologies: Research after the child* (pp. 33–46). Springer.

Lenz Taguchi, H., & Palmer, A. (2013). A more 'livable' school? A diffractive analysis of the performative enactments of girls' ill-/well-being with(in) school environments. *Gender and education*, 25(6), 671–87. https://doi.org/10.1080/09540253.2013.829909

Lenz Taguchi, H., & St. Pierre, E. A. (2017). Using concept as method in educational and social science inquiry. *Qualitative inquiry*, 23(9), 643–8. https://doi.org/10.1177/1077800417732634

Lesko, N. (1988). The curriculum of the body: Lessons from a Catholic high school. In L. G. Roman, L. Christian-Smith, & E. Ellsworth (Eds.), *Becoming feminine: The politics of popular culture* (pp. 123–42). Falmer Press.

Lorimer, J. (2013). More-than-human visual analysis: Witnessing and evoking affect in human-non human interactions. In R. Coleman, & J. Ringrose (Eds.), *Deleuze and research methodologies* (pp. 61–78). Edinburgh University Press.

Lyttleton-Smith, J., & Robinson, K. (2019). 'I like your costume': Dress-up play and feminist trans-theoretical shifts. In J. Osgood, & K. Robinson (Eds.), *Feminists researching gendered childhoods: Generative entanglements* (pp. 61–84). Bloomsbury.

Mac An Ghaill, M. (1996). Deconstructing heterosexualities with school arenas. *Curriculum studies*, 4(2), 191–209.

MacLure, M. (2009). Broken voices, dirty words: On the productive insufficiency of voice. In A. Y. Jackson, & L. A. Mazzei (Eds.), *Voice in qualitative inquiry: Challenging conventional, interpretive, and critical conceptions of qualitative research* (pp. 97–115). Routledge.

MacLure, M. (2010). The offence of theory. *Journal of education policy*, 25(2), 277–86. https://doi.org/10.1080/02680930903462316

MacLure, M. (2013a). Researching without representation? Language and materiality in post-qualitative methodology. *International journal of qualitative methods*, 26(6), 658–67. https://doi.org/10.1080/09518398.2013.788755

MacLure, M. (2013b). The wonder of data. *Cultural studies – Critical methodologies*, 13(4), 228–32. https://doi.org/10.1177/1532708613487863

MacLure, M. (2015). The 'new materialisms': A thorn in the flesh of critical qualitative inquiry. In G. Cannella, M. S. Perez, & P. Pasque (Eds.), *Critical qualitative inquiry: Foundations and futures* (pp. 93–112). Left Coast Press.

MacLure, M. (2017). Qualitative methodology and the new materialisms: 'A little of Dionysus's blood?'. In N. K. Denzin, & M. D. Giardina (Eds.), *Qualitative inquiry in neoliberal times* (pp. 48–58). Routledge.

Malone, K., Logan, M., Siegel, L., Regalado J., & Wade-Leeuwen, W. (2020). Shimmering with Deborah Rose: Posthuman theory-making with feminist ecophilosophers and social ecologists. *Australian journal of environmental education*, 36, 129–45. https://doi.org/10.1017/aee.2020.23

Manning, E. (2013). *Always more than one: Individuation's dance.* Duke University Press.

Marling, K. (2004). *Debutante: Rites and regalia of American Debdom.* University Press of Kansas.

Massey, D. (1992). Politics and space/time. *New left review*, 196, 65–84.

Massey, D. (1994). *Space, place, and gender.* University of Minnesota Press.

Massumi, B. (1987). Translator's foreword: Pleasures of philosophy & notes on the translation and acknowledgements. In G. Deleuze, & F. Guattari (Eds.), *A thousand plateaus: Capitalism and schizophrenia* (B. Massumi Trans.) (pp. ix–xix). University of Minnesota Press.

Massumi, B. (2002). *Parables for the virtual: Movement, affect, sensation.* Duke University Press.

Massumi, B. (2005). 'Fear (The Spectrum Said)'. *Positions*, 13, 31–48.

Massumi, B. (2015). *Politics of affect.* Polity Press.

May-Ron, R. (2016). Rejecting the glass slipper: The subversion of Cinderella in Margaret Atwood's *The edible woman*. In M. Hennard Duthiel de la Rochère, G. Lathey, M. Wozniak, C. Bacchilega, R. Bottigheimer, & K. Hoffmann (Eds.), *Cinderella across cultures: New directions and interdisciplinary perspectives* (pp. 143–61). Wayne State University Press.

Mazzarella, S. (1999). The 'Superbowl of all Dates': Teenage girl magazines and the commodification of the perfect prom. In S. Mazzarella, & N. O. Pecora (Eds.), *Growing up girls: Popular culture and the construction of identity* (pp. 97). Peter Lang.

Mazzei, L. A. (2013a). Materialist mappings of knowing in being: Researchers constituted in the production of knowledge. *Gender and education*, 25(6), 776–85. https://doi.org/10.1080/09540253.2013.824072

Mazzei, L. A. (2013b). A voice without organs: Interviewing in posthuman research. *International journal of qualitative studies in education*, 26(6), 732–40. https://doi.org/10.1080/09518398.2013.788761

Mazzei, L. A. (2016). Voice without a subject. *Critical studies – Critical methodologies*, 16(2), 151–61. https://doi.org/10.1177/1532708616636893

Mazzei, L. A. (2017). Following the contour of concepts towards a minor inquiry. *Qualitative inquiry*, 23(9), 675–85. https://doi.org/10.1177/1077800417725356

Mazzei, L. A., & Jackson, A. Y. (2009). The limit of voice. In A. Y. Jackson, & L. A. Mazzei (Eds.), *Voice in qualitative inquiry: Changing conventional, interpretive, and critical conceptions in qualitative research* (p. 1). Routledge.

Mazzei, L. A., & Jackson, A. Y. (2012). Complicating voice in a refusal to 'let participants speak for themselves'. *Qualitative inquiry*, 18(9), 745–51. https://doi.org/10.1177/1077800412453017

Mazzei, L. A., & Jackson, A. Y. (2016). Voice in the agentic assemblage. *Educational philosophy and theory*, 1–8. https://doi.org/10.1080/00131857.2016.1159176

McClelland, S., & Fine, M. (2017). Sexualities education in schools. In L. Allen, & M. Rasmussen (Eds.), *The Palgrave handbook of sexuality education* (pp. 211–15). Palgrave Macmillan.

McCormack, D. (2008). Engineering affective atmospheres on the moving geographies of the 1897 Andrée expedition. *Cultural geographies*, 15, 413–30. https://doi.org/10.1177/1474474008094314

Meyer, M. (2012). *Cinder*. Feiwel & Friends.

Minard, R. (1975). *Womenfolk and fairy tales*. Houghton Mifflin.

Morris, P., White, J., Morrison, H., & Fisher, K. (2013). High heels as supernormal stimuli: How wearing high heels affects judgements of female attractiveness. *Evolution and human behaviour*, 34, 176–81.

Mulcahy, D. (2012). Affective assemblages: Body matters in the Pedagogic practices of contemporary school classrooms. *Pedagogy, culture and society*, 20(1), 9–27. https://doi.org/10.1080/14681366.2012.649413

Mulcahy, D. (2016). 'Sticky' learning: Assembling bodies, objects and affects at the museum and beyond. In J. Coffey, S. Budgeon, & H. Cahill (Eds.), *Learning bodies: The body in youth and childhood studies* (pp. 207–22). Springer. https://doi.org/10.1007/978-981-10-0306-6

Murray, S. (2012, June 17). Whole new ball game. *Sunday*.

Murris, K., & Bozalek, V. (2019). Diffraction and response-able reading of texts: The relational ontologies of Barad and Deleuze. *International journal of qualitative studies in education*, 32(7), 872–86. https://doi.org/10.1080/09518398.2019.1609122

Myers, C. (2020). Interview with Casey Y. Myers. In C. Diaz-Diaz, & P. Semenec (Eds.), *Posthumanist and new materialist methodologies: Research after the child* (pp. 101–10). Springer.

Niccolini, A. (2016). Animate affects: Censorship, reckless pedagogies, and beautiful feelings. *Gender & education*, 28(2), 230–49. https://doi.org/10.1080/09540253.2015.1121205

Niccolini, A., & Pindyck, M. (2015). Classroom acts: New materialisms and haptic encounters in an urban classroom. *Reconceptualising educational research methodology*, 6(3), 1–23.

Niccolini, A., & Ringrose, J. (2019). Feminist posthumanism. In P. Atkinson, S. Delamont, A. Cernat, J. Sakshaug, & R. Williams (Eds.), *Sage research methods*. Sage.

O'Donoghue, D. (2006). Situating place and space in the making of masculinities in schools. *Journal of curriculum and pedagogy*, 3(1), 15–33.

Orme, J. (2016). I'm sure it all wears off by midnight: Prince Cinders and a fairy's queer invitation. In M. Hennard Duthiel de la Rochère, G. Lathey, M. Wozniak, C. Bacchilega, R. Bottigheimer, & K. Hoffman (Eds.), *Cinderella across cultures: New directions and interdisciplinary perspectives* (pp. 215–31). Wayne State University Press.

Osgood, J., & Guigni, M. (2015). Putting posthumanist theory to work to reconfigure gender in early childhood: When theory becomes method becomes art. *Global studies of childhood*, 5(3), 346–60. https://doi.org/10.1177/2043610615597

Osgood, J., & Robinson, K. (Eds.). (2019). *Feminists researching gendered childhoods: Generative entanglements.* Bloomsbury.

Otterstad, A. M., & Waterhouse, A. (2016). Beyond regimes of signs: Making art/istic portrayals of haptic moments/movements with child/ren/hood. *Discourse: Studies in the cultural politics of education*, 37(5), 739–53. https://doi.org/10.1080/01596306.2015.1075727

Paechter, C. (2006). Constructing femininities/constructing femininity. In B. Skelton, B. Francis and L. Smulyan (Eds.), *The Sage handbook of gender and education* (pp. 365–77). Sage.

Pascoe, C. (2007). *Dude you're a fag: Masculinity and sexuality in high school.* University of California Press.

Perrault, C. (1697). *Cendrillon: Histoires; ou, Contes du temps passé: Avec des Moralitez.* Claude Barbin.

Pomerantz, S. (2006). 'Did you see what she was wearing?' The Power and Politics of Schoolgirl Style. In Y. Jiwani, C. Steenbergen, & C. Mitchell (Eds.), *Girlhood: Redefining the limits* (pp. 173–90). Black Rose Books.

Pomerantz, S. (2007). Cleavage in a tank top: Bodily prohibition and the discourses of school dress codes. *Alberta journal of educational research*, 53(4), 373–86.

Pomerantz, S. (2008). *Girls, style and school identity.* Palgrave Macmillan.

Pyyry, N. (2015). 'Sensing with' photography and 'thinking with' photographs in research into teenage girls' hanging out. *Children's geographies*, 13(2), 149–63. https://doi.org/10.1080/14733285.2013.828453

Quinlivan, K., & Town, S. (1999). Queer pedagogy, educational practice and lesbian and gay youth. *Qualitative studies in education*, 12(5), 509–24.

Raby, R. (2010). 'Tank tops are ok but I don't want to see her thong': Girls' engagements with secondary school dress codes. *Youth and society*, 41(3), 333–56.

Raby, R. (2012). *School rules: Obedience, discipline, and elusive democracy.* University of Toronto Press.

Rasmussen, M. (2004). Safety and subversion: The production of sexualities and genders in school spaces. In M. Rasmussen, E. Rofes, & S. Talburt (Eds.), *Youth and sexualities: Pleasure, subversion and insubordination in and out of schools* (pp. 131–52). Palgrave Macmillan.

Rasmussen, M. (2006). *Becoming subjects: Sexualities and secondary schooling.* Routledge.

Rautio, P. (2020). Post-qualitative inquiry: Four balancing acts in crafting alternative stories to live by. *Qualitative inquiry*, 1–3. https://doi.org/10.1177/1077800420933297

Reay, D. (2001). 'Spice girls', 'nice girls', 'girlies', and 'tomboys': Gender discourses, girls' cultures and femininities in the primary classroom. *Gender and education*, 13(2), 153–66. https://doi.org/10.1080/09540250120051178

Renold, E. (2005). *Girls, boys and junior sexualities: Exploring children's gender and sexual relations in the primary school.* RoutledgeFalmer.

Renold, E., & Allan, A. (2006). Bright and beautiful: High achieving girls, ambivalent femininities, and the feminization of success in the primary school. *Discourse: Studies in the cultural politics of education*, 27(4), 457–73. https://doi.org/10.1080/01596300600988606

Renold, E., & Ivinson, G. (2014). Horse-girl assemblages: Towards a post-human cartography of girls' desire in an mining valleys community. *Discourse: Studies in the cultural politics of education*, 35(3), 361–76. https://doi.org/10.1080/01596306.2014.888841

Renold, E., & Ringrose, J. (2008). Regulation and rupture: Mapping tween and teenage girls' resistance to the heterosexual matrix. *Feminist theory*, 9(3), 313–38.

Renold, E., & Ringrose, J. (2011). Schizoid subjectivities?: Re-theorizing teen girls' sexual cultures in an era of 'sexualisation'. *Journal of sociology*, 47(4), 389–409.

Renold, E., & Ringrose, J. (2017a). Pin-balling and boners: The posthuman phallus and intra-activist sexuality assemblages in secondary school. In L. Allen, & M. Rasmussen (Eds.), *The Palgrave handbook of sexuality education* (pp. 631–54). Palgrave Macmillan.

Renold, E., & Ringrose, J. (2017b). Re-animating what else sexuality education research can do, be and become. In L. Allen, & M. Rasmussen (Eds.), *The Palgrave handbook of sexuality education* (pp. 547–54). Palgrave Macmillan.

Revelles-Benavente, B., Ernst, W., & Rogowska-Stangret, M. (2019). Feminist new materialisms: Activating ethico-politics through genealogies in social science. *Social sciences*, 8(296), 1–3. https://doi.org/10.3390/socsci8110296

Richardson, K. (2020). *The season: A social history of the debutante.* W. W. Norton & Company.

Riggs, A. (2016). Multiple metamorphoses, or 'new skins' for an old tale. In M. H. Duthiel de la Rochère, G. Lathey, M. Wozniak, C. Bacchilega, R. Bottigheimer, & K. Hoffman (Eds.), *Cinderella across cultures* (Detroit ed., pp. 180–96). Wayne State University Press.

Ringrose, J., & Coleman, R. (2013). Looking and desiring machines: A feminist Deleuzian mapping of bodies and affects. In J. Ringrose, & R. Coleman (Eds.), *Deleuze and research methodologies* (pp. 125–44). Edinburgh University Press.

Ringrose, J., & Rawlings, V. (2015). Posthuman performativity, gender and 'school bullying': Exploring the material-discursive intra-actions of skirts, hair, sluts and poofs. *Confero*, 3(2), 1–37. https://doi.org/10.3384/confero.2001-4562.150626

Ringrose, J., & Renold, E. (2014). 'F**k Rape!': Exploring affective intensities in a feminist research assemblage. *Qualitative inquiry*, 20(6), 772–80. https://doi.org/10.1177/1077800414530261

Ringrose, J., & Renold, E. (2016). Cows, cabins and tweets: Posthuman intra-active affect and feminist fire in secondary school. In C. A. Taylor, & C. Hughes (Eds.), *Posthuman research practices in education* (pp. 220–41). Palgrave Macmillan.

Ringrose, J., Warfield, K., & Zarabadi, S. (Eds.). (2019). *Feminist posthumanisms, new materialisms and education*. Routledge.

Robinson, K. (2008). In the name of 'childhood innocence': A discursive exploration of the moral panic associated with childhood and sexuality. *Cultural studies review*, 14(2), 113–29.

Rose, D. B. (2022). *Shimmer: Flying fox exuberance in worlds of Peril*. Edinburgh University Press.

Rowe, K. E. (1986). Feminism and fairy tales. In J. Zipes (Ed.), *Don't bet on the prince: Contemporary feminist fairy tales in North America and England* (pp. 209). Routledge.

Roy, E. A. (2016, April 11). Schoolgirls in New Zealand told to lengthen skirts to 'stop distracting male staff and pupils'. *Guardian UK*.

Rutherford, B. (2016, June 23). Christchurch's Hornby High School tells girls short skirts 'distracting' for male staff, students. *The New Zealand Herald*.

Sauzet, S. (2015). Thinking through picturing. In P. Hinton, & P. Treusch (Eds.), *Teaching with feminist materialisms* (pp. 37–52). ATGENDER.

Schoultz, R. (2016, April 10). Students told skirts need to be lowered to 'stop boys from getting ideas'. *The New Zealand Herald*.

Seigworth, G., & Gregg, M. (2010). An inventory of shimmers. In M. Gregg, & G. Seigworth (Eds.), *The affect theory reader* (pp. 1–25). Duke University Press.

Shannon, E. R. (2015). Disney princess panopticism: The creation of girlhood femininity. *Girls studies: An undergraduate research journal*, 1(1), 1–11.

Shuttleworth, K. (2012, March 4). Same-sex ball query gets blanks. *The New Zealand Herald*.

Smelik, A. (2018). New materialism: A theoretical framework for fashion in the age of technological innovation. *International journal of fashion studies*, 5(1), 33–54.

Smith, E. O. (1999). High heels and evolution: Natural selection, sexual selection and high heels. *Psychology, evolution and gender*, 1(3), 245–77.

Smith, L. A. (2012). *Gender and the school formal* [Unpublished PhD thesis]. University of Otago.

Smith, L. A. (2014). Gender, romance and the school ball. *New Zealand journal of educational studies*, 49(1), 73–86.

Smith, L. A. (2015). Queer students and same-sex partners at the school formal. In A. Gunn, & L. A. Smith (Eds.), *Sexual cultures in Aotearoa New Zealand education* (pp. 82–98). Otago University Press.

Smith, L. A., Nairn, K., & Sandretto, S. (2016). Complicating hetero-normative spaces at school formals in New Zealand. *Gender, place and culture*, 23(5), 589–606. https://doi.org/10.1080/0966369X.2015.1034245

Snaza, N., & Weaver, J. A. (Eds.). (2015). *Posthumanism and educational research*. Routledge.

Springgay, S. (2016). 'Approximate-rigorous abstractions': Propositions of activation for posthumanist research in education. In N. Snaza, & J. A. Weaver (Eds.), *Posthumanism and educational research* (pp. 76–88). Routledge.

Springgay, S., & Truman, S. (2017). On the need for methods beyond proceduralism: Speculative middles, (in)tensions, and response-ability in research. *Qualitative inquiry*, 24(3), 203–14. https://doi.org/10.1177/1077800417704464

Springgay, S., & Zaliwska, Z. (2015). Diagrams and cuts: A materialist approach to research-creation. *Cultural studies – Critical methodologies*, 15(2), 136–44. https://doi.org/10.1177/1532708614562881

St. Pierre, E. A. (2008). Decentering voice in qualitative inquiry. *International review of qualitative research*, 1(3), 319–36.

St. Pierre, E. A. (2013a). The appearance of data. *Cultural studies – Critical methodologies*, 13(4), 223–7. https://doi.org/0.1177/1532708613487862

St. Pierre, E. A. (2013b). The posts continue: Becoming. *International journal of qualitative studies in education*, 26(6), 646–57. https://doi.org/10.1080/09518398.2013.788754

St. Pierre, E. A., Jackson, A. Y., & Mazzei, L. A. (2016). New empiricisms and new materialisms: Conditions for new inquiry. *Cultural studies – Critical methodologies*, 16(2), 99–110. https://doi.org/10.1177/1532708616638694

Stender Petersen, K. (2014). Interviews as intraviews: A hand puppet approach to studying processes of inclusion and exclusion among children in kindergarden. *Reconceptualising educational research methodology*, 5(1), 32–45.

Stewart, K. (2010). Afterword: Worlding refrains. In M. Gregg, & G. Seigworth (Eds.), *The affect theory reader* (pp. 339–54). Duke University Press.

Strom, K., Ringrose, J., Osgood, J., & Renold, E. (2019). PhEmaterialism: Response-able research and pedagogy (editorial). *Reconceptualising educational research methodology*, 3(2), 1–39.

Swann, B. (2016). *The claiming of Cinderella*. Bella Swan Erotica.

Tait, M. (2013, June 28). Warning over same-sex ball dates. *The New Zealand herald*.

Tait, M. (2014, March 20). Scramble to be belle of ball. *The New Zealand Herald*.

Tay, K. (2007). *How to be the belle of the ball*. http://www.stuff.co.nz/life-style/6220/How-to-be-the-Belle-of-the-school-ball

Taylor, C. A. (2013). Objects, bodies and space: Gender and embodied practices of mattering in the classroom. *Gender and education*, 25(6), 688–703. https://doi.org/10.1080/09540253.2013.834864

Taylor, C. A. (2016). Edu-crafting a cacophonous ecology: Posthumanist research practices for education. In C. A. Taylor, & C. Hughes (Eds.), *Posthuman research practices in Education* (pp. 5–24). Palgrave Macmillan. https://doi.org/10.1057/9781137453082

Taylor, C. A., & Hughes, C. (Eds.). (2016). *Posthuman research practices in education*. Palgrave Macmillan.

Taylor, C. A., & Ivinson, G. (2013). Material feminisms: New directions for education. *Gender & education*, 25(6), 665–70. https://doi.org/10.1080/09540253.2013.834617

Todd, Z. (2016). An indigenous feminist's take on the ontological turn: 'Ontology' is just another word for colonialism. *Journal of historical sociology*, 29(1), 4–22. https://doi.org/10.1111/johs.12124

Truman, S. (2019). Feminist new materialisms. In P. A. Atkinson, S. Delamont, M. A. Hardy, & M. Williams (Eds.), *The SAGE encyclopedia of research methods*. SAGE. https://doi.org/10.4135/9781526421036

Valenti, J. (2015, 14 May). The only thing shameful about 'revealing' prom dresses are adults who stress over them. *The guardian*.

van der Tuin, I. (2008). Deflationary Logic: Response to Sara Ahmed's 'Imaginary Prohibitions: Some preliminary remarks on the founding gestures of 'new materialism'. *European journal of women's studies*, 15(4), 411–6. https://doi.org/10.1177/1350506808095297

van der Tuin, I. (2011). 'New feminist materialisms'. *Women's studies international forum*, 34, 271–7.

Wade. 2011, June 15. Same-sex date banned at school ball. *The New Zealand Herald*.

Walkerdine, V. (1990). *Schoolgirl fictions*. Verso.

Walter, N. (1999). *The new feminism*. Virago.

Warfield, K. (2016). Making the cut: An agential realist examination of selfies and touch. *Social media + society*, 2, 1–10. https://doi.org/10.1177/2056305116641706

Warfield, K. (2018). Im(matter)ial bodies: A material and affective rethinking of selfies for digital literacy resources. *Language and literacy*, 20(3), 73–88.

Warner, M. (2014). *Once upon a time: A short history of fairy tale*. Oxford University Press.

Weaver, J. A., & Snaza, N. (2016). Against methodocentrism in educational research. *Educational philosophy and theory*. https://doi.org/10.1080/00131857.20161140015

Weedon, C. (1987). *Feminist practice & poststructuralist theory*. Blackwell.

White, G. (2007). *Light fantastic: Dance floor courtship in New Zealand*. HarperCollins.

Wilson, E. (2004). *Psychosomatic: Feminism and the neurological body*. Duke University Press.

Yolen, J. (1977). America's Cinderella. *Children's literature in education*, 8(1), 21–9.

Youdell, D. (2004). Wounds and reinscriptions: Schools, sexualities and performative subjects. *Discourse*, 24(4), 477–94.

Youdell, D. (2005). Sex-gender-sexuality: How sex, gender and sexuality constellations are constituted in secondary schools. *Gender and education*, 17(3), 249–70.

Youdell, D. (2006). *Impossible bodies, impossible selves: Exclusions and student subjectivities*. Springer.

Zembylas, M. (2007). *Five pedagogies, a thousand possibilities: Struggling for hope and transformation in education*. Sense Publishers.

Zipes, J. (2016). The triumph of the Underdog: Cinderella's Legacy. In M. Hennard Duthiel de la Rochère, G. Lathey, M. Wozniak, C. Bacchilega, R. Bottigheimer, & K. Hoffman (Eds.), *Cinderella across cultures: New directions and interdisciplinary perspectives* (pp. 358–401). Wayne State University Press.

Zlatunich, N. (2009). Prom dreams and prom reality: Girls negotiating 'perfection' at the high school prom. *Sociological inquiry*, 79(3), 351–175.

Index

accountability 22, 24, 151
affect theory 34–5, 57, 77, 130
affective atmosphere 77–83
agential realism 11, 13, 17
   agency 21, 31, 56
   agential cuts 27–8, 30, 54–5, 89, 146–7
   agential inseparability 11, 27
   differentiation 30
   dis/continuity 19–20, 25
   entanglement 11, 12, 26–7
   ethics 21–2, 146
   intra-action 11, 26–7, 29, 31
   material-discursive 10, 20, 28, 97
   materialization of bodies 29, 51–5, 86, 148
   onto-epistemology 9, 12, 25–6, 144–6
   phenomena 28–30, 52, 54, 146
   posthuman performativity 28–9, 32, 50–3, 97
   power 22
   subjectivity 38
agency 21, 31, 37–8, 46, 87, 101
Ahmed, Sara 82, 107, 115, 131–2
Alldred, Pam 35–7, 57, 102, 114, 133
Allen, Louisa 6, 25, 30, 35–7, 144–5, 149–50
anthropocentric gaze 43, 94
anthropocentricism 7, 10, 35, 43, 56
assemblage 32–8
atmosphere 76–83

Barad, Karen 11
beauty as affective-material process 104–10
beauty-body practices 89–92, 101–10
Bennett, Jane 32, 38, 56, 96
Best, Amy 4, 45, 113, 120
bodies 12–13, 48–58
   agency of bodies 55–8, 87, 101
   Baradian approach to bodies 51–5, 86

   as becoming 53–5, 57, 85
   Butler's materialization of the body 49–50
   as phenomena 52, 54, 86–9, 103–4
   surveillance 3, 49–50, 55, 125
Butler, Judith 2, 18–19, 28, 49–50

causality 13, 31, 34, 101, 143
cause and effect logic 34, 41, 105, 110
Cinderella 1, 40–3
critique 22–3, 31, 149
critiques of new materialism 21, 23, 30
cutting together-apart 20, 27

data snaps 43, 145
debutante balls 1
Deleuze and Guattari 32–3, 53
desire 36–7, 114, 117
difference 24, 29–30
diffraction 24, 25, 43, 147
diffractive reading 24, 32, 43
dis/continuity 19–20, 25

effort (as affect) 72–3, 79, 81
emotion (as affect) 35, 73, 132
entanglement 11, 12, 26–7
ethico-onto-epistemology 9, 17, 145–6
ethics 8–11, 20, 22, 26, 146, 151–52

fairy-tale 40–4, 66
femininities 13, 54
feminist new materialism 7–9, 21
feminist poststructuralism 4–5, 18–20, 25, 47
Foucault, Michel 2–3, 28, 49
Fox, Nick 35–7, 57, 102, 114, 133

happiness 79–83
heteronormativity 3, 19, 37, 47–8, 113, 116
high heels 92–102, 127–33

Index

identity 5, 13, 29–31
identity formation 29–31
indeterminacy 31, 33, 139, 148
indigenous ontologies 18
intra-action 11, 26–9, 31

justice 21–2, 149–50

'ladylike' discourses 100
linguistic turn 2, 8–9

material-discursive 10, 20, 28, 97
materiality of language 68, 149
matter 17–18, 20, 28–9, 51
mattering 20, 29, 32, 39
media representations 3–4, 44–5, 143
more-than-human 11

nature/culture divide 6, 10, 51
new materialisms 8, 17–18, 30
new materialist ontology of sexuality 6–7, 11, 25, 35, 151
newness 18, 25, 43, 144
nice girl femininity 121
non-representation 27, 145

onto-epistemology 9, 12, 25–6, 144–6

participants 13–14, 36
phenomena 28–30, 146
photographs
    anthropocentric gaze 43, 94
    as material-discursive phenomena 123–7
    new materialist approach to photographs 71, 74
    relational materialist reading 77–8, 91–2, 95, 147
post-anthropocentrism 114, 146–9

posthuman ethics 9–11, 20, 22, 146
posthumanism 9
posthuman performativity 28–9, 32, 50–3, 97
posthuman voice 33
power 86, 102
pre-balls 73–6
princess femininity 41, 66, 106
prom magazines 44–5

queer theory 4, 19, 47

representational logic 27
resistance as affective movement 102
response-ability 8, 22, 151
re-turning 64
romance 47, 113, 136–8

sexuality
    as discursively produced 2–3, 6, 19
    girlhood sexualities 3, 139
    as intra-actively becoming 6, 12, 36–8, 114
    sexuality-assemblages 36–8, 114, 118, 132–3
    sexual identity 30, 36
sexual subjectivity 12, 139
shimmer 24, 42, 43, 78
Smith, Lee 4, 19, 47–8, 138
social media 65, 125
space 62–4, 133–9
spacetimemattering 61–4, 68–76, 136, 151
subjectivity 10, 92
surveillance of girls' bodies 3, 49–50, 55, 125

temporal entanglements 19, 25, 62–5, 68–76
time 61

www.ingramcontent.com/pod-product-compliance
Lightning Source LLC
Chambersburg PA
CBHW052125300426
44116CB00010B/1787